The Charles Center area of downtown Baltimore

Maryland

WORKING WONDERS

Gary Gately • M. L. Martin

This book was produced in cooperation with the Maryland Department of Business and Economic Development. Cherbo Publishing Group gratefully acknowledges its important contribution to *Maryland: Working Wonders*.

 cherbo publishing group, inc.

president	JACK C. CHERBO
chief operating officer	ELAINE HOFFMAN
editorial director	CHRISTINA M. BEAUSANG
managing feature editor	MARGARET L. MARTIN
senior profiles editor	J. KELLEY YOUNGER
profiles editors	NEVAIR KABAKIAN
	LIZA YETENEKIAN SMITH
associate editors	SYLVIA EMRICH-TOMA
	JENNY KORNFELD
editorial assistant/proofreader	MARK K. NISHIMURA
profiles writers	B. D. CAMPBELL
	SYLVIA EMRICH-TOMA
	JENNY KORNFELD
	TINA G. RUBIN
creative director	PERI A. HOLGUIN
senior designer	THEODORE E. YEAGER
designer	NELSON CAMPOS
senior photo editor	WALTER MLADINA
photo editor	KAREN MAZE
digital color specialist	ART VASQUEZ
sales administrator	JOAN K. BAKER
client services supervisor	PATRICIA DE LEONARD
senior client services coordinator	LESLIE E. SHAW
client services coordinator	KENYA HICKS
executive assistant	JUDY ROBITSCHEK
administrative assistant	BILL WAY
regional development manager	GLEN EDWARDS
eastern regional manager	MARCIA WEISS
publisher's representatives	RICHARD NAFE
	KAY ZIEGLER

Cherbo Publishing Group, Inc.
Encino, California 91316
© 2009 by Cherbo Publishing Group, Inc.
All rights reserved. Published 2009.

Printed in Canada
By Friesens

Subsidiary Production Office
Santa Rosa, CA, USA
888.340.6049

Library of Congress Cataloging-in-Publication data
Gately, Gary M.
A pictorial guide highlighting Maryland's historical tourism and the state's economic and social advantages.

Library of Congress Control Number
2009930017
ISBN 978-1-882933-25-9
Visit the CPG Web site at
www.cherbopub.com

The information in this publication is the most recent available and has been carefully researched to ensure accuracy. Cherbo Publishing Group, Inc. cannot and does not guarantee either the correctness of all information furnished it or the complete absence of errors, including omissions.

To purchase additional copies of this book, contact Joan Baker at Cherbo Publishing Group: jbaker@cherbopub.com or phone 818.783.0040 ext. 27.

Dedication and Acknowledgments

Gary Gately dedicates this book to his wife, Lorraine, and to his sons, Joseph and Paul, and wishes to thank the staff at the Maryland Department of Business and Economic Development for their kind assistance throughout the production of this publication.

Margaret Martin dedicates this book to her son, Paul. She wishes to thank the staff at the Maryland Department of Business and Economic Development—in particular David Tillman, Sherri Diehl, and Johanna Colburn—for their support and assistance with *Maryland: Working Wonders*.

Blackwater National Wildlife Refuge, Cambridge

TABLE OF CONTENTS

Left to right: Drum Point Lighthouse at the Calvert Marine Museum, Solomons; Maryland's legendary blue crab; catch of the day on the Chesapeake Bay.

Left to right: Taking on the role of British Marines in a War of 1812 reenactment at Jefferson Patterson Park and Museum, St. Leonard; playing 18th-century period instruments at the Market Fair, Fort Frederick; monument to the 130th Pennsylvania Volunteer Infantry at Antietam National Battlefield, Sharpsburg

Left to right: Reaching new heights in the Allegheny Mountains; sailing competition on the Chesapeake Bay; taking the plunge on the Potomac River.

Dimensions Healthcare System
3001 Hospital Drive, Cheverly, MD 20785
Contact: Suzanne Almalel, Vice President,
Public Affairs and Government Relations
Phone: 301-618-3859 / Fax: 301-618-2547
E-mail: suzanne.almalel@dimensionshealth.org
Web site: www.dimensionshealth.org
"The Human Dimension in Medicine"

Prince George's Hospital Center
3001 Hospital Drive, Cheverly, MD 20785
Phone: 301-618-2000

Laurel Regional Hospital
7300 Van Dusen Road, Laurel, MD 20707
Phone: 301-725-4300 or 410-792-2270

Bowie Health Campus
15001 Health Center Drive, Bowie, MD 20716
Phone: 301-262-5511

Gladys Spellman Specialty Hospital & Nursing Center
2900 Mercy Lane, Cheverly, MD 20785
Phone: 301-618-2010

Larkin Chase Nursing and Rehabilitation Center
15005 Health Center Drive, Bowie, MD 20716
Phone: 301-805-6070

Glenridge Medical Center
7582 Annapolis Road, Lanham, MD 207846
Phone: 301-618-1550 or 301-322-2326

Senior Health Center
Cora B. Wood Senior Center, Suite 108
3601 Taylor Street, Brentwood, MD 20722
Phone: 301-927-4987

Integral Systems, Inc.
6721 Columbia Gateway Drive, Columbia, MD 21046
Phone: 443-539-5008
Web site: www.integ.com

Johns Hopkins Medicine
733 North Broadway, Suite 104, Baltimore, MD 21287
Phone: 410-955-5000
Web site: www.hopkinsmedicine.org

861 Baltimore Blvd. Westminster, MD 21157 Phone 1.410. 875. 0900 Fax 1.410.875.0830

Knorr Brake Corporation
861 Baltimore Boulevard, Westminster, MD 21157-7021
Phone: 410-875-0900 / Fax: 410-875-0830
Web site: www.knorrbrakecorp.com

The Knowland Group™ Inc.
Knowland™ Group Operations/Call Center
600 Beam Street, Salisbury, MD 21801
Michael McKean, CEO
Phone: 410-860-2270 or 888-841-2289 / Fax: 410-860-2777
E-mail: mmckean@knowlandgroup.com
Web site: www.knowlandgroup.com

Knowland™ Washington Office
Knowland Group™ Inc.
1616 Anderson Road, McLean, VA 22102

Knowland™ Lewes Office
Knowland Group™ Inc.
P.O. Box 476, Lewes, DE 19958

LEGG MASON
GLOBAL ASSET MANAGEMENT

Legg Mason, Inc.
100 International Drive, Baltimore, MD 21202
Web site: www.leggmason.com

McCormick & Company, Inc.
18 Loveton Circle, Sparks, MD 21152
Contact: Corporate Communications
Phone: 410-771-7301 or 800-533-8767 / Fax: 410-527-8289
Web site: www.mccormickcorporation.com

continued on next page

BUSINESS VISIONARIES

continued from previous page

MECU of Baltimore, Inc.
7 East Redwood Street, Baltimore, MD 21202
Bert J. Hash Jr., President and CEO
Phone: 410-752-8313 / Fax: 443-927-3804
E-mail: bhash@mecu.com
Web site: www.mecu.com
"Baltimore's Credit Union"

MedImmune, LLC
One MedImmune Way, Gaithersburg, MD 20878
Contact: Perla Copernik, Associate Director, Corporate Public Relations
Phone: 301-398-0000 / Fax: 301-398-9000
E-mail: PR@medimmune.com
Web site: www.medimmune.com
"Advancing Science for Better Health"

The Mergis Group
Phone: 410-752-5244 / Fax: 410-752-5924
Web site: www.mergisgroup.com

Baltimore Office
120 East Baltimore Street, Suite 2220, Baltimore, MD 21202
Michael Bettick, Senior Vice President
Phone: 410-783-8523
E-mail: mikebettick@mergisgroup.com

Columbia Office
9891 Broken Land Parkway, Woodmere 2, Suite 401,
Columbia, MD 21046
Tom Sabia, Managing Director
Phone: 410-290-5755
E-mail: tomsabia@mergisgroup.com

Bethesda Office
4550 Montgomery Avenue, Suite 320N, Bethesda, MD 20814
Stacey O'Neill, Managing Director
Phone: 301-654-2542
E-mail: staceyoneill@mergisgroup.com

The MIL Corporation
MIL Corporate Headquarters
4000 Mitchellville Road, Suite 210A, Bowie, MD 20716
Phone: 301-805-8500 / Fax: 301-805-8505
Web site: www.milcorp.com
"People That Make the Difference."

MIL Lexington Park Office
46655 Expedition Drive, Suite 100, Lexington Park, MD 20653
Phone: 301-863-9566 / Fax: 301-863-9597

MIL Integration Facility
21660 Great Mills Road, Lexington Park, MD 20653
Phone: 301-863-4600 / Fax: 301-863-4636

Satellite Offices
Rosslyn, VA
Charleston, SC
Rapid City, SD
Ridgecrest, CA
Lakehurst, NJ
Denver, CO

Middle River Aircraft Systems
103 Chesapeake Park Plaza, Baltimore, MD 21220
Contact: Norton DePinho, Director of Business Development
Phone: 410-682-1938 / Fax: 410-682-1930
E-mail: norton.depinho@ge.com
Web site: www.mras-usa.com

Murthy Law Firm
10451 Mill Run Circle, Suite 100, Owings Mills, MD 21117
Phone: 410-356-5440 / Fax: 410-356-5669
E-mail: law@murthy.com
Web site: www.murthy.com
"We know immigration matters!"

NBRS Financial Bank
6 Pearl Street, Rising Sun, MD 21911
Jack H. Goldstein, Chairman and CEO
Phone: 410-658-5504 / Fax: 410-658-6215
E-mail: jgoldstein@nbrs.com
Web site: www.nbrs.com
"Everything You're Banking For!"

PROTEUS Technologies
Corporate Headquarters
133 National Business Parkway, Suite 150,
Annapolis Junction, MD 20701
Contact: Karen Locke, Director of Communications
Phone: 443-539-3400 / Fax: 443-539-3370
E-mail: klocke@proteus-technologies.com
Web site: www.proteus-technologies.com
"Transforming the Future of IT"

Northrop Grumman Corporation Electronic Systems
1580-A West Nursery Road, Linthicum, MD 21090
Phone: 410-765-1000 / Fax: 410-993-6698
E-mail: commes@ngc.com
Web site: www.es.northropgrumman.com

Reliable Churchill LLLP
7621 Energy Parkway, Baltimore, MD 21226
Phone: 410-439-5000; 800-492-5150 / Fax: 410-439-3496
Web site: www.reliable-churchill.com
"Your Distributor of Choice"

Pharmaceutics International, Inc. (PII)
10819 Gilroy Road, Hunt Valley, MD 21031
Steve J. King, Senior Vice President
Phone: 410-584-0001 / Fax: 410-584-0007
E-mail: sjking@pharm-int.com
Web site: www.pharm-int.com
"Formulate for Success"

Riggs, Counselman, Michaels & Downes, Inc. (RCM&D)
555 Fairmount Avenue, Baltimore, MD 21286
Robert T. Cawley, President
Phone: 800-346-4075
Web site: www.rcmd.com
"Providing tailored solutions to unique insurance needs
for over a century"

Salisbury University
1101 Camden Avenue, Salisbury, MD 21801
Phone: 410-543-6030
TTY: 410-543-6083
Web site: www.salisbury.edu
"A Maryland University of National Distinction"

Price Modern LLC
2604 Sisson Street, Baltimore, MD 21211
Robert S. Carpenter, President
Phone: 410-366-5500 or 800-366-5501 / Fax: 410-235-8382
E-mail: robert.carpenter@pricemodern.com
Web site: www.pricemodern.com

Price Modern of Washington
4400 Forbes Boulevard, Suite A, Lanham, MD 20706
Phone: 301-459-8111 / Fax: 301-459-3715

Price Modern of Raleigh
3000 Perimeter Park Drive, Morrisville, NC 27560
Phone: 919-325-0002 / Fax: 919-829-0103

SECU Credit Union
971 Corporate Boulevard, Linthicum, MD 21090-2337
Contact: Peggy Young, Vice President, Marketing
Phone: 410-487-7328 or 800-879-7328 or 888-833-7328
E-mail: peggy.young@SecuMd.com
Web site: www.SecuMd.org
"Better Banking. Better Service."

continued on next page

BUSINESS VISIONARIES

continued from previous page

Shah Associates

Shah Associates
Vinod K. Shah, M.D., President and CEO
E-mail: vkshah@shah-associates.com
Web site: www.shah-associates.com
"A Tradition of Excellence in Health Care"

Breton Medical Group
22576 MacArthur Boulevard, Suite 354,
California, MD 20659
Phone: 301-737-0500 / Fax: 301-737-3351

By the Mill Road Medical Center
23263 By the Mill Road, P.O. Box 540,
California, MD 20619
Phone: 301-863-5835 / Fax: 301-863-5489

Calvert Medical Office Building
110 Hospital Road, Suite 303,
Prince Frederick, MD 20678
Phone: 410-535-4333 / Fax: 410-535-0495

Charlotte Hall Medical Center
37767 Market Drive, Second Floor,
Charlotte Hall, MD 20622
Internal Medicine—Phone: 301-884-7322 /
Fax: 301-884-8663
Pediatrics—Phone: 301-884-7330 / Fax: 301-884-7530

Clinton Medical Center
9131 Piscataway Road, Suite 610, Clinton, MD 20735
Phone: 301-868-2106 / Fax: 301-868-6757

Fort Washington Medical Center
11701 Livingston Road, Suites 101, 103, 108, 203,
Fort Washington, MD 20744
Phone: 301-292-7270 / Fax: 301-292-0740

Lexington Park Medical Center
22335 Exploration Park, Lexington Park, MD 20653
Internal Medicine—Phone: 301-863-7041 /
Fax: 301-863-8927
Pediatrics—Phone: 301-863-9000 / Fax: 301-863-5170

Mechanicsville Medical Center
28103 Three Notch Road, Suite 101,
Mechanicsville, MD 20659
Phone: 301-884-4666 / Fax: 301-884-5852

Medical Arts Center
22650 Cedar Lane Court, Leonardtown, MD 20650
Phone: 301-475-5021 / Fax: 301-997-0264

Philip J. Bean Medical Center
24035 Three Notch Road, Hollywood, MD 20636
Phone: 301-373-7979 / Fax: 301-373-6900

Shanti Medical Center
26840 Point Lookout Road, Leonardtown, MD 20650
Internal Medicine—Phone: 301-475-5577 /
Fax: 301-884-7419
Family Practice—Phone: 301-475-8885 /
Fax: 301-884-7419

Solomons Medical Center
14090 H. G. Truman Road, Suite 2100, Solomons, MD 20688
Phone: 410-394-2700 / Fax: 410-394-2701

Waldorf Medical Center
12070 Old Line Center, Suite 100, Waldorf, MD 20602
Phone: 301-705-7870 / Fax: 301-705-7628

Wildewood Center
23415 Three Notch Road, # 2050, California, MD 20619
Phone: 301-863-8605 / Fax: 301-863-8091

Shimadzu Scientific Instruments, Inc.
7102 Riverwood Drive, Columbia, MD 21046
Contact: Kevin McLaughlin
Phone: 800-477-1227 / Fax: 410-381-1222
E-mail: webmaster@shimadzu.com
Web site: www.ssi.shimadzu.com

TeleCommunication Systems, Inc.
Corporate Headquarters
275 West Street, Annapolis, MD 21401
Phone: 410-263-7616 / Fax: 410-263-7617
Web site: www.telecomsys.com

THALES

Thales Communications, Inc.
22605 Gateway Center Drive, Clarksburg, MD 20871
Contact: Sheila R. Gindes, Marketing Communications Manager
Phone: 240-864-7000 / Fax: 240-864-7920
E-mail: sheila.gindes@thalescomminc.com
Web site: www.thalescomminc.com
"Lives depend on what we do—we will always act accordingly"

T. Rowe Price Associates, Inc.
4515 Painters Mill Road, OM-3260, Owings Mills, MD 21117
Phone: 800-638-7890 / Fax: 410-345-3400
Web site: www.troweprice.com

Under Armour, Inc.
1020 Hull Street, Baltimore, MD 21230
Phone: 888-4-ARMOUR (888-427-6687)
Web site: www.underarmour.com
"To make all athletes better through passion, science, and
the relentless pursuit of innovation."

The University of Maryland BioPark
Baltimore, Maryland
University of Maryland, Baltimore
620 West Lexington Street, 4th Floor, Baltimore, MD 21201
Contact: Jane Shaab, Assistant Vice President,
Economic Development
Phone: 410-706-8282 / Fax: 410-706-1066
E-mail: jshaab@umaryland.edu
Web site: www.umbbiopark.com

Washington County Health System
251 East Antietam Street, Hagerstown, MD 21740
James P. Hamill, President and CEO
Phone: 301-790-8000
E-mail: hamilj@wchsys.org
Web site: www.washingtoncountyhospital.com

FOREWORD

A Message from Governor Martin O'Malley

Dear Friends,

It is my pleasure to offer you our informative new book, *Maryland: Working Wonders*, which showcases the strong and diverse business community and the unparalleled quality of life we have in our state. We are very proud of our historic, cultural, and corporate treasures, and we hope that you will enjoy learning more about everything that Maryland has to offer.

Our long-term economic development strategy is key to keeping Maryland's economy strong and outperforming the nation and other states in areas like unemployment and job creation. Home to a wide array of highly valuable resources that are crucial to businesses in today's global, knowledge-based marketplace, Maryland boasts the best public schools in America, a highly educated and highly skilled workforce, and many of the nation's top-ranked institutions of higher learning and research. In addition, we are strategically located near many of the country's top federal facilities and offer a diverse business community that features traditional manufacturing side-by-side with the most advanced technology and life science research in the nation. We are working hard every day to build on these unique assets, helping businesses to flourish in our state and create jobs for all Maryland families.

I hope you will find this publication to be a valuable resource, and we invite you to call on us at 1-888-CHOOSEMD or www.choosemaryland.org to learn more about the benefits of starting and growing your business in the great state of Maryland.

Sincerely,

Martin O'Malley
Governor

1631

1634

1631
William Claiborne, Jamestown's official surveyor, establishes the first European settlement in what will become Maryland, on Kent Island.

1632
Cecilius Calvert receives a grant from King Charles I for the first proprietary colony, Maryland, named for the king's wife, Henrietta Maria.

1634
Maryland's first colonists arrive on the *Ark* and the *Dove* and establish the fourth permanent European settlement in British North America, at St. Mary's City.

1649
The Maryland Act Concerning Religion is passed, granting a measure of religious freedom to both Catholics and Protestants in the colony.

1684
Maryland's earliest dated building, the Third Haven Meeting House, is erected in Easton.

1685
William Nuthead establishes the second printing press in the American colonies, in St. Mary's City, Maryland's capital at the time.

1696
King William's School is founded in Annapolis. In 1784 it will be consolidated with St. John's College, whose founders include Maryland's four signers of the Declaration of Independence.

William Claiborne

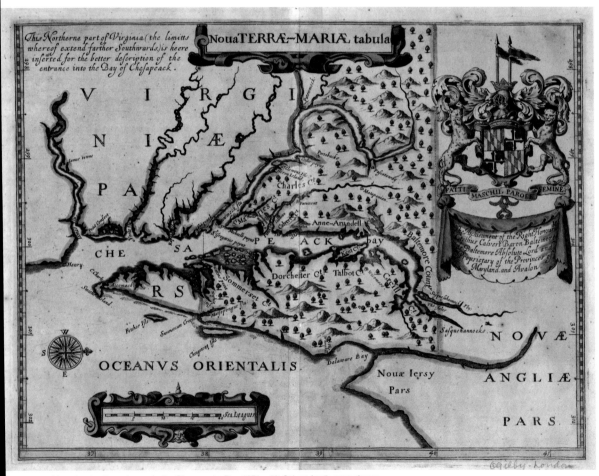

Map showing the entrance to the Chesapeake Bay, 1671, with Calvert family coat of arms

DID YOU KNOW...

- Diverse in geography and population, Maryland has been called "America in Miniature," a moniker that also refers to the important role it has played throughout the nation's history.

- During the Great Ice Age, no glaciers entered what is now Maryland, resulting in its being the only state in the country to have no natural lakes.

- With the nation's highest median household income ($68,080 in 2007), Maryland is the wealthiest state in the country.

- In the early 19th century, with dueling banned in Washington, D.C., gentlemen would meet in a field in nearby Bladensburg to resolve their differences. The field became the most popular dueling site in the country.

- On July 4, 1828, the race to connect the Ohio Valley with the East Coast began as Charles Carroll laid the cornerstone of the Baltimore and Ohio Railroad and President John Quincy Adams broke ground in Little Falls for the Chesapeake and Ohio Canal.

1706

Whetstone Point near Fort McHenry is designated an official Port of Entry, the first of five such ports that will merge to become the Port of Baltimore.

Baltimore viewed from Whetstone Point, late 18th century

1721

Gustavus Hesselius paints *The Last Supper* for the St. Barnabas Church in Prince George's County, the first recorded public artwork commissioned in America.

1743

The Maryland Jockey Club, North America's oldest sporting organization, is founded.

1767

Astronomer Charles Mason and surveyor Jeremiah Dixon are hired to settle a boundary dispute between the Calverts of Maryland and the Penns of Pennsylvania. The Mason-Dixon line will become the de facto divider between the Northern and the Southern states.

1782

Baltimore's Lexington Market opens. Today it is the oldest continuously operating market in the country.

1784

Rising above Bladensburg in a tethered hot-air balloon, 13-year-old Edward Warren makes the nation's first manned flight.

Laying out the Mason-Dixon line

Baltimore and Ohio Railroad, 1832

- The only earned doctorate degree held by a U.S. president was awarded to Woodrow Wilson in 1886 by The Johns Hopkins University, where Wilson studied government and history and wrote his first book.

- As Ocean City was unsuccessfully petitioning the government to pay for a man-made inlet to help its commercial fishing industry, the Great Hurricane of 1933 cut through the town—and through the red tape—creating a natural inlet.

- It took nearly two months for Maryland widow Mary Pickersgill to make the 30-by-42-foot flag that flew above Fort McHenry. Eight miles downriver, during the battle of September 14, 1814, Francis Scott Key saw it waving through the "bombs bursting in air" and was inspired to write his poem "Star-Spangled Banner."

- The cabin of Josiah Henson, whose autobiography was the inspiration for Harriet Beecher Stowe's novel *Uncle Tom's Cabin*, is located in Montgomery County. Purchased by the county, the cabin opened for limited visitation in 2006.

UNCLE TOM'S CABIN;

OR,

LIFE AMONG THE LOWLY.

BY

HARRIET BEECHER STOWE.

VOL. I.

ONE HUNDRED AND FIFTH THOUSAND.

Page from the first edition of *Uncle Tom's Cabin*

- The Colonies' first all-female jury was convened in Patuxent in 1656 in the trial of a woman accused of killing her infant. Chosen for their knowledge of pregnancy and birth, the jury acquitted the woman, believing her story that she had never been pregnant.

- During the War of 1812, the people of St. Michaels defended their town from the British Navy by extinguishing the town's lights and hanging lanterns in treetops, which caused the British to overshoot their target, saving the small town.

1788

1806

Thomas Moore

1788
Maryland cedes to Congress 10 square miles of land as a possible site for the nation's capital, as does Virginia a year later. In 1791 President Washington chooses the Maryland property as the site.

1790
Hampton Mansion, at the time the largest residence in the country, is built near Towson.

1796
Joshua Johnson, a native of Baltimore, is listed on the city's directory as a portrait painter, the first African American to earn a living at this occupation.

1800
Alex. Brown & Sons, the first investment bank in the country, is founded in Baltimore.

1803
Thomas Moore of Montgomery County patents his invention, which he calls the "refrigerator."

1806
Congress and President Thomas Jefferson authorize the first federal highway, the National Road, running from Cumberland to Vandalia, Illinois, connecting the East to the Northwest Territory.

1807
The University of Maryland School of Medicine, the country's first public medical school, is founded.

1813
In Baltimore, Rembrandt Peale commissions architect Robert Cary Long to build the Peale Museum, the first building in the nation designed specifically to house a museum.

1814
President James Madison takes command at the Battle of Bladensburg. He is the first and only commander-in-chief to fight on a battlefield while in office.

1814
Captive on a British ship in Baltimore Harbor, Francis Scott Key observes "through the rockets' red glare" the U.S. flag flying over Fort McHenry, a sight that inspires his poem "Star-Spangled Banner," which will become the lyrics of the national anthem.

Flag that flew over Fort McHenry, inspiration for "Star-Spangled Banner"

MARITIME MARYLAND

- Nearly 200 miles long, the Chesapeake Bay contains two of the country's five major ports. It is North America's largest estuary and the world's third largest.

- The first naval battle in Colonial America took place in Maryland on April 23, 1635, when a territorial feud over Kent Island between Virginia and Maryland settlements erupted in a skirmish at the mouth of the Pocomoke River.

- With the reestablishment of a national navy in 1794, Congress commissioned six frigates, among them the *Constellation*, which was built at the shipyards in Baltimore. Victorious in its first battle, it served the navy for over 50 years.

First naval battle in Colonial America, 1635

1815
Construction begins in Baltimore on the first monument to George Washington. Its designer is Robert Mills, the first architect born and trained in the United States; he will later design the Washington Monument in the nation's capital.

Chesapeake and Ohio Canal

1825
The Chesapeake and Ohio (C&O) Canal Company is formed to construct the C&O Canal, which will parallel the Potomac River between Washington, D.C., and Cumberland.

1826
The Maryland Institute for the Promotion of the Mechanic Arts, fore-runner of the Maryland Institute College of Art and today the nation's oldest art college, is established in Baltimore.

1829
The Carrollton Viaduct, America's first stone railroad bridge and the world's oldest railroad bridge still in use, is completed in southwest Baltimore as part of the Baltimore and Ohio Railroad.

1830
The Baltimore and Ohio Railroad, the first commercial railroad in the United States, begins offering service between Baltimore and Ellicott's Mill with the *Tom Thumb*, America's first locomotive.

1832
The Democratic Party holds its first national convention—and the first presidential convention—in Baltimore. It will hold five more conventions there consecutively until 1856.

Carrollton Viaduct

When it was completed in 1829, the Chesapeake and Delaware Canal shortened the route from Philadelphia to Baltimore by 300 miles. Connecting the Chesapeake Bay and the Delaware River, it is one of the busiest canals in the world.

The Chesapeake Bay was the first estuary to be targeted for restoration and protection by Congress. In 1983 federal, state, and local governments from throughout the bay's watershed formed the Chesapeake Bay Program, a partnership dedicated to restoring the bay.

Later renamed the William Preston Lane Jr. Memorial Bridge, the Chesapeake Bay Bridge opened in 1952, connecting the state's eastern and western shores for the first time. Over four miles long, it was the third-longest bridge in the world when it opened.

One of the top-producing ports in the country, the Port of Baltimore annually handles some 40 million tons of cargo. The closest Atlantic port to the Midwest, it ranks first among the nation's ports in several categories, including automobile exports.

William Preston Lane Jr. Memorial Bridge

Skipjacks, which were designed on the Eastern Shore in the 1890s for dredging oysters, form the last commercial sailing fishing fleet in North America. In 2003 at 117 years old, the oldest member of the fleet became a National Historic Landmark.

To commemorate John Smith's exploration of the Chesapeake Bay and its tributaries in the early 17th century, the Captain John Smith Chesapeake National Historic Trail was inaugurated in 2006. It is the first national water trail in the country.

1840

1859

Samuel Morse's telegraph

1840
Baltimore is the site of the world's first dental school, the Baltimore College of Dental Surgery, today part of the University of Maryland.

1844
Samuel Morse sends the first official telegraph with the message "What hath God wrought?" from Washington, D.C., to Baltimore.

1850
The Naval Academy, established in Annapolis in 1845 by Secretary of the Navy George Bancroft, is renamed the U.S. Naval Academy. Its illustrious alumni will include Nobel Prize–winning President Jimmy Carter and U.S. Senator and 2008 Republican presidential nominee John McCain.

1859
John Brown establishes headquarters at the Kennedy Farmhouse in Washington County, where he and his followers plan their raid on the Federal Armory at Harpers Ferry, which takes place in October.

1868
Classes begin at the Peabody Conservatory of Music, the nation's first academy of music.

1873
The first Preakness Stakes—which will become the second jewel in the Triple Crown of Thoroughbred horse racing—is held in Baltimore at Pimlico, the second-oldest race course in America.

1876
The Johns Hopkins University opens, revolutionizing education with a curriculum that combines teaching and research.

Copyright 1893 by Small, Maynard & Company

John Brown

View of the U.S. Naval Academy in Annapolis, circa 1870

REVOLUTIONARY TIMES

- Maryland's nickname "Old Line State" is generally attributed to George Washington, who credited the heroism of the Maryland Line troops with saving the Continental Army at the 1776 Battle of Long Island.

- The Maryland State House in Annapolis, the oldest state capitol in continuous legislative use, was constructed between 1772 and 1779 and served briefly as the nation's capitol. It was here that the Treaty of Paris was signed, officially ending the Revolutionary War and declaring the United States a sovereign nation.

- In the early 1770s, Baltimore printer and publisher William Goddard, frustrated by the Crown post's blocking delivery of his newspapers, organized a system of private carriers for the purpose. His plan was later adopted by Congress and became the basis for the U.S. Postal System.

- Rebels met in Montgomery County in 1774 to pass the Hungerford Resolves protesting Britain's punitive reaction to the Boston Tea Party. That same year citizens in Chestertown and Annapolis demonstrated their patriotism by holding their own "tea parties."

William Goddard

hns Hopkins

1878
Purportedly the offspring of Newfoundland dogs found in a shipwreck off the Maryland coast and bred with local coonhounds, the Chesapeake Bay retriever is registered by the American Kennel Club.

1882
Enoch Pratt gives the city of Baltimore a library system and a $1 million endowment, the basis for the Enoch Pratt Free Library, one of the country's oldest such library systems.

1884
Ottmar Mergenthaler, a resident of Baltimore, patents his invention the linotype, which modernizes the printing industry.

1889
With the opening of The Johns Hopkins Hospital and, in 1893, The Johns Hopkins University School of Medicine, Johns Hopkins Medicine is born in Baltimore. Its innovations will include a teaching hospital, admitting women, developing renal dialysis and CPR, and advancing genetic engineering.

The Johns Hopkins Hospital, circa 1903

- Four Marylanders signed the Declaration of Independence: Charles Carroll of Carrollton, Samuel Chase of Princess Anne, William Paca of Abingdon, and Thomas Stone of Charles County.

- Baltimore became one of the nation's early capitals when it hosted the Second Continental Congress, from December 1776 to February 1777. The congress had been forced out of Philadelphia when British troops drew near.

- Maryland was the last colony to ratify the Articles of Confederation, which created a national, centralized government. John Hanson, a delegate from Maryland, served as the Congress of the Confederation's first president.

- With the resignation of his commission as commander-in-chief of the army to the Congress assembled in Annapolis in 1783, George Washington averted a military dictatorship, established the principle that a military power is subservient to its civilian government, and confirmed republican ideals.

- At the Annapolis Convention in 1786, representatives reviewed problems found in the Articles of Confederation. Their recommendations led to a meeting the next year in Philadelphia—the Constitutional Convention— where the U.S. Constitution was written.

- In 1788 Maryland ratified the U.S. Constitution, thus becoming the seventh state to join the new nation. The vote was not unanimous; however the arguments presented by the Antifederalists spurred discussions that led to the Bill of Rights.

Washington resigning his commission, Maryland State House, 1783

Clara Barton. A war time photograph by Brady.

Clara Barton

1895
Rival inventors of the modern submarine, Simon Lake and John Holland, work simultaneously on their early models, the *Argonaut* and the *Plunger* respectively, at Baltimore Harbor's Columbia Iron Works dry dock.

1897
Clara Barton moves the American Red Cross headquarters, which also serves as her home, to Glen Echo, where she remains the rest of her life.

1902
Maryland passes the nation's first state workmen's compensation law.

1907
Albert Michelson, a U.S. Naval Academy graduate and professor, becomes the first American to win a Nobel Prize, in Physics, for his studies on the speed of light.

1909
The Wright brothers begin giving flying lessons to military personnel at College Park Airport, today the world's oldest airport in continuous use.

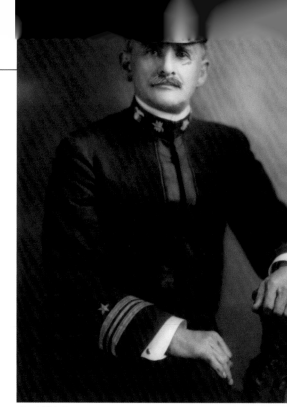

Albert Michelson

MARYLAND IN THE CIVIL WAR

Baltimore riot, 1861

Lincoln at Antietam, 1862

- The first bloodshed of the war occurred on Baltimore streets when a mob of Southern sympathizers attacked Union soldiers, killing 13, in what became known as the Baltimore riot.

- To curb the secessionist movement in Maryland, Lincoln declared martial law and suspended habeas corpus, guns at Federal Hill and Fort McHenry were pointed at Baltimore, and hundreds of civilians were arrested.

Berliner helicopter

1917
S. Duncan Black and Alonzo G. Decker open a facility in Towson where they manufacture power drills that feature their newly patented pistol grip and trigger switch.

1920
Though the sixth state to have ratified the 18th Amendment, Maryland is the only one not to pass a prohibition enforcement law, its governor citing the amendment as an invasion of state's rights.

1922
President Warren G. Harding becomes the first president to be heard on the radio when his address at a dedication of a memorial to Francis Scott Key at Fort McHenry is broadcast.

1916
The Baltimore Symphony Orchestra is established as a branch of the municipal government, the only major American orchestra so founded.

1924
Emile and Henry Berliner conduct the world's first controlled helicopter flight, at College Park Airport.

Frederick Douglass

- Frederick Douglass served as a consultant to Lincoln during the war, advising the president to make the abolition of slavery a goal of the war and to allow blacks to join the military.

- All Confederate attempts to invade the North went through Maryland, with the first halted at Antietam, the second successful in breaking through to Gettysburg, and the third stalled at Monocacy.

- With over 20,000 casualties, the Battle of Antietam was the bloodiest single-day battle in American history.

- The first photographs of war dead were taken by Alexander Gardner following the Battle of Antietam. Displayed in a New York gallery, the pictures changed the prevailing view of war from bloodless and romantic to gory and morbid.

- The Union victory at Antietam provided Lincoln with the support he needed to make freeing slaves a goal of the war. In his preliminary version of the Emancipation Proclamation, announced five days later, Lincoln granted freedom to slaves in any rebel state that refused to rejoin the Union.

Battle of Antietam

- The Battle of the Ironclads took place in Chesapeake Bay, and damaged vessels were repaired in the Port of Baltimore shipyards.

- Slavery was abolished in Maryland on November 1, 1864, when the state's third constitution—ratified specifically for this purpose—went into effect.

1925

1938

1925

Dr. Florence Sabin, known as the "first lady of American science" and whose education and career started at The Johns Hopkins University School of Medicine, is the first woman elected to the National Academy of Science.

1933

Fort McHenry becomes part of the National Park System. It is the only site within the system designated as both a national monument and historic shrine.

1935

Construction begins on the city of Greenbelt, the first federally funded planned community, a New Deal project to create affordable housing and jobs.

Seabiscuit leading War Admiral in the Preakness, 1938

1938

One in three Americans tune in to the "race of the century" held at Pimlico, where Seabiscuit triumphs against the 1937 Triple Crown–winner, War Admiral.

City of Greenbelt, circa 1935

MARYLAND TRAILBLAZERS

Benjamin Banneker (1731–1806)
One of the few free black men living in Baltimore County, Banneker was a well-known and respected mathematician, astronomer, and inventor. He accurately predicted a solar eclipse, assisted in the surveying of Washington, D.C., and published an annual almanac.

Charles Carroll (1737–1832)
Annapolis-born Carroll sat on the Continental Congress in 1775 and served in the first U.S. Senate. The only Catholic to sign the Declaration of Independence, he outlived all the other signers.

Elizabeth Ann Seton (1774–1821)
The first U.S.-born saint, Seton established the country's first free school and first community of apostolic women, in Emmitsburg, where she is buried at the basilica that bears her name.

Johns Hopkins (1795–1873)
Hopkins, born in Anne Arundel County, quit school at 12 and went on to become a wealthy merchant and banker. In 1867 he incorporated The Johns Hopkins University and The Johns Hopkins Hospital, which would become world-renowned centers of academic and medical research.

Charles Carroll

James Rouse

President Franklin Roosevelt (center) at Shangri La (now Camp David), 1942

1939
James Rouse—whose career as a developer will include pioneering enclosed malls, planned communities, and urban renewal—opens the Moss-Rouse Company, a mortgage banker, in Baltimore.

1940
President Franklin Roosevelt dedicates the new National Institutes of Health campus in Bethesda.

1941
The first camp for conscientious objectors, part of the Civilian Public Service, is established in Patapsco.

1942
FDR establishes Shangri La, a presidential retreat in the Catoctin Mountains in Frederick County, renamed Camp David by President Dwight D. Eisenhower.

arriet Tubman

Harriet Tubman (1822?–1913)
Born in Dorchester County and a runaway slave herself, Tubman returned to Maryland nearly 20 times in 10 years to lead other slaves to freedom on the Underground Railroad. In the Civil War she worked as both spy and nurse and was later a strong supporter of the women's suffrage movement.

Frederick Douglass (1817–1895)
Born into slavery in Tuckahoe, the abolitionist, author, and editor challenged slavery in his weekly newspaper, the *North Star* (later called the *Frederick Douglass Papers*) and was a consultant to President Lincoln. His works include *Narrative of the Life of Frederick Douglass, an American Slave* and *Life and Times of Frederick Douglass.*

Frances E. W. Harper (1825–1911)
A participant in the abolition, temperance, and women's suffrage movements, Harper, of Baltimore, was a noted social reformer, orator, and author. One of the earliest published African Americans, she wrote fiction, essays, speeches, and poetry.

Matthew Henson

Matthew Henson (1866–1955)
As part of Robert Peary's team of explorers, this native of Charles County was the first man to reach the North Pole, planting the U.S. flag at the top of the world in 1909.

Thurgood Marshall

Thurgood Marshall (1908–1993)
Before becoming the first black U.S. Supreme Court justice, Baltimore-born Marshall had argued 32 cases before the Court for the NAACP, prevailing in 29, including the landmark *Brown v. Board of Education,* which declared racial segregation in public schools unconstitutional.

Clarence Mitchell Jr. (1911–1984)
A civil rights activist from Baltimore, Mitchell was the NAACP's chief lobbyist from 1950 to 1979, helping to usher in key civil rights legislation. Dubbed the "101st Senator," Mitchell was presented with the Presidential Medal of Freedom in 1980.

1944   1946

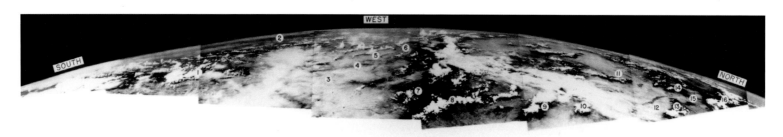

1· MEXICO	3· LORDSBURG, NEW MEXICO	6· SAN CARLOS RESERVOIR	9· SAN MATEO MTS.	12· ALBUQUERQUE, NEW MEXICO
2· GULF OF CALIFORNIA	4· PELONCILLO MTS.	7· MOGOLLON MTS.	10· MAGADALENA MTS.	13· SANDIA MTS.
	5· GILA RIVER	8· BLACK RANGE	11· MT. TAYLOR	14· VALLE GRANDE MTS.
				15· RIO GRANDE
				16· SANGRE DE CRISTO RANGE

ROCKET FIRED AT WHITE SANDS PROVING GROUND, JULY 26,1948   **DISTANCE FROM CAMERA TO HORIZON-700 MILES**

AREA SHOWN APPROXIMATELY 800,000 SQ.MILES   **DISTANCE ALONG HORIZON-2700 MILES**

INSTRUMENTATION AND PHOTOGRAPHY BY APPLIED PHYSICS LABORATORY OF THE JOHNS HOPKINS UNIVERSITY FOR THE BUREAU OF ORDNANCE, U.S.NAVY

View of earth's curvature taken with a camera built at The Johns Hopkins University's Applied Physics Laboratory, 1946

Dr. Alfred Blalock

1944

Dr. Alfred Blalock, a surgeon at The Johns Hopkins University School of Medicine, and his laboratory technician Vivien Thomas perform the world's first operation for the congenital heart defect Tetralogy of Fallot or "blue baby syndrome."

1946

A camera from The Johns Hopkins University's Applied Physics Laboratory captures the first photographs of earth's curvature from space.

1956

The Baltimore Urban Renewal and Housing Agency, the first such agency in the nation, is formed to direct the waterfront revitalization that will transform Baltimore's downtown.

MEN OF LETTERS

● Edgar Allan Poe (1809–1849)
Baltimore served as Poe's home for several years, provided literary inspiration, and is where the author is buried. Celebrated for establishing the short story, Poe also pioneered science fiction, the detective story, and the horror story.

● Upton Sinclair (1878–1968)
Best known for his novel *The Jungle*, whose graphic descriptions of the meat-packing industry's practices led to federal food-inspection reforms, Sinclair was also a political activist. He won the Pulitzer Prize in 1943 for his novel *Dragon's Teeth*.

Edgar Allan Poe

Upton Sinclair

1957
Fort Meade becomes home to the newly formed National Security Administration.

1966
The Baltimore Orioles sweep the Los Angeles Dodgers in four games to win their first World Series.

1967
The innovative master-planned community of Columbia is founded, a Rouse Company development designed with input from social scientists.

1968
The North Baltimore Aquatic Club—whose students will include Olympic swimmers Katie Hoff and Michael Phelps and many other record breakers and Olympic contenders—is founded.

1969
Maryland's governor, Spiro Agnew, becomes the 39th vice president of the United States.

1970
Baltimore defeats Cincinnati's Big Red Machine as the Orioles win their second World Series.

1973
Maryland establishes the nation's first statewide Emergency Medical Services system, which is directed by the University of Maryland Medical Center's R. Adams Cowley, a pioneer in the treatment of shock trauma.

Baltimore Orioles, 1966

Henry Louis Mencken (1880–1956)
An influential social and literary critic, Mencken began his nearly 50 years in journalism in 1899 at the *Baltimore Morning Herald*. He wrote newspaper columns and a number of books and founded and edited *American Mercury* magazine.

James M. Cain (1892–1977)
A native of Annapolis and former newspaperman, Cain wrote the classic crime novels *Double Indemnity* and *The Postman Always Rings Twice*.

Dashiell Hammett

Dashiell Hammett (1894–1961)
Hammett, of St. Mary's County, was a prolific author whose detective stories *The Maltese Falcon* and *The Thin Man* were made into classic films. In 1951 he was sentenced to jail for contempt of court during the House Un-American Activities Committee investigations and was later blacklisted by Hollywood.

F. Scott Fitzgerald (1896–1940)
The author's many ties to Maryland include his ancestor Francis Scott Key. From 1932–34 he lived and wrote in the Baltimore area while his wife, Zelda, underwent treatment at The Johns Hopkins Hospital. He and Zelda are buried in Rockville, his father's hometown.

John Barth (1930–)
The Cambridge-born writer is best known for his book *The Sot-Weed Factor*, a picaresque and satirical novel of Colonial Maryland. He won the National Book Award for *Chimera*, an examination and retelling of famous mythological stories.

Tom Clancy (1947–)
Born in Baltimore, Clancy is a master of the thriller and one of the best-selling authors of all time. His works include *The Hunt for Red October*, *Clear and Present Danger*, *Patriot Games*, and *The Sum of All Fears*.

Tom Clancy

1975

1982

1975
The Calvert Cliffs Nuclear Power Plant in Lusby begins generating electricity.

1978
Ground is broken for the National Aquarium in Baltimore.

Water filtration system at the newly opened National Aquarium in Baltimore, 1981

1982
Garrett Park outlaws the production, transportation, and storage of nuclear weapons within its boundaries and becomes the first nuclear-free zone in the country.

1985
The widest underwater vehicular tunnel in the world, Fort McHenry Tunnel opens.

Calvert Cliffs Nuclear Power Plant, Lusby, 1979

ENTERTAINING MARYLANDERS

Edwin Booth (1833–1893)
One of the greatest tragic actors and interpreters of Shakespeare's *Hamlet*, Booth was born near Bel Air. His real life was touched by tragedy in 1865 when his brother, John Wilkes Booth, assassinated President Lincoln.

Billie Holiday (1915–1959)
Born Eleanor Fagan in Baltimore, "Lady Day" sang with the Count Basie and Artie Shaw orchestras before recording with Benny Goodman. In addition to her unique singing style, she had a gift for composing and wrote the classics "Strange Fruit" and "God Bless the Child."

James Hubert "Eubie" Blake (1883–1983)
Born in Baltimore to former slaves, Blake wrote over 350 songs throughout his 80-year career as a composer and pianist. Working with Noble Sizzle, Blake co-produced *Shuffle Along*, the first Broadway musical written and directed by African Americans.

Eubie Blake

1986
The National Association for the Advancement of Colored People (NAACP), the nation's oldest civil rights organization, moves its headquarters from New York City to Baltimore.

1996
Dr. Robert Gallo, a co-discoverer of HIV, founds the Institute of Human Virology, a unique organization that serves as a laboratory, research institute, and patient care facility.

1997
Dr. John Gearhart of The Johns Hopkins University School of Medicine successfully develops the first human embryonic stem cell lines.

1998
Sergey Brin, a graduate of the University of Maryland, College Park, co-creates and launches the online search engine Google.

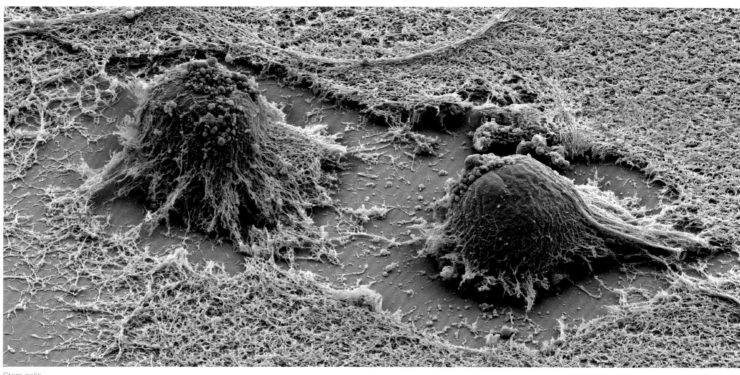

Stem cells

m Henson

Jim Henson (1936–1990)
While a freshman at the University of Maryland, College Park, Henson had his own television show, *Sam and Friends*, on the local NBC affiliate. The program featured Kermit the Frog, probably the most famous of Henson's Muppets.

Frank Zappa (1940–1993)
A musician and prolific composer, the Baltimore native and Rock and Roll Hall of Famer was equally at home in classical, jazz, rock, and electronic music. With his band, the Mothers of Invention, and as a solo artist, he produced more than 60 albums.

Cass Elliot (1941–1974)
Born Ellen Naomi Cohen in Baltimore, Elliot shot to fame as a member of the 1960s pop group the Mamas and the Papas and later enjoyed a successful solo career.

Barry Levinson (1942–)
Baltimore native and award-winning director Barry Levinson made his directorial debut with *Diner*, the first in his "Baltimore trilogy," which includes *Tin Men* and *Avalon*. He also directed *Rain Man*; *Good Morning, Vietnam*; and *The Natural*.

Goldie Hawn

Goldie Hawn (1945–)
This native of Tacoma Park was a standout as the bubbly blond on *Rowan & Martin's Laugh-In* and later won an Academy Award for her performance in *The Cactus Flower*. Her other credits include *Private Benjamin*, *Death Becomes Her*, and *The First Wives Club*.

John Waters (1946–)
Called "the Pope of Trash," the Baltimore-born filmmaker has become known for movies that target middle-class values, feature offbeat characters, and revel in the grotesque. His films include *Pink Flamingos*, *Hairspray*, and *Pecker*.

Parker Posey (1968–)
Known as the "Queen of the Indies," the Baltimore native has starred in *Waiting for Guffman*, *The House of Yes*, and *Best in Show*.

Edward Norton (1969–)
Raised in Columbia, the planned community developed by his grandfather James Rouse, the actor received the Golden Globe and an Oscar nomination for *Primal Fear*, his feature film debut, and earned a second Oscar nomination for *American History X*—all before the age of 30.

2000

2000

The Bethesda-based National Human Genome Research Institute and Rockville-based Celera Genomics jointly announce that they have simultaneously yet separately succeeded in mapping the human genome sequence.

Dr. Francis Collins, director, National Human Genome Research Institute

2001

Baltimore Ravens, Super Bowl XXXV

2001

The Baltimore Ravens earn their first Super Bowl victory when they defeat the New York Giants at Super Bowl XXXV.

2002

The Kunta Kinte–Alex Haley Memorial is dedicated in Annapolis. Haley traces his ancestry back to Kinte, who arrived in Annapolis from West Africa in 1767 and was the central character in Haley's novel *Roots*.

OLD LINE PLAYERS

George Herman "Babe" Ruth (1895–1948)
Born in Baltimore, the Sultan of Swat learned to play baseball at St. Mary's Industrial School for Boys and was hired by the Orioles in 1914. In 1919 he began a 25-year stint with the Yankees. His record .847 slugging average stood for 78 years until broken by Barry Bonds.

George Herman "Babe" Ruth

Jim McKay (1921–2008)
Raised in Baltimore, the legendary sports commentator began his career with the *Baltimore Evening Sun* and went on to host *ABC's Wide World of Sports* for nearly 20 years, receiving the Emmy for his coverage of the murder of Israeli athletes at the 1972 Olympic Games. McKay was part owner of the Orioles and founded the Maryland Million Thoroughbred race.

John Constantine "Johnny" Unitas (1933–2002)
One of the greatest quarterbacks of all time, Unitas played for the Baltimore Colts from 1956–72, leading the team to victory in Super Bowl V. The Pro Football Hall of Famer is buried in Timonium.

Baltimore/Washington International Thurgood Marshall Airport

2006

J. D. Power and Associates and *Aviation Week* rank the Baltimore/Washington International Thurgood Marshall Airport third among North America's medium-sized airports in overall passenger satisfaction.

2007

Baltimore native Nancy Pelosi becomes the first female Speaker of the House of Representatives.

2008

The Milken Institute moves Maryland from fourth to second place on its State Technology and Science Index, highlighting the state's expanding knowledge economy.

2008

Maryland announces the BIO 2020 Initiative through which the state will invest $1.1 billion in its bioscience industry over 10 years—the largest per capita bioscience investment made by any state to date.

Nancy Pelosi

Brooks Robinson (1937–)
In his 23 seasons with the Orioles, the multi-award–winning third baseman was named MVP in the 1970 World Series for his remarkable fielding. In 1983 he was inducted into the Hall of Fame and in 1999 was named to the 25-member All Century Team.

Jim Palmer (1945–)
Considered one of baseball's finest pitchers, Palmer played his entire career with the Orioles, leading them to victory in the 1966, 1970, and 1983 World Series. A three-time Cy Young Award winner and member of the Hall of Fame, he went on to a successful broadcasting career.

Cal Ripken Jr. (1960–)
Born in Havre de Grace, the Baseball Hall of Famer, MVP, and Gold Glove recipient played for the Orioles for 21 years and holds MLB's record for most consecutive games played (2,632). Today Ripken heads Ripken Professional Baseball, whose teams include the Aberdeen IronBirds, based in his hometown.

Pam Shriver (1962–)
One of only five women with more than 100 career titles, the Baltimore native gained fame as a doubles player, winning 79 titles with teammate Martina Navratilova. She later went into broadcasting and was inducted into the International Tennis Hall of Fame in 2002.

Michael Phelps

Michael Phelps (1985–)
Born and trained in Baltimore, swimmer Michael Phelps won a record eight gold medals and contributed to seven world records at the 2008 Olympic Games in Beijing. He currently holds more Olympic gold medals (14) than any other athlete.

Fredua "Freddy" Adu (1989–)
The son of immigrants from Ghana, Adu grew up in Rockville and Potomac, where he still lives. At 14 he became the youngest soccer player to go pro and the youngest in Major League Soccer history to score a goal. A member of the U.S. Men's National Team, he also plays for France's AS Monaco.

Kimberly "Kimmie" Meissner (1989–)
The Towson native and current Bel Air resident won the 2006 World Figure Skating Championships and is only the second U.S. woman to land a triple axle in a competition, at the 2005 U.S. National Figure Skating Championships.

Fredua "Freddy" Adu

MARYLAND MOMENTUM:
A COMPELLING FORCE

PART**ONE**

A STATE OF WONDERS

Maryland has been called America in Miniature, a nickname conferred on the state as much for the diversity of its geography as for the variety of its industries. The moniker also refers to Maryland's role in so many of the nation's pivotal events, be they historic, political, or economic. From every corner of the state, history calls—from the battlefield at Antietam to the halls of government at Annapolis, from the flag at Fort McHenry to the cobblestone streets of Fells Point, from the birthplace of Harriet Tubman to the resting place of Edgar Allan Poe. And Maryland continues to make history—as a global leader in education, research, health care, bioscience, advanced technology, transportation and logistics, and many other fields.

Maryland's success story is due in large part to forward-thinking policies and programs that promote business development, embrace technology, and invest in education. As a result, Maryland ranks at or near the top of surveys and studies in numerous areas of accomplishment.

In recent years the state has put billions of dollars into education, and the investment is paying off. In January 2009, both *Education Week* and the management consulting firm MGT of America named Maryland's K–12 public school system the best in the nation. Within weeks the College Board announced that the percentage of Maryland students achieving "college mastery level" on the 2008 Advanced Placement exams was the highest in the country. According to the U.S. Department of Commerce, Maryland is second in the level of educational achievement, with more than 35 percent of its citizens over age 25 holding at least a bachelor's degree. It is no wonder then that the state has one of the nation's most educated workforces.

Maryland is also a leading player in the New Economy, promoting and investing in technology. In 2008 it ranked second in the State New Economy Index for, among other criteria, the number of knowledge jobs and its support for technological innovation. The Milken Institute put Maryland in the top 10 in its 2008 State Technology and Science Index, ranking the state first in human capital development and second in inputs for research and development and in technology concentration and dynamism. And Maryland's BIO 2020 Initiative will solidify the state as a leader in stem cell research and other bioscience fields.

Entrepreneurship is also highly valued, and numerous incentives and benefits support the business community. Maryland is a top venture capital investor and ranks first in the percentage of businesses that are majority owned by women and sixth in the number of companies owned by African Americans. In 2008 the accounting firm of Ernst & Young found that for the fifth year in a row Maryland companies paid the lowest share of local and state taxes of all the states.

Further enhancing the state's reputation is its enviable quality of life. Residents earn the highest median income in the country—$68,080 in 2007, more than 30 percent above the national average. They enjoy year-round recreation and sports, exciting arts and culture, and varied and beautiful scenery. Maryland truly is a state of wonders.

At the Heart of It All: Central Maryland

Central Maryland is indeed the nexus of the state, home to both the state capital, Annapolis, and one of the nation's great cities, Baltimore; but the region is also one of serene waterfront villages, scenic country roads, and charming hamlets.

Baltimore's maritime heritage defines the city and made Baltimore a vital player in the nation's early history. The city's location along the natural harbor formed by the Patapsco River basin made it a center for trade, transportation, and shipbuilding—and a prime target of the British in two wars. When the Erie Canal and the Mississippi River threatened to replace Baltimore as a transportation hub, the city reinvented itself—and transformed the way the nation did business—with the founding of the world's first long-distance railroad. There followed remarkable advances in technology, and Baltimore became an industrial powerhouse. Through the years it experienced highs

and lows until the 1950s when a revitalization project renewed downtown, and in the 1980s Baltimore underwent yet another renaissance with the Inner Harbor development.

Today Baltimore is a decidedly modern city but where one is never far from history. It was in Baltimore Harbor that Francis Scott Key, captive on a British warship, watched the "bombs bursting in air" over Fort McHenry as the British attacked in the 1814 Battle of Baltimore. His paean to America's steadfastness, "Star-Spangled Banner," became the lyrics of the national anthem. Today visitors may take a self-guided tour at Fort McHenry National Monument and Historic Shrine where, in addition to the "Star-Spangled Banner" story, they will learn about the fort's role in the Civil War and the two world wars. Mary Pickersgill, who sewed the flag that inspired Key's poem, lived and worked at what is now the Star-Spangled Banner Flag House, built in 1793. Living history interpreters offer guided tours of the house.

The city's shipbuilding legacy is explored in Fells Point, a waterfront neighborhood of cobblestone streets lined with restored 18th- and 19th-century brick buildings where the great shipyards of Baltimore once stood and which at one time was the second-largest port of immigration in the country. The Fells Point Maritime Museum looks at the community's seafaring history through artifacts, paintings, and ship models. Fells Point is also home to Broadway Market, established in 1784, upscale boutiques and shops, and dozens of pubs and restaurants.

To the west of Fells Point is the Inner Harbor, where visitors may tour the 1854 U.S.S. *Constellation*, the last all-sail warship built by the U.S. Navy. Its Museum Gallery displays artifacts and belongings of the ship's crew. The Baltimore Maritime Museum oversees three other historic vessels docked at the harbor: the U.S.C.G.C. *Taney*, the last warship afloat that survived the attack on Pearl Harbor; the U.S.S. *Torsk*, which sank the last enemy warships torpedoed in World War II; and the 1930 lightship *Chesapeake*.

Baltimore's central role in the creation of the American railroad industry is explored at the Baltimore & Ohio Railroad Museum. The 40-acre facility features a stunning roundhouse and the world's oldest and most comprehensive American railroad collection, including 19th-century locomotives and railroad cars. The B&O also displays vintage railroading clocks, pocket watches, dining-car china, and communication devices.

The railroad and maritime industries were the catalysts for many other industries that grew and thrived in Baltimore. Located in a former oyster cannery, the Baltimore Museum of Industry has recreated machine, printing, garment-making, and metal workshops, and showcases such Maryland firsts as the typesetting machine, the disposable bottle cap, and modern radar. Outside, along the harbor's dock, is the BMI-maintained U.S.S. *Baltimore*, the only steam tugboat operating on the East Coast.

The Maryland Historical Society Museum chronicles the state's history through permanent and changing exhibits. The museum's 350,000 objects include paintings, maritime-related artifacts, decorative arts, silver, quilts, costumes, ceramics, dolls, and toys.

Maryland's African American heritage is the theme of the Reginald F. Lewis Museum of Maryland African American History and Culture. Named for the pioneering Baltimore-born lawyer and entrepreneur, the museum features a permanent exhibition that focuses on African American families and communities; labor and the black experience; and arts, culture, and faith. The National Great Blacks in Wax Museum celebrates black heritage through life-size wax figures of such luminaries as Frederick Douglass, Thurgood Marshall, and President Barack Obama.

For many years, Baltimore served as the port of entry for immigrants, many seeking religious freedom. The Jewish Museum of Maryland brings together art, historical photographs, clothing, ceremonial items, rare books, documents, oral histories, and memorabilia. It is the only museum in the country to house two synagogues, the 1845 Lloyd Street Synagogue and the 1876 B'nai Israel Synagogue. In addition, the museum displays archaeological and architectural relics recently discovered on the premises.

Baltimore was also pivotal in the history of Catholicism in the United States. It was a Marylander, John Carroll, who in 1784 was named by the pope to be the first bishop of the United States. In 1806 Carroll laid the cornerstone for

Baltimore Cathedral, the first Roman Catholic cathedral in the nation. The neo-classical building, designed by architect Benjamin Henry Latrobe and completed in 1821, is today the Basilica of the National Shrine of the Assumption of the Blessed Virgin Mary. In 2006 it reopened after a two-year renovation to restore it to its original design. In 1808 Elizabeth Ann Seton, the first American-born saint, moved with her three daughters to the Federal-style Mother Seton House, where she started Baltimore's first Catholic school.

The homes of two of Baltimore's most famous residents are open to the public. Baseball great George Herman "Babe" Ruth was born in the upstairs bedroom of a tiny row house, where today are exhibited such artifacts as a catcher's mitt and a jersey he used as a boy. Edgar Allan Poe lived in a five-room brick row house at 203 Amity Street, most likely from 1832 to 1835, with his aunt and his young cousin and future bride, Virginia Eliza Clemm. Among the items on display are his telescope, his lap desk, and the only known portrait of his wife.

Part of the University of Maryland, site of the country's first dental school, is the Dr. Samuel D. Harris National Museum of Dentistry, whose displays include George Washington's lower denture (ivory, not wooden), a play dentist office, vintage toothpaste commercials, and interactive exhibits that teach how to keep a smile healthy. Near Camden Yards is the fascinating Geppi's Entertainment Museum with its vast collection of toys and comics dating to the 18th century.

The region is also home to two renowned gardens. In the northern Baltimore neighborhood of Guilford, Sherwood Gardens is considered by many to be the continent's most famous tulip garden, with 80,000 of the bulbs planted annually. At Ladew Topiary Gardens in Monkton in Baltimore County, visitors can take self-guided tours through the 15 themed topiary and flower gardens on 22 acres of an estate once owned by gardener Harvey S. Ladew.

Baltimore County also boasts the Hampton National Historic Site, whose mansion has undergone little change since its completion in 1790. The terraced gardens and slave quarters also remain, as do thousands of original artifacts.

To the west of Baltimore County is Howard County, whose Center of African-American Culture, in Columbia, features a research and reading library with approximately 4,000 books. Also in the county, on the B&O line, is Ellicott City Station, the oldest railroad depot in the nation.

In the northeast corner of the region lies Cecil County, where the C&D Canal Museum in Chesapeake City traces the history of the canal linking the Chesapeake and Delaware bays. Housed in the original pumphouse, the museum displays the waterwheel and steam pumping engines.

West of Cecil County is Harford County, where maritime history comes alive at the Havre de Grace Maritime Museum. The town also boasts the state's oldest lighthouse in continuous use, Concord Point Lighthouse, built in 1827. At Jerusalem Mill in Gunpowder Falls State Park, visitors are treated to blacksmithing demonstrations and other activities that recreate18th-century village life.

The legacy of Carroll County as an agricultural center is explored at the Carroll County Farm Museum in Westminster, a 19th-century farmhouse displaying period equipment and other items. The Union Mills Homestead and Grist Mill has been a working mill since 1797 and is on the National Register of Historic Places.

Anne Arundel County is home to Annapolis, where under the dome of the Maryland State House, lawmakers convene in the oldest state capitol in continuous use by a state legislature. Annapolis, chartered in 1608, served briefly as the nation's first peacetime capital when the Continental Congress met there from November 1783 through August 1784. During that period, George Washington resigned his commission as commander-in-chief of the Continental Army, and Congress ratified the Treaty of Paris, officially ending the Revolutionary War. Visitors may tour the Old Senate Chamber where these historic events took place.

Many signers of the Declaration of Independence resided in Annapolis. Lawyer Samuel Chase built what is said to be one of the first three-story Georgian town houses in the colonies, in 1769. He sold it, unfinished, in 1771 to Edward Lloyd IV, a politician and planter, who adorned the home with two large interior chimneys, ornamental plaster ceilings and doorways, and an elaborate dining room. Today the upper floors of the Chase-Lloyd House are used as a rest home, while the ground floor is a museum open to visitors. The Georgian-style William Paca House, built between 1763 and 1765, is a five-part mansion with two acres of formal gardens. In 1965 the Historic Annapolis Foundation saved the home from demolition and restored it. The Charles Carroll House was constructed around 1725 by Charles Carroll the Settler, the state's first attorney general. It was the

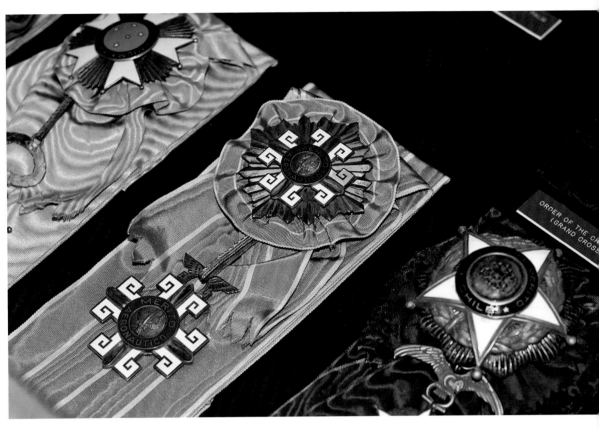

birthplace of his grandson Charles Carroll of Carrollton, the only Catholic to sign the Declaration of Independence, who expanded the house in the 1770s.

Other period homes include the 1774 Hammond-Harwood House, built by wealthy tobacco planter and General Assembly delegate Matthias Hammond. Designed by William Buckland, who also designed the Chase-Lloyd House, the Anglo-Palladian structure is a fine example of Colonial-era academic architecture. Historic London Town and Gardens, a 23-acre park on the South River in Edgewater, contains part of the late-17th- and early-18th-century town and is an active archaeological excavation site. London Town includes the William Brown House, a Georgian-style house built between 1758 and 1764.

Annapolis is also home to the Banneker-Douglass Museum, Maryland's official repository of African American material culture. It is named for native sons Benjamin Banneker, astronomer and editor, and Frederick Douglass, journalist, author, and statesman. Through artifacts, photos, art, historical documents, and

rare books, the museum chronicles African American history in Maryland dating to 1633. The Kunta Kinte–Alex Haley Memorial marks the spot where Haley's African ancestor arrived in the New World. The memorial features a sculpture of Haley reading to three children of different ethnic backgrounds and a wall of sculpted bronze plaques engraved with messages encouraging universal reconciliation.

Also in Annapolis is the U.S. Naval Academy. Its museum has an extensive collection of art, artifacts, and memorabilia that covers 2,000 years of naval history and includes ancient coin medals, warship models, ship instruments and gear, flags, uniforms, manuscripts, and much more. Exhibits also pay tribute to such renowned naval leaders as David Farragut, Chester Nimitz, and William Halsey.

Crossroads of History: The Capital Region

Not to be confused with the state capital, the Capital Region refers to the three counties that are in the Washington, D.C., vicinity: Frederick, Montgomery, and Prince George's.

The county seat of Frederick County, Frederick is a blend of history and charm. Visitors can take walking tours—some by candlelight—through its 50-block historic district, full of restaurants, shops, galleries, and antique stores. Frederick was a crossroads of the Civil War, and many of its most popular sites date from that era including the Barbara Fritchie House and Museum in the reconstructed home of the Civil War heroine immortalized by poet John Greenleaf Whittier.

The fascinating National Museum of Civil War Medicine displays surgical instruments, prosthetic devices, and the only remaining surgeon's tent from the war. Nearby is the Monocacy National Battlefield, site of a July 9, 1864, battle that was won by the Confederates; but because of fierce fighting by Union forces, the rebels' plans to invade Washington, D.C., were foiled. In Emmitsburg, in the northern part of the county, is National Fallen Firefighters Memorial Park on the campus of the National Fire Academy. The centerpiece is a bronze Maltese Cross with an eternal flame, symbolizing groups that help in disasters. The names of firefighters killed in the line of duty since 1981 are listed on plaques around a plaza. A short drive away, the National Shrine of Saint Elizabeth Ann Seton, the former home of the first American-born saint, lets visitors journey through the life and legacy of Mother Seton, whose remains are in the basilica.

rural. Gardening and horticulture aficionados head to the award-winning, 50-acre Brookside Gardens in Wheaton Regional Park to stroll through its many themed and formal gardens.

Montgomery County borders the nation's capital (in fact, much of what was originally Montgomery County was ceded to the District of Columbia in 1791) and is home to some of the U.S. government's largest institutions, including the National Institutes of Health, which houses the world's largest medical library, in Bethesda. The Clara Barton National Historic Site, once the headquarters of the American Red Cross and warehouse for relief work supplies, tells the story of the life of Clara Barton, the "angel of the battlefield" who helped wounded soldiers during the Civil War and in 1881 founded the Red Cross. She lived in the Glen Echo home, built in 1891, until her death in 1912. The Great Falls Tavern on the C&O Canal in Potomac began welcoming guests in 1831 and continues to this day as both a hotel and a visitor center. Mule-drawn barges take visitors on a canal ride while the area offers views of the beautiful Great Falls themselves. Despite its proximity to Washington, much of the county remains

Like Montgomery County, Prince George's County also gave up some of its land to create Washington and it too is home to government facilities, including the National Archives at College Park, the NASA Goddard Space Flight Center in Greenbelt, and Andrews Air Force Base in Camp Springs. Indeed, the county's role in aviation history is important. College Park Airport is the world's oldest airport in continuous use, founded in 1909 following Wilbur Wright's arrival there to train military pilots. The College Park Aviation Museum displays both memorabilia and historic and reproduction aircraft. The county also offers its share of historic homes. In Laurel, the Georgian-style Montpelier Mansion is surrounded by acres of parkland. The home, believed to have been built between 1781 and 1785, was originally owned by Major Thomas Snowden and his wife, Anne, known to have hosted George Washington. The house features a rare example of an 18th-century summer house.

The Mountain Side of Maryland: Western Maryland

The Allegheny Mountains run through the three counties of Western Maryland, an area of unsurpassed beauty and limitless recreation and the site of many of the nation's pivotal historic events. A journey through Washington, Allegany, and Garrett counties is a journey through time.

In Washington County near Sharpsburg lies Antietam National Battlefield, site of the bloodiest one-day battle in American history, which saw 23,000 casualties. The battle, which took place on September 17, 1862, changed the course of the Civil War when the Confederate army was forced to withdraw to Virginia, ending its attempt to invade the North. The outcome brought Lincoln the public support he needed to issue his preliminary Emancipation Proclamation. Strolling the grounds of the mostly undisturbed battlefield, one can almost feel the presence of the ghosts of the war dead. The Statue of Hope at Rose Hill

Cemetery in Hagerstown marks the gravesites of more than 2,000 Confederate soldiers who died at Antietam and those who died three days earlier at the Battle of South Mountain. At the Kennedy Farmhouse in Sharpsburg, abolitionist John Brown planned his pre–Civil War raid on the federal armory at Harpers Ferry. Brown and his followers stockpiled weapons and stayed at the two-story farmhouse in the summer of 1859.

West of Hagerstown in Big Pool is Fort Frederick State Park, Maryland's frontier defense in the French and Indian War, where the stone wall and two barracks have been restored to their 1758 appearance. The fort also served as a prison during the American Revolution. Today visitors will find a boat launch, cross-country skiing, campsites, fishing, canoeing, and a hiking trail. The Hagerstown Aviation Museum highlights the area's history as an aircraft manufacturing hub with exhibits of engines, equipment, and electronics.

Further west, into Allegany County, is the town of Cumberland, where George Washington slept in a one-room cabin while serving as a young aide to General Edward Braddock. George Washington's Headquarters—the cabin, completed in 1755—is the only structure remaining of what was once Fort Cumberland. Cumberland's Canal Place Heritage Area offers numerous historical attractions, including the Cumberland C&O Canal National Historical Park Visitor Center showcasing history through exhibits on canal-boat building and the town's role as a transportation center. Cumberland is where the first National Road, the railroad, and the canal converged. Visitors may also board a full-scale replica of the *Cumberland* canal boat. The district is also home to the Queen City Transportation Museum where exhibits include a Conestoga wagon and a Ford Model T. From Canal Place, riders may board the Western Maryland Scenic Railroad, which chugs through the mountains between Cumberland and Frostburg.

Garrett County is best known for Deep Creek Lake State Park. The Deep Creek Lake Discovery Center explores the region's history of coal mining and timber logging and offers hikes and educational programs.

Land of Timeless Appeal: The Eastern Shore

On the Eastern Shore, flat farmland seems to stretch to the horizon, interrupted by waterfront towns Norman Rockwell could have painted. In Kent County along the Chester River is Chestertown, designated one of 12 Distinctive Destinations by the National Trust for Historic Preservation in 2007. The town features the Geddes-Piper House, a late-18th-century furnished town house, and a replica of the 1768 schooner *Sultana*. To the southwest on the Chesapeake Bay lies Rock Hall, where the town's fishing, oystering, and crabbing history is the theme at the Waterman's Museum. Filled with fascinating photographs from the 19th and early 20th centuries, the 1890 African American Schoolhouse Museum in Worton also features artifacts and oral histories.

Queen Anne's County is known as the Gateway to the Eastern Shore, for it is where the William Preston Lane Jr. Memorial Bridge (also known as the Bay Bridge) connects "mainland" Maryland to this region. Upon crossing east on the bridge, one arrives at Kent Narrows and the Chesapeake Exploration Center. The center is home to a museum on the history of the Chesapeake. From there, the Chesapeake Bay Scenic Byway wends its way through charming towns that have changed little over time.

St. Michael's, in Talbot County, is one of the most popular destinations on the Eastern Shore. Its Chesapeake Bay Maritime Museum chronicles the seafaring life in compelling detail. On the grounds of the 18-acre waterfront museum are a restored 1879 lighthouse, a skipjack, a working boatyard, an impressive collection of decoys, and a waterman's shanty complete with tools of the trade. A marker at a farm in Trappers Corner near Easton designates the place where abolitionist Frederick Douglass was born.

The mission of the Choptank River Heritage Center in Caroline County's West Denton is to preserve the region's river heritage and culture. Its Joppa Wharf Museum includes the renovated wharf, restored skipjacks, and exhibits on river trade and transportation. In Denton, the Museum of Rural Life pays tribute to agriculture, for three centuries the county's only industry, through four historic dwellings which once housed the farm's owners and workers.

A plaque marks the birthplace of Harriet Tubman, who was born into slavery in Bucktown near Cambridge, in Dorchester County, and worshipped at the town's small Bazzel Methodist Church. Tubman, called "the Moses of her people," helped more than 300 slaves escape to freedom through the Underground Railroad, and the county has many sites related to the Underground Railroad and to the civil rights movement.

Salisbury University in Salisbury, Wicomico County, hosts the Nabb Research Center for Delmarva History and Culture and is also home to the Ward Museum of Wildfowl Art, with the largest public collection on the planet of antique and decorative decoys.

Also of interest to history buffs is Somerset County with its many examples of 18th- and 19th-century architecture. In Crisfield, displays at the J. Millard Tawes Historical Museum depict the history of the lower Eastern Shore with exhibits on the area's Native Americans and early colonists, seafood harvesting and fishing, and the fine art of decoy carving and painting.

Generations of Marylanders have been coming to Ocean City, in Worcester County, to enjoy its immaculate beaches, lively boardwalk, amusement parks, and neon-soaked strips. But the county also features numerous historic homes, many of which are also museums. Ocean City is also the site of the U.S. Life-Saving Station Museum, whose exhibits include vintage bathing suits, artifacts from shipwrecks, and an aquarium.

Charm of the Chesapeake: Southern Maryland

Throughout much of its history, Southern Maryland relied on tobacco—and to a lesser extent on seafood—to sustain it; and while new homes have replaced the tobacco fields, most of the region retains its rural charm.

Historic St. Mary's City, the state's birthplace and from 1634 to 1695 its capital, looks much as it did when the first colonists stepped ashore. Located in St. Mary's County, the town features the reconstructed State House of 1676, a working Colonial farm, and the *Maryland Dove*, a replica square-rigged ship. The National Historic Landmark is also an active Colonial archaeological site. In Drayden, the foundation of the Drayden African-American Schoolhouse rests on tree trunks, a construction method popular throughout Southern Maryland since the 17th century. Sotterley Plantation in Hollywood provides glimpses of life on an early-18th-century plantation. Visitors can admire the Chinese Chippendale stairway, stand on the portico and take in the countryside, and tour grounds that look much as they

have for two centuries. The Patuxent River Naval Air Museum in Lexington Park chronicles U.S. Navy research, development, testing, and evaluation. Exhibits include flight trainers, models, unmanned air vehicles, equipment, and helicopters and planes.

The Thomas Stone National Historic Site in Port Tobacco in Charles County is the site of Haberdeventure, the 322-acre property of one of the signers of the Declaration of Independence. Stone purchased the plantation house in 1770, and today the restored structure includes exhibits on Native Americans, European colonization, and slavery. A house with a less reputable past is the Dr. A. Samuel Mudd Home in Waldorf, where Lincoln's assassin, John Wilkes Booth, stopped to have his broken leg treated before continuing his escape.

At Jefferson Patterson Park and Museum in St. Leonard in Calvert County, visitors can explore archaeological sites and trails dating back 9,000 years. Here the 1814 Battle of St. Leonard Creek took place, the largest naval battle in state history. The town of Solomons is the county's most popular tourist destination with its excellent sailing and fishing opportunities and its stunning waterfront. Not to be missed is the Calvert Marine Museum, chronicling the history of the Patuxent and the Chesapeake, and the historic 1883 Drum Point Lighthouse. Solomons also provides a starting point for exploring the Captain John Smith National Historic Trail. This, the country's first all-water trail, follows Smith's journey along the Chesapeake and its tributaries.

State of the Arts: Maryland's Cultural Scene

Maryland is the first state in the nation to sponsor Arts and Entertainment Districts, promoting the arts through tax incentives and other means. From world-class and unusual museums to performing arts venues to studios and galleries, the arts come alive in all corners of the state.

by Andy Warhol. The American Visionary Art Museum, one of the more recent additions to the city's cultural scene, offers a one-of-a-kind look at art by self-taught artists.

Performance venues in Baltimore include the restored 1914 Hippodrome Theatre at the France-Merrick Performing Arts Center, which reopened in 2004 as a venue for Broadway touring shows; the Lyric Opera House; and the Joseph Meyerhoff Symphony Hall, home of the world-renowned Baltimore Symphony Orchestra. Classic and contemporary plays are produced at Baltimore's CenterStage midtown. The Peabody Institute, affiliated with The Johns Hopkins University, trains students in music and dance and each year puts on more than 800 musical and dance programs in Baltimore and in other cities across the country. Baltimore is also home to the Arena Players, the country's oldest African American regional theater; and the Eubie Blake National Jazz Institute and Cultural Center, which promotes the history of African American art and culture through classes, an art gallery, and musical theater and jazz performances. Annapolis is home to the Annapolis Opera, the Annapolis Symphony Orchestra, and the Ballet Theater of Maryland.

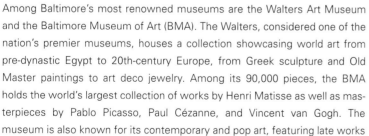

Among Baltimore's most renowned museums are the Walters Art Museum and the Baltimore Museum of Art (BMA). The Walters, considered one of the nation's premier museums, houses a collection showcasing world art from pre-dynastic Egypt to 20th-century Europe, from Greek sculpture and Old Master paintings to art deco jewelry. Among its 90,000 pieces, the BMA holds the world's largest collection of works by Henri Matisse as well as masterpieces by Pablo Picasso, Paul Cézanne, and Vincent van Gogh. The museum is also known for its contemporary and pop art, featuring late works

In Southern Maryland, the Black Box Theatre at the Indian Head Center for the Arts in Indian Head presents a variety of performing artists in an intimate, 80-seat venue. Marbury's Mattawoman Creek Art Center showcases visual arts in a lovely waterfront setting.

Playing Outdoors: Recreation and Spectator Sports

Leisure activities abound in Maryland, where one is never far from a park, river, beach, or mountaintop for all manner of outdoor recreation. The state has limitless options for those who seek active recreation or prefer to enjoy sports from the stands.

In the Capital Region are the Olney Theatre Center for the Arts in Olney; Silver Spring Stage, in Silver Spring; and in Bethesda, the Round House Theatre and the Strathmore. The latter offers art exhibitions, concerts, and literary lectures and events in the Mansion at Strathmore, the Music Center at Strathmore, and on the center's 11-acre grounds. The Weinberg Center for the Arts, a theater built in 1926 and owned by the city of Frederick, offers dramatic, musical, artistic, and educational programs.

Western Maryland has a vibrant arts scene. The Maryland Symphony, a professional orchestra, performs in the historic and restored 1915 Maryland Theatre in downtown Hagerstown. The city of Cumberland is home to the Saville Gallery, showcasing local, regional, and national artists, and to the Cumberland and New Embassy theaters offering Broadway plays and musicals.

On the Eastern Shore, the Avalon Theatre in Easton presents performances and events as varied as symphony, bluegrass, comedy, and art festivals. In Rock Hall, the Mainstay cultural and artistic center is located in a century-old building and serves up jazz, blues, classical, and folk concerts.

Recreational adventures in Central Maryland include everything from kayak fishing in Baltimore's Canton Waterfront Park to rafting on the world's only

mountain-top whitewater course at the new Adventure Sports Center International (ASCI) in McHenry. ASCI offers different levels of rafting and kayaking either with a guide or on one's own. With its naval history, it comes as no surprise that Annapolis is considered the nation's sailing capital. For golf enthusiasts, there is the Waverly Woods Golf Club in Marriottville, named one of the top 10 courses in the mid-Atlantic by *Golf Magazine*, and the Pete Dye–designed Bulle Rock course in Havre de Grace, host of the LPGA Championship.

The Capital Region's courses include Frederick Golf Course in Frederick, the Blue Mash Golf Course in Laytonsville, and the Congressional Country Club in Bethesda, the new home of the Constellation Energy Senior Players Championship. Other recreational activities include trout fishing in Cunningham Falls State Park in Thurmont, camping in the Catoctin Mountains, and hiking and biking on the region's numerous trails.

The mountainous Western Maryland region is home to the state's only ski resort, Wisp Resort in McHenry in the Deep Creek Lake area. The resort also offers snowboarding and tubing. Deep Creek Lake abounds in trout, bass, and walleye, while the area's rivers offer opportunities for flyfishing, whitewater rafting, and kayaking. Hikers explore the Appalachian Trail, while golfers test their skills at Rocky Gap Lodge and Golf Resort in Cumberland, the only Jack Nicklaus Signature Course in Maryland.

The Eastern Shore is famous for the resort town of Ocean City, which boasts one of the top East Coast beaches for swimming and other water sports. Sandy Point State Park has a beach along the Chesapeake Bay, while Chesapeake Beach offers a quieter getaway for swimming and sunbathing enthusiasts. For scenic hiking there is Tuckahoe State Park, while Assateague Island State Park offers a chance to see its famous wild ponies.

In Southern Maryland, Smallwood State Park and St. Mary's River State Park are excellent spots for bass fishing, while would-be paleontologists can hunt for fossils on a hike through Calvert Cliffs State Park.

When it comes to spectator sports, Maryland scores big. The NFL Baltimore Ravens, who won the Super Bowl in 2001, make their home at M&T Bank Stadium. Completed in 1998, the stadium seats 71,008. Oriole Park at Camden Yards, home of the Baltimore Orioles, set the standard for new Major League Baseball parks when it opened in 1992. Oriole Park's retro design blends elements of classic ballparks such as Fenway in Boston and Wrigley Field in Chicago. The Baltimore Blast brought the excitement of indoor soccer to Baltimore in 1980. The team, playing in the 1st Mariner Arena, won the Major Indoor Soccer League Championship in 1984, 2003, 2004, 2006, and 2008. Minor League Baseball thrives in Maryland with teams playing across the state, including the Bowie Baysox, a Class AA affiliate of the Orioles; the Frederick Keys and the Delmarva Shorebirds, both Class A Orioles affiliates; and the Aberdeen IronBirds, a Class A, short-season Orioles affiliate which plays at Ripken Stadium, named for Aberdeen native and Orioles legend Cal Ripken Jr. Other teams include the Hagerstown Suns, a Class A Washington Nationals affiliate, and the new kids on the block, the Southern Maryland Blue Crabs of Waldorf. Lacrosse fans follow the Washington Bayhawks and can learn about the sport at the Lacrosse Museum and National Hall of Fame in Baltimore, which showcases photographs, vintage equipment and uniforms, trophies, and memorabilia. Fans of Thoroughbred racing flock to Pimlico Race Course in Baltimore, home of the Preakness Stakes, the second jewel of the Triple Crown and Maryland's biggest single-day sporting event.

Pleasurable Pursuits: Shopping, Dining, and Entertainment

With a history like Maryland's, it is not surprising that the state is a favorite destination for lovers of antiques. The state's agricultural background also makes it a leading wine producer, and wine tours are a popular outing. From big-city multiuse complexes to Main Street and from downtown Baltimore to the shorelines and the mountains, the state offers something for everyone.

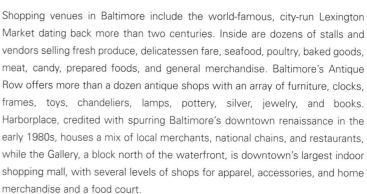

Shopping venues in Baltimore include the world-famous, city-run Lexington Market dating back more than two centuries. Inside are dozens of stalls and vendors selling fresh produce, delicatessen fare, seafood, poultry, baked goods, meat, candy, prepared foods, and general merchandise. Baltimore's Antique Row offers more than a dozen antique shops with an array of furniture, clocks, frames, toys, chandeliers, lamps, pottery, silver, jewelry, and books. Harborplace, credited with spurring Baltimore's downtown renaissance in the early 1980s, houses a mix of local merchants, national chains, and restaurants, while the Gallery, a block north of the waterfront, is downtown's largest indoor shopping mall, with several levels of shops for apparel, accessories, and home merchandise and a food court.

Another popular shopping center in Central Maryland is Arundel Mills, close to Baltimore/Washington International Thurgood Marshall Airport in Anne Arundel County. It bills itself as part discount mall, part lifestyle center, with entertainment that ranges from movies to restaurants to a medieval-themed dinner theater. In Howard County, Historic Savage Mill, located in an historic complex of buildings once used as a textile mill, is now home to antique shops, home furnishing stores, artist studios, specialty shops, and restaurants. Running from the north of Baltimore along I-83 into Pennsylvania is the Mason-Dixon Wine Trail leading to eight wineries, half of them in Maryland.

Located on Baltimore's Inner Harbor are three of the city's most popular attractions. The National Aquarium in Baltimore sets the standard by which other aquariums are measured, with its more than 16,000 aquatic residents and its fascinating exhibits. At the Maryland Science Center, visitors can dig for fossils beneath enormous dinosaurs; touch a mini tornado form; and look inside the cells of the heart, brain, and bones. The center also is home to an IMAX Theater and the Davis Planetarium. Just north of the harbor is Port Discovery, Baltimore's children's museum, offering three floors of permanent and rotating interactive exhibits. A 10-minute drive north from the harbor in Druid Hill Park is the Maryland Zoo, home to more than 1,500 birds, mammals, amphibians, and reptiles housed in settings that mimic their native habitats.

FREDERICK

● Frederick

MONTGOMERY

● Rockville

Upper Marlboro
●

PRINCE
GEORGE'S

0   12.5   25   50   Miles

Frederick County

Picturesque Frederick County, Maryland—nestled along the foothills of the Appalachian mountains and home to such historical notables as Francis Scott Key, Barbara Fritchie, and Governor Thomas Johnson—provides fertile ground for innovation, creativity, and opportunity for residents and business owners alike.

FREDERICK COUNTY, MARYLAND
OFFICE OF
ECONOMIC
DEVELOPMENT

Frederick is Maryland's largest county (663 square miles) and is strategically located within an hour of two major metropolitan areas, Washington, D.C., and Baltimore, Maryland. A culturally rich heritage, thriving arts community, beautiful countryside, and an enviable quality of life complement the county's diverse economic base and vibrant business climate.

Entrepreneurial Spirit

The business sector is growing in Frederick County; the number of companies opening shop has increased 15 percent in the last five years—that is more than 800 new businesses representing 10,000 jobs. More than 95 percent of local companies are considered small businesses, and for them Frederick County offers the Entrepreneur

Support Network, which provides a wide range of free services; the Frederick Innovative Technology Center, a business incubator program; and assistance from the Small Business Development Center. Industry-wise, four primary business sectors are targeted: bioscience, advanced technology, manufacturing, and agriculture. An economic engine that helps drive Frederick County's success is Fort Detrick, a medical research and biological defense installation where more than 8,000 workers are employed. Billions of dollars in construction funds will be invested in the base during the next decade as the National Interagency Biodefense Campus is established.

Magnificent Municipalities

The City of Frederick, a thriving business base and Great American Main Street community, is home to the aforementioned Fort Detrick as well as several international firms including BP Solar, MedImmune, the National Cancer Institute, and Wells Fargo. Frederick also has an established reputation as an "Arts City." This is due in part to the large number of performance-arts companies and venues that feature a wide variety of live entertainment. Frederick's award-winning Carroll Creek Park further enhances a thriving downtown and serves as a model for economic revitalization efforts nationwide. There are 12 incorporated municipalities in Frederick County, each with its own rich historic, cultural, and economic identity.

Top-shelf Education

Frederick County is home to top-notch educational programs and institutions, including a nationally recognized public school system, three esteemed colleges, and several superb private and special-education schools. For many years, students in the Frederick County Public School System have surpassed the national average on their SATs, and the system has been a recipient of the U.S. Department of Education's prestigious National Blue Ribbon Schools of Excellence Award. The local graduation rate is an astounding 96 percent, while the dropout rate of .73 percent is the lowest in Maryland. A comprehensive array of higher education options is offered by three local colleges: Hood College, Mount St. Mary's University, and Frederick Community College.

National History

Settlement began in history-rich Frederick County in the 1730s. The county was the site of perhaps the first open defiance of British rule serving as a prelude to the Revolutionary War. The local circuit court repudiated the unpopular Stamp Act, thus fueling the fire of national revolt. Later, Frederick County was at the crossroads of America's Civil War, serving as the site of the Battle of South Mountain and the Battle of Monocacy, which in essence saved Washington, D.C., from a strong Confederate attack. Local towns were occupied by troops from both sides in the days before the internationally known, nearby battles of Antietam and Gettysburg. Following these deadly skirmishes, the county became a major hospital center; today the story of care and compassion in the wake of battle is told at the National Museum of Civil War Medicine in downtown Frederick. Other prominent national sites include Camp David, the Mother Seton Shrine, Francis Scott Key's grave and monument, the Barbara Fritchie house, and the Monocacy National Battlefield.

On the Horizon

Great business opportunities lie ahead for Frederick County, especially with the expansion of Fort Detrick. The bioscience and advanced-technology fields are booming throughout the state and nation, and Frederick County is prepared to capitalize on this trend and grow and prosper.

Innovation, creativity, and opportunity are abundant assets in this beautiful, thriving county, whose slogan is "no matter what your perspective, it all points to Frederick, Maryland." *For further information, visit www.discoverfrederickmd.com.*

Opposite page, clockwise from top left: A wonderful recreational and cultural resource, Downtown Frederick's Carroll Creek Park also serves as an economic development catalyst, offering office and commercial/retail space and residential units. Maryland's second-largest city, Frederick is a treasure trove of historic sites, museums, art galleries, specialty shops, and restaurants. Much of Frederick County is rolling farmland with open pastureland and bountiful orchards. This page, left to right: The Weinberg Center for the Arts serves as the hub for the Frederick County arts and entertainment community. During winter, Frederick County becomes an outdoor wonderland.

Montgomery County

Montgomery County is a thriving center of commerce as well as a great place to live and to work. In addition to being Maryland's most populous jurisdiction, it is one of the nation's most affluent counties and a major contributor to jobs in the state.

Montgomery County enjoys a rich history. The county was formed in 1776 by the splitting of Frederick County. In 1791 portions of Montgomery County, including Georgetown, were ceded to form the new District of Columbia, along with portions of Prince George's County, as well as parts of Virginia that were later returned to Virginia.

Consequently, the county borders Washington, D.C., and is located roughly 30 miles southwest of Baltimore. Montgomery County's ideal location makes it convenient to just about anywhere in the world. It also provides quick access to major interstate highways and rail transportation hubs and three major airports, including Baltimore/Washington International Thurgood Marshall Airport, Dulles

International Airport, and Ronald Reagan Washington National Airport. Well-maintained interstate highways offer easy access to significant markets in the north and south.

Montgomery County is the heart of Maryland's biotechnology community, which ranks third-largest in the nation. Over 200 biotech companies and industry leaders such as Human Genome Sciences and MedImmune/AstraZeneca are located in the county.

The county is home to or near a wealth of federal research and regulatory agencies, including the Food and Drug Administration, the National Aeronautics and Space Administration, the National Institute of Standards and Technology, the National Institutes of Health, the National Oceanic and Atmospheric Administration, the

Nuclear Regulatory Commission, the U.S. Department of Defense, and the U.S. Department of Energy.

Montgomery County's 32,400 businesses employ more than 386,000 workers in areas including information technology, telecommunications, biotechnology, software development, aerospace engineering, and various professional services. Montgomery County is a place for dynamic companies, and that is why it is headquarters to a number of companies, including several Fortune 500 companies such as American Capital Strategies, Coventry Health Care, Discovery Communications, LLC, GEICO, Host Hotels and Resorts, Hughes Network Systems, Lockheed Martin, Marriott International Corporation, and United Therapeutics.

The county is also home to world-famous educational and research organizations, including the Johns Hopkins University's Montgomery County campus, the Center for Advanced Research in Biotechnology, the Institute for Genomic Research, and the Universities at Shady Grove. Not surprisingly, Montgomery County also boasts the highest percentage (29.2 percent) of residents over 25 years old who hold an advanced degree.

But Montgomery County is not all work and no play. One-third of the county is open space, including the 93,000-acre Agricultural Reserve and more than 28,000

acres of parkland and green space. Five large regional parks complement more than 350 other parks, including one state park, two national parks, and numerous local and neighborhood parks featuring a combined 636 acres of lakes.

Montgomery County residents have access to nine public golf courses, 22 private golf courses, and more than a dozen country clubs, including the Tournament Players Club at Avenel. Swimming is available at nine public pools and 50 private community pools. Public and private tennis courts are available throughout the county. Year-round amateur and professional sports available in the area include football, baseball, tennis, hockey, soccer, and lacrosse, as well as Thoroughbred racing.

The county is home to several world-class cultural institutions. Strathmore Performing Arts Center houses a 1,978-seat concert hall, which welcomes world-renowned performers, and includes a state-of-the-art education center. The American Film Institute's Silver Theatre and the Round House Theatre's Black Box are leading the arts revival in Silver Spring, and the new Bethesda Theatre now brings Broadway-caliber shows to the county. In addition, a variety of visual, performing, and literary arts are coordinated by the Montgomery County Arts Council.

The county is proud of its efforts to preserve its rich and valuable farmland. Agricultural activities occupy about one-third of Montgomery County's land area, and the county's diverse agricultural industry—577 farms and 350 horticultural enterprises—produces more than $251 million in economic contribution and employs more than 10,000 residents.

Montgomery County combines abundant resources for the knowledge economy and a richly diverse and educated population with an excellent quality of life. The county is poised for even greater success in the future. *For further information, visit www.SmartMontgomery.com.*

Opposite page, clockwise from top left: One-third of Montgomery County is open space, including the 93,000-acre Agricultural Reserve and more than 28,000 acres of parkland and green space. The Montgomery County Conference Center features more than 35,000 square feet of meeting and exhibit space, including a 130-seat amphitheater. The Rockville Innovation Center is one of five business and technology incubators that make up the county's Business Innovation Network, which offers the critical combination of highly flexible, modern office and laboratory space and business support services to emerging start-up companies. This page: Strathmore Performing Arts Center houses a 1,978-seat concert hall, which welcomes world-renowned performers, and includes a state-of-the-art education center.

Prince George's County

Prince George's County is not just a destination—it is a vibrant, livable community. The county is rich in attractions, culture, history, and diversity and is considered to be a driving force for economic development in the mid-Atlantic region. It is also one of the fastest-growing and most prosperous places in the United States. As the second-wealthiest county in Maryland, and the nation's wealthiest minority-majority county with a highly educated workforce, and with a population that has been booming for more than 30 years, it has the resources and leadership essential to achieve economic success.

The location of Prince George's, which has a common border with Washington, D.C., comes with a number of constant key advantages. All major modes of transportation are within or near the county, including two international airports, one national airport, passenger rail service, major freight carriers, and bus and rail commuter service. Highway access is beyond exceptional, which makes it a perfect location for a Foreign Trade Zone. In 2007 Prince George's County was granted a boundary modification of Foreign Trade Zone #63 (FTZ #63), which had been dormant for more than 25 years. The modification created a $65 million project (Steeplechase 95), that includes approximately one million square feet of business space, including 16 acres slated for retail. Therefore, the zone has become another economic engine for the county.

The Steeplechase 95 International Business Park is located within FTZ #63. It has also been designated as an Enterprise Zone and State Priority Funding Area. Therefore, businesses can realize a number of tax benefits. The Foreign Trade Zone status on the industrial portion of the property allows customs duty savings for companies engaged in international trade. The Foreign Trade Zone designation will help foreign companies forge partnerships with U.S. businesses and support the distribution of products along the entire Atlantic Coast. Real estate and employment tax credits are also available to companies locating in the development through the Enterprise Zone program.

The county is also an intellectual center with its many colleges and universities, several of which offer research and workforce partnerships with the private sector. The largest is the University of Maryland at College Park, a comprehensive research institution that counts two Nobel Prize winners among its staff. Flanking the University of Maryland is M Square, which is slated to become the largest research park in the state of Maryland and one of the largest in the country.

One major draw to the county is its attractions. The county has more than 26,000 acres of parkland, operated by the Maryland National-Capital Park and Planning Commission. The acreage includes parks, picnic areas, athletic fields, historic sites, museums, community centers, recreation facilities, and a large percentage of land that has been left undeveloped to serve as green buffers and to provide natural open spaces. Visitors and residents of Prince George's County can cheer for the NFL's Washington Redskins at FedEx Field; ride the tallest spinning rapids ride in the mid-Atlantic at Six Flags America, which has more than 100 rides, slides, shows, and attractions; and enjoy the arts at the Clarice Smith Performing Arts Center, among many other cultural facilities. Other attractions include NASA/Goddard

Space Flight Center, the National Archives at College Park, Andrew's Air Force Base, and the U.S.D.A.'s Agricultural Research Center.

Prince George's County is also making a name for itself in the world of retail, much of which is being planned as a part of mixed-use developments. Many new homes in the county are part of these integrated communities. Among the developments is the estimated $2 billion National Harbor, a spectacular 350-acre project on the Potomac River that includes the largest hotel and convention center on the Eastern Seaboard, offices, high-end retail shops, timeshares, and 2,500 residences. The Gaylord National Hotel & Convention Center, the world's fourth-largest hotel, opened its doors at the National Harbor in 2008. Now visitors can take a water taxi from Alexandria, Mount Vernon, and Washington directly to the riverfront community, the newest destination in the mid-Atlantic region.

With a focus on the future, Prince George's County is making a name for itself in the Washington, D.C., area and the world as an excellent place to live, work, play, and do business. *For further information, visit www.co.pg.md.us.*

Opposite page, top to bottom: National Harbor offers 350 acres of shopping, dining, entertainment, and office and residential space on the shores of the Potomac River. The Prince George's County Administration Building houses the County Executive, the County Council, and the Maryland National-Capital Park and Planning Commission offices. This page: FedEx Field is the home of the NFL's Washington Redskins.

61

Central Maryland

BALTIMORE CITY AND ANNE ARUNDEL, BALTIMORE, CARROLL, CECIL, HARFORD, AND HOWARD COUNTIES

The hub of Maryland, this region is home to both the state capital, Annapolis, and to the great city of Baltimore. Its strategic location and its comprehensive transportation system of ports, highways, airports, and railroads offer easy access to Washington, D.C., and Philadelphia. This accounts for the presence of large industrial and commercial centers, major corporations, aerospace and defense facilities, and government agencies. But it is not just for business that people come to Central Maryland. They are drawn by the area's historic sights, its five Arts and Entertainment Districts, its abundant and varied recreational offerings, and its world-class museums, performing arts, and sports venues. From its quaint fishing villages and charming country towns to its exciting urban cities, Central Maryland has something for everyone.

CARROLL

Westminster

CECIL

Elkton

HARFORD

BALTIMORE

Bel Air

Towson

Baltimore
City

HOWARD

Ellicott City

ANNE
ARUNDEL

Annapolis

0   12.5   25   50 Miles

Anne Arundel County

Anne Arundel County has been called the Land of Pleasant Living and for good reason. The one-half million county residents enjoy more than 500 miles of Chesapeake Bay shoreline and over 60,000 acres of protected green space and agricultural land. The county is also known for being the home of the U.S. Naval Academy and some of the state's most charming sights.

The Land of Pleasant Living

The historic City of Annapolis, located in Anne Arundel County overlooking the Severn River, is still reminiscent of the booming 18th-century seaport it once was. The cozy brick streets in the downtown Annapolis district lead past buildings with architecture that has stood for more than 300 years. The Maryland State House, for example, is one of the oldest state capitol buildings still in legislative use in the United States.

Many boating enthusiasts, sail or power, choose the county for their home because of its water access. Nature lovers appreciate the more than 70 parks in the county, which include wetlands sanctuaries, biking and hiking trails, fishing spots, boat rentals, and historic sites. Surrounded by nature at its best, county residents can also enjoy the culture and amenities of the many local cultural organizations, including the Maryland Hall—which houses the Annapolis Opera, the Annapolis Symphony Orchestra, and the Ballet Theater of Annapolis—and the Chesapeake Center for the Performing Arts.

Attracting Businesses and Residents

Businesses and families are drawn to Anne Arundel County for its strategic location in the Baltimore–Washington, D.C., corridor, the fourth-largest marketplace in the country with a population of eight million. Anne Arundel County's AAA bond rating from Standard & Poor's and a "positive" outlook from Moody's Investors Service

and Fitch Ratings reflect the county's strong economy and above-average wealth statistics. The investment made in the county by its world-class businesses has contributed to this strong economic base.

Anne Arundel County is a major business hub, and few areas can match its transportation infrastructure. Three international airports are located in the region, including Baltimore/Washington International Thurgood Marshall Airport (BWI Marshall) in Anne Arundel County. The county also has an extensive commercial and commuter rail system; close proximity to the Port of Baltimore, one of the country's largest deepwater ports; and access to major interstate highways, making it possible for distribution operations in the county to reach one-third of the U.S. market overnight.

Anne Arundel County has a labor pool with one of the highest concentrations of scientists and engineers in the country. With over 30 top-flight colleges and universities in the region, businesses in Anne Arundel County are in an ideal position to capture a young, educated workforce. A superior quality of life helps attract and retain a highly skilled workforce. Once families locate in the area, they are reluctant to leave the excellent school systems, health care access, and recreational opportunities on the Chesapeake Bay that Anne Arundel County affords.

Representing Diverse Industries

Anne Arundel County has a diverse business community, with a strong presence in both the private and the public sectors. Leaders in aerospace and defense, manufacturing, health care, and technology have chosen Anne Arundel County for their headquarters and regional offices. The National Security Agency (NSA)

is located at Fort George G. Meade in Anne Arundel County. Within the gates of Fort Meade, the U.S. Department of Defense employs an estimated 36,000 people. Top national defense contractors like Northrop Grumman, General Dynamics, Booz Allen Hamilton, Boeing, Computer Sciences Corporation, and Lockheed Martin have locations in Anne Arundel County to be near NSA and other defense agencies located in nearby Washington, D.C. Fort Meade and the surrounding area are experiencing rapid growth as a result of the Defense Base Closure and Realignment Commission (BRAC) process of consolidation, which is expected to bring an estimated 22,000 jobs to the region.

Anne Arundel County also has a strong technology base that continues to grow. To encourage technology growth, the Chesapeake Innovation Center (CIC), the county's early-stage business incubator, nurtures emerging technology companies. The CIC's unique TechBridge program connects innovative technology companies with the CIC Partners—Northrop Grumman, ARINC, Boeing, and the National Security Agency.

Anne Arundel County has something for everyone. Each year, more businesses, new residents, and scores of visitors learn what locals have known for decades— that Anne Arundel County is a great place to do business, a great place to live, and a great place to visit.

For further information, visit www.aacounty.org.

Opposite page, top: The historic City of Annapolis, reminiscent of the 18th-century seaport town it once was, has the oldest state capitol building still in legislative use. Opposite page, bottom: Graduation ceremonies at the U.S. Naval Academy include the traditional hat toss. This page, left: Southwest Airlines is the leading carrier at the Baltimore/Washington International Thurgood Marshall Airport in Anne Arundel County. This page, right: Thomas Point Lighthouse provides a scenic backdrop for the many sailing enthusiasts in Annapolis.

Baltimore City

Baltimore City is located 38 miles north of the U.S. capital, Washington, D.C., and 95 miles south of Philadelphia. Among U.S. cities, it ranks 18th in population. Baltimore offers a unique quality of life, driven by a waterfront location, with beaches and mountains nearby. Baltimore regularly ranks among the best cities in the country when it comes to hospitals, art destinations, or places to live.

Baltimore is a big city with small-town neighborhoods. Ask anyone in Baltimore, "What makes our city special?" The answer heard time and time again is "the people and the neighborhoods." Baltimore has its share of historic and popular landmarks; but to its residents, the city is defined by an intricate set of boundaries that collectively create its 225-plus unique neighborhoods. Residents enjoy the world-class amenities as well as locally owned neighborhood businesses. Whether charming or eclectic, with the feel of suburbia or the fast pace of downtown life, Baltimore's diverse communities are one of its greatest assets.

Whether strolling the world-famous Inner Harbor; attending the Preakness, the second jewel in horse racing's Triple Crown, or a Ravens or Orioles game; or visiting one of the dynamic museums, there is much to do in Baltimore City. Part of America's heritage was born in Baltimore—the city played a crucial role in the War of 1812 when soldiers, stationed at Fort McHenry, successfully held off a British attack on Baltimore. That victory for Baltimore was commemorated in a poem by Francis Scott Key, whose words became the lyrics of the U.S. national anthem.

Art lovers should be sure to stop at the Baltimore Museum of Art, Maryland's largest art museum; the American Visionary Art Museum, which displays original works of art created by self-taught artists; and the Walters Art Museum, which proudly boasts 55 centuries of art from around the world. The Reginald F. Lewis Museum of Maryland African American History and Culture, the National

KENT

Chestertown

QUEEN
ANNE'S

Centreville

Denton

Easton

TALBOT   CAROLINE

Cambridge

DORCHESTER

WICOMICO

Salisbury

Princess Anne   WORCESTER

SOMERSET   Snow Hill

0   12.5   25   50   Miles

79

Paul Zapp

Caroline County

Tucked away in the heartland of Maryland's Eastern Shore sits Caroline County, an area rich in heritage and nature's bountiful resources. Caroline is an ideal destination for outdoor enthusiasts, history connoisseurs, and those who appreciate the simple charm of small-town living.

The Great Outdoors: A Scenic Chesapeake Landscape

Endless outdoor opportunities exist within the more than 8,000 acres of state parks, nature preserves, and trails of Caroline County. Adkins Arboretum boasts 400 acres of streams, woodlands, wetlands, and meadows brimming with the diverse flora and fauna native to the Delmarva Peninsula. Martinak and Tuckahoe state parks allow for fishing, camping, picnicking, and bird-watching. Park-going anglers may enjoy the opportunity to reel in bass, sunfish, perch, and catfish from the Tuckahoe and Choptank rivers and Watts Creek. With miles of winding country roads weaving through its quaint, Chesapeake towns, Caroline County provides the perfect backdrop for cycling or a leisurely Sunday drive.

Recreation Opportunities

Though the county is landlocked, the Marshyhope, Tuckahoe, and Choptank rivers flow through Caroline's fertile Chesapeake farmland, making the county a haven for those seeking adventures on the water. More than 15 public-access points provide access to those who wish to explore the pristine watershed of the Chesapeake Bay.

For those seeking adventure in the sky, Highland Aerosports in Ridgely offers hang-gliding lessons. Newcomers can get a bird's-eye view of Caroline County, soaring in tandem flight at altitudes as high as 10,000 feet. The experienced glider can catch a solo aerotow skyward to glide with the geese that spangle in the autumn Chesapeake sky on their annual southward migration.

Caroline County also offers sportsmen an array of clay-shooting courses, preserves, and retreats such as Bridgetown Manor, a three-story manor house in Henderson with over 25,000 acres of prime hunting properties on the Eastern Shore.

Heritage and History

The stunning landscapes that make up Caroline County are steeped in a resonant history. Underground Railroad pathways traversed by Harriet Tubman and Frederick Douglass weave through the county. A self-guided driving tour called "Finding a Way to Freedom" provides a trip back in time to explore the many lesser-known sites. Freedom seekers found assistance and shelter in Caroline County as they traveled along the Underground Railroad to points north. Caroline County is also unique in that it has existed for over 300 years dependent solely on an agriculturally based economy. Several museums and landmarks such as the Mason-Dixon Line, the Museum of Rural Life, Linchester Mill, and the Choptank River Heritage Center tell stories of early American rural life and highlight Caroline County's agricultural history.

Preserving the Past for the Future

Although Caroline County has an abundant history, her eyes are on the future. A dynamic community is working to preserve the invaluable history and heritage of the area. The Caroline County Historical Society has restored numerous remarkable buildings, including the James H. Webb Log Cabin and the Linchester Mill. The Caroline Economic Development Corporation manages redevelopment and revitalization efforts within the county, creating jobs within the community and strengthening industry. The Denton Development Corporation is currently involved in numerous projects, including the development of an Arts and Entertainment District and the redevelopment of the waterfront on the Choptank River that will include a heritage visitors' center and public riverfront facilities. Recognizing the immeasurable value of the arts, the Caroline County Council of Arts works to ensure that an abundance of art performances are available to residents, including weekly concerts and a performing-

arts series. The Chesapeake Culinary Center, a nonprofit and community-driven organization, offers adults and youth educational programs in the culinary arts.

Unmatched Quality of Life

Caroline County offers a matchless quality of life, serving visitors and residents an impressive selection of gourmet culinary offerings. The Lily Pad Café, an epicurean bistro located in Denton, gives visitors the opportunity to savor a delectable meal in a historic 1883 schoolhouse. A mouth-watering fusion of Irish and American foods, properly-poured Guinness, live music, and a friendly ambience can all be found at the Market Street Public House in the heart of Denton. The baseball-themed Batter Up Restaurant in Ridgely serves up classic 1950s-style diner dishes, including old-fashioned patty melts and milkshakes. Harry's at the Goldsborough House in Greensboro features an extensive and elegant menu prepared by widely acclaimed chefs. This Greensboro gem also serves as a bed-and-breakfast. For a tranquil evening overlooking the Choptank River in Denton, relax at the Bryant-Todd House Inn with luxurious, European style accommodations.

Caroline County also provides residents with year-round festivals and events. From the Caroline County Fair, Holiday Parades, Strawberry Festival, and Denton's Spring Gala to Summerfest and the annual Wheat Threshing, Steam & Gas Engine Show, an endless stream of exciting events keeps Caroline's calendars full. Fans of jousting, Maryland's official state sport, can even watch riders compete at the annual Ridgely Jousting Tournament. There is something for everyone here. With its beautiful natural resources, genuine people, scenic Chesapeake landscape, and intriguing history, Caroline County is the quintessential place to visit, explore, work, play, and call home. *For details, visit www.tourcaroline.com.*

Dorchester County

Dorchester County, Maryland, is just a short drive from many large cities, but miles apart in attitude. In an increasingly homogenized society where highways go past the same fast-food stops and gas stations, towns across the country look identical. But Dorchester County is quite a refreshing change.

While remaining true to its roots, the county is also positioned to compete in the 21st century. Boasting 1,700 miles of shoreline, Dorchester County has sought to preserve the natural resources long enjoyed by generations, including the early Native Americans. This unspoiled region offers opportunities to bird-watch, cycle, kayak, fish, golf, and more.

Dorchester County also has a rich national history. It is the birthplace of Harriet Tubman, who was born a slave and spent her adult life as a conductor on the Underground Railroad, guiding slaves northward to freedom. Dorchester County offers many opportunities to experience the places that are significant to this early Civil Rights pioneer and Underground Railroad hero.

Home to 790 businesses, Dorchester County continues to diversify to create a business environment conducive to prosperous economic growth. To that end, the county plans to develop the new Business and Technology Park, which will focus on technology-related industry sectors, to serve the county and the region. The new park will support the county's vision of maintaining a diverse industry base that includes agriculture, aquaculture, manufacturing, and technology businesses, where all industry sectors will fuel future economic growth. The new technology park will be the third industrial park in the county. The first was the Chesapeake Industrial Park, developed in the City of Cambridge in the mid 1980s. Shortly thereafter, a second park was developed in the northern part of the county in the town of Hurlock. A key component of the new technology park will be the

county's first-ever business incubator, which will provide temporary space for innovative aspiring entrepreneurs.

Businesses located in Dorchester County may be eligible for a number of local, state, and federal economic development incentive programs such as workforce training assistance, business tax credits, and low-interest loans. With Dorchester County's close proximity to Washington, D.C., the Federal HUBZone status is one of the county's important attributes, providing procurement opportunities for qualified small businesses that provide products and services to the federal government. The county's economic development staff assists existing and relocating businesses determine which programs they qualify for and help them navigate through the application process.

By seamlessly partnering with education, county and regional businesses, and local municipalities, the county stands to achieve an amazing economic transformation.

Dorchester County is truly fertile ground for new major business investment, entrepreneurship start-up opportunities, and expansion projects for existing businesses.

The City of Cambridge, which is the county's largest municipality and is also the county seat, is experiencing a major revitalization of its downtown business district. Additionally, the new Hyatt Regency Chesapeake Bay Golf Resort, Spa and Marina, also located in Cambridge, has yielded positive returns and given the county greater exposure as a tourist destination. The arts have long been an important part of Dorchester County, and the Arts and Entertainment District in historic downtown Cambridge offers opportunities to stop at a studio and chat with an artist, take in a gallery exhibit, and view unique artwork created locally.

County residents treasure the unique Chesapeake Bay traditions and gracious living of Maryland's Eastern Shore. One may savor fresh seafood in a fine or casual dining atmosphere, enjoying local cuisine with a modern infusion and warm hospitality riverside, downtown, or in a remote village. Visitors and local residents may experience Dorchester's heritage in the beautiful architecture of its churches, and explore some of the country's oldest cemeteries.

Dorchester County is a place that celebrates its love of history. It is an excellent location for business expansion or relocation. Now more than ever, this is a thrilling time to be in Dorchester County. Local art truly flourishes; food and drink speak new languages; business booms. Dorchester County welcomes first-time and returning visitors to enjoy the area and to discover why Dorchester County is the perfect place for a home or business.

For further information, visit www.docogonet.com.

Opposite page, clockwise from top left: The annual Taste of Cambridge draws crowds to the historic downtown area from around the Eastern Shore and beyond for a street festival featuring a crab cook-off, crab-picking contests, music, and more. One of Maryland's few deepwater ports, Cambridge draws all manner of boats, from skipjacks and schooners to cruise ships and motorboats. Chesapeake College, a community college located in Wye Mills, also offers a satellite campus in Cambridge. This page, left to right: Blackwater National Wildlife Refuge on Maryland's Eastern Shore is a bird watcher's paradise; its woodlands house more than 85 species of birds. A Few of My Favorite Things, a quaint Cambridge shop, features a range of gourmet items. Downtown Cambridge offers unique shops and restaurants, plus great places to relax.

Kent County

Every county in the nation believes that it is an ideal place to live, work, and play; however, Kent County, Maryland, has the proof. Kent County was voted the "Best Place to Live in Rural America" by *The Progressive Farmer* magazine. That award is all the more impressive considering that Kent County is the smallest county by population, and the second-smallest by land mass, in Maryland.

Knowing that many of the traditions of this great nation were formed in and around Kent County is a source of great pride. A prime example of this heritage is represented by Washington College. Located in the county seat of Chestertown, Washington College was the first college founded (in 1782) in the newly formed United States of America. This renowned liberal arts school of 1,500 students, which is also the county's second-largest employer, has worked closely with county businesses to provide innovative means to train and motivate future businesspeople, many who remain in the area after graduation. To have such a center of higher learning locally clearly establishes a base of culture and knowledge in the county.

Kent County is serious about its quality of life. County residents highly prize driving on well-maintained roads where they enjoy a delightful view of over 178,000 acres of prime Maryland farmland and where the roads carry them past 268 miles of shoreline and safely lead them through five delightful towns steeped in centuries of history. The Eastern Neck National Wildlife Refuge provides a 2,285-acre nature reserve, and the waterways and local heritage are made into living experiences for more than 10,000 students of all ages every year on the decks of the 1768-reproduction sailing schooner *Sultana*.

Tens of thousands of tourists visit the county and participate in such annual events as the Chestertown Tea Party, a reenactment of a local 1770s tea tax rebellion.

KENT COUNTY COURTHOUSE

103

Additional activities include an annual wildlife show, Sultana Downrigging, the Rock Fish Tournament, a New Year's Eve celebration, and the Kent County Fair.

In order to maintain the rural character of the county, and leverage the existing agricultural land usage, the county's Economic Development Office has undertaken a major vineyard expansion effort. This effort extends throughout the tri-county region and the entire Eastern Shore of Maryland, and it is expected that these efforts will substantially increase the number of regional vineyards and ultimately

result in the establishment of a string of wineries, creating a tourism destination that will benefit the entire region.

The county utilizes its unique geographic characteristics, historic building availability, and cultural heritages to attract film industry professionals. It maintains an inventory of several hundred potential film locations on its Web site at www.kentcounty.com/bus/film.php. The program is aimed at assisting the Maryland Film Office of the Maryland Department of Business and Economic Development and national and international film industry location specialists in finding ideal movie and commercial locations quickly and easily. Residents throughout the county have willingly placed their properties in this inventory and anxiously await the day that they can see their site in the movies.

Close proximity to quality medical facilities is crucial to any community, and the Chester River Health System fills that requirement with high honors. This health system is currently the largest employer in the county and attracts numerous medical professionals to a number of subspecialty office locations. The health system's partnership with the University of Maryland Medical System has brought distinct benefits to the partnership and has offered collaborative opportunities to enhance health care services and access to the region.

Kent County's business community consists of large manufacturing concerns, leading cement-products providers, major health care providers, biotechnology firms, farming, wholesale nursery, and extensive marine-related industries. It also includes small local artist businesses, entrepreneurial endeavors such as book publishing, and a strong theater and arts climate. The Economic Development Office galvanizes business interests using the county's intrinsic resources: its land, water, people, and heritage. Kent County encourages business owners to consider their weekend lifestyle, consider their business lifestyle, and then combine them in Kent County, Maryland. *For further information, visit www.kentcounty.com.*

Opposite page, clockwise from top left: Although the smallest county in Maryland, Kent County's crop output is the second-highest in the state, creating many beautiful landscapes. Kent County's Rock Hall is steeped with waterman culture and a thriving boating industry with its deepwater access. The county was awarded top honors in the fourth annual edition of the "Best Places to Live in Rural America" rankings by *The Progressive Farmer* magazine. This page: The Court House, in downtown historic Chestertown, is a relaxing, shady spot for summer lunch breaks yet home to a wandering ghost, as it made national news when a surveillance tape captured a black apparition on the back stairs.

Queen Anne's County

When traversing the Chesapeake Bay Bridge from Annapolis, one can catch a glimpse of what sets Queen Anne's County apart from other counties on the Eastern Shore. Known as the "Gateway to the Eastern Shore," the county is a member of the Baltimore–Washington, D.C., Metropolitan Statistical Area, a status that is pleasantly complemented by its rural charm.

Much of what attracts people to Queen Anne's County, such as the working waterfront and the pastoral views, sustains its economy. The county is reliant upon its natural resource–based industries and, as such, has worked diligently to permanently preserve 70,000 acres of agriculturally zoned land, some of which is waterfront. Preservation plays a key role in maintaining the farming heritage, restoring the Chesapeake Bay, and supporting the sustainability of the county's largest industry sector, agriculture. Queen Anne's County is the largest producer of wheat, corn, and soybeans in Maryland and supports Delmarva's commercial poultry industry in the production of feed. Additionally, hunting, commercial crabbing, and oystering contribute to the local economy. The county's other major industries include hospitality, health care, financial services, and manufacturing.

The majority of Queen Anne's County's workforce of approximately 26,000 is employed in management, professional, and service occupations. Many residents and companies benefit from the resources available at Chesapeake College. Queen Anne's County's proximity to major metropolitan markets, its highly skilled workforce, and its excellent quality of life make it an ideal location to live, work, and play.

Queen Anne's County is a year-round destination that draws tourists, sportsmen, and nature lovers worldwide. Its 414 miles of shoreline offer unparalleled views of spectacular sunsets and access to a plethora of water-related activities. During the summer, there are opportunities to enjoy an excursion on a charter boat, kayaking on the Corsica and Chester rivers, and sailing on the Chesapeake. Golfers choose

from four golf courses, including the nationally acclaimed Queenstown Harbor. The natural beauty of Queen Anne's County can be experienced by hiking, biking, golfing, hunting, or birding on any one of the numerous well-maintained public and privately held lands, such as the Wye Island Wildlife Refuge, Chesapeake Bay Environmental Center, and Tuckahoe State Park. The county maintains 2,633 acres of public parks, including 21 public landings. One prime example is Terrapin Park, a 276-acre nature park featuring a 3.25-mile oyster-chaff walking trail that meanders through wildflower meadows, wetlands, tidal ponds, woodlands, and sandy beaches. The park connects to the six-mile Cross Island Trail and the Chesapeake Bay Business Park, a campus-like park that is home to approximately 80 companies. Recognizing that the preservation of open space is important not only to its residents but also to the business community, Queen Anne's County is unique in that each of its business parks incorporates a public space.

Traveling the Chesapeake Bay Scenic Byway is like stepping back in time as the history and culture of Queen Anne's County is preserved in small towns and picturesque countryside. Quaint towns and villages, such as Stevensville, Queenstown, Centreville, Church Hill, and Sudlersville, offer fine examples of early American architecture in structures that are still in use. Many of these sites are available for touring from May through October. The Chesapeake Bay Exploration Center, in the Kent Narrows, is home to the county's visitor center, which includes a museum with an interactive exhibit entitled *Our Chesapeake Legacy* exploring the natural history of the bay. The Queen Anne's Museum of Eastern Shore Life, located at the 4-H Park near Centreville, commemorates the county's rich heritage by collecting, preserving, and displaying artifacts relating to the Eastern Shore's natural resource-based industries. In June 2009, Queen Anne's County hosted

the 60th Annual Delmarva Chicken Festival at the 4-H Park. Other special events include holiday house tours, Queen Anne's County Fair, the Taste of the Narrows, Tuckahoe Outlaw Days, annual birding events, local theater productions at the Church Hill Theater and Chesapeake College, and numerous art shows sponsored by local civic groups.

Since its settlement by the English in 1631, people have been attracted to Queen Anne's County because of its ability to hold onto its past while embracing the future.

For further information, visit www.qac.org.

Above, left to right: The Chesapeake Bay Business Park, in Stevensville, is home to many internationally known companies such as PRS Guitars and Vapotherm. Queen Anne's County produces enough wheat per year to make 156 million loaves of bread. Queen Anne's County offers many examples of 18th- and 19th-century architecture that have remained in continuous use, such as those at Lawyer's Row in Centreville.

Somerset County

Somerset County is nature's masterpiece. Capturing the unrivaled beauty of Maryland's Eastern Shore, Somerset County is graced by a simpler, less hectic pace. The rivers, marshes, and islands of the area and, of course, the magnificent Chesapeake Bay have supported traditions of fishing, hunting, and sailing for over 300 years. As a water-oriented county, rural Somerset has two municipalities—the City of Crisfield, once known as the Seafood Capital of the World, and the Town of Princess Anne, which serves as the county seat of Somerset.

Recreation and Culture

Located in Westover is the Great Hope Golf Course, an 18-hole course on a 213-acre site. Football, baseball, basketball, softball, racquetball, swimming, dance, volleyball, weight lifting, soccer, biking, karate, yoga, aerobics, and after-school programs are among the recreation activities offered by Somerset County Recreation and Parks and the new Garland Hayward Park. Other recreation options in the county include water activities, hunting, and the natural beauty of Janes Island State Park, which offers numerous amenities including a campground and the availability of cabin rental. The Somers Cove Marina, located in Crisfield, is a state-owned marina with more than 500 slips.

The Crisfield/Somerset County Airport is located approximately three miles outside the city limits. Its two runways measure 2,500 feet and 3,300 feet respectively.

Somerset County History and Tourism

Somerset County, established in 1666, is surrounded by history and by exquisite 18th- and 19th-century architecture of which many examples are listed on the National Register of Historical Places. The Teackle Mansion, an early-19th-century structure on Maryland's Eastern Shore, was built between 1802 and 1819 as the home of Littleton Dennis Teackle (1777–1848), a prominent merchant and statesman, and his wife Elizabeth Upshur Teackle (1783–1835).

The 54th governor of the State of Maryland, J. Millard Tawes, resided in Crisfield. In addition to Governor Tawes, Crisfield was also home to the Ward Brothers, Lem and Steve, pioneers well known for their exquisite detail in wood-carving decoys. One of the signers of the Declaration of Independence, Samuel Chase, was born near Princess Anne in Somerset County.

Annual Events

Annual events offered are Old Princess Anne Days, the Crisfield Hard Crab Derby, the Skipjack Race of Deal Island, the annual J. Millard Tawes Crab and Clam Bake, Somerset County Fair, Colonial Christmas Candlelight Tour, Fairmount Academy 1800s Festival, Waterman's Folklife Festival, Pro-Am Fishing Tournament, Native American Indian Festival and Powwow, Soft Shell Spring Fair, July 4th Celebration, and Watermen's Festival.

Economic Development Projects and Incentives

Crisfield and Princess Anne are the two major business and industrial centers of the county. Major employers are Lankford/Sysco Food Services, McCready Hospital, Eastern Correctional Institute, University of Maryland Eastern Shore, Mountaire Farms, PNC, Perdue, and the Sherwin-Williams Company/Rubberset.

Somerset is a major seafood processor and poultry producer and provides a rich agricultural harvest including soybeans, corn, tomatoes, and wheat. The county's Economic Development Commission is working on developing services in and around Princess Anne to assist the University of Maryland Eastern Shore and commercial interests in the waterfront of Crisfield. Plans are moving forward with a marine/barge terminal and alternative-energy projects (biomass, ethanol, etc.). The establishment of the Wal-Mart Distribution Center and the Crisfield Industrial Park are also progressing. Projects that have materialized are the Bio Diesel Facility and Poole & Associates.

Somerset County has a 499-acre enterprise zone located within the City of Crisfield, and a 1,297-acre enterprise zone in the Town of Princess Anne.

In addition, Somerset is participating in the One Maryland Program, which offers significant tax credits for capital investments that create jobs.

The Chesapeake Bay forms the county's western boundary, Virginia its southern. The county is located approximately 100 miles from the Baltimore–Washington, D.C., Wilmington-Philadelphia, and Norfolk–Hampton Roads metropolitan areas.

Education and Health Care

The University of Maryland Eastern Shore (UMES), a historically black college, offers graduate degrees in the following fields: Marine-Estuarine and Environmental Sciences at the M.S. and Ph.D. levels; Toxicology at the M.S. and Ph.D. levels; and an M.S. in Applied Computer Science, Guidance and Counseling, Agricultural and Extension Education, Physical Education, Physical Therapy, or Special Education.

The Board of Education is located in Westover, approximately seven miles south of Princess Anne. The nine public schools in the school system include one technology and career center, two high schools, an intermediate school, and five elementary and primary schools. Approximate enrollment is an estimated 2,910.

McCready Hospital is the first stop for health care for the people of Somerset County and adjoining areas. McCready specializes in providing the basic medical, emergency, surgical, and diagnostic services one might need over a lifetime. In addition, they have a sophisticated referral network of specialists and regional medical centers.

For further information, visit www.somersetcountyedc.org.

Opposite page, clockwise from top: The University of Maryland Eastern Shore was founded in 1886 as the Delaware Conference Academy and became a member of the University System of Maryland in 1988. The 65-acre Princess Anne Industrial Park is an ideal location for small-to-medium businesses. The annual J. Millard Tawes Crab and Clam Bake in Crisfield is an outdoor all-you-can-eat affair featuring crabs, clams, fish, and more. This page, left to right: Kayaking is a popular pastime along the miles of isolated shoreline and marshland at Janes Island State Park in Crisfield. Smith Island is Maryland's only offshore island in the Chesapeake Bay, and is accessible only by boat.

Talbot County

Talbot County fronts the Chesapeake Bay and is located midway down the Delmarva Peninsula, an area just east of metropolitan Washington, D.C., referred to locally as Maryland's Eastern Shore. The area is recognized as *the* green spot on the mid-Atlantic seaboard, largely attributable to the poultry industry's demand for grain.

Talbot County seeks to balance demands for growth with its desire for minimal environmental impact by focusing future development efforts on emerging technology companies that require a place to explore environmental sciences and who are interested in the overlap of natural sciences, engineering, and social sciences. The county believes that solutions to 21st-century environmental issues will require large, multidisciplinary teams to analyze complex environmental problems and will require large natural areas in which to conduct these studies. There is room for 21st-century sciences in Talbot County.

Talbot County's population has steadily increased at 1.4 percent per year for the last 25 years. The county is host to five incorporated towns—Easton, Oxford,

Queen Anne, St. Michaels, and Trappe—as well as several smaller villages. The economy remains healthy, partly as a result of a stable and diverse industrial base of agriculture, manufacturing production, financial and professional services, medical and health care services, and general aviation. A skilled workforce representing 38.7 percent of the population is employed in management and professional services jobs. Talbot County Public Schools supports a mission of graduating all its students as "lifetime learners;" Chesapeake College and area four-year institutions partner in supporting this mission by offering degree and workforce development programs. The Chesapeake Bay Regional Technical Center for Excellence brokers federal laboratory technology transfer from the mid-Atlantic region to area businesses. The Cooperative Oxford Laboratory provides an interdisciplinary laboratory campus,

which includes the U.S. Coast Guard, the Maryland Department of Natural Resources, the National Oceanic and Atmospheric Administration (NOAA), and National Ocean Service reporting to the Center for Coastal Environmental Health and Biomolecular Research. The Cooperative Oxford Laboratory is the only federal laboratory of its kind located on the Chesapeake Bay.

The Town of Easton serves as the county seat and is also the cultural, commercial, financial, and medical hub for the mid-Shore region. Its seven industrial parks are occupied by national and international manufacturers which continue to expand and are supported by a regional employment base of 84,000 workers. Easton Utilities Commission, owned and operated by the Town of Easton, operates as an enterprise and provides electricity, water, wastewater treatment, natural gas, cable television, Internet, and advertising services for the town. The Town of Easton, in conjunction with the State of Maryland, invested $36 million to provide for expansion of the town's wastewater sewer treatment facility which is expected to support development requirements through 2030. Shore Health System/University of Maryland Medical System is the largest employer in Talbot County and serves the Upper Shore with the Memorial Hospital at Easton.

Easton Airport, a general aviation airport, is located at the northern entrance to the Town of Easton. It has 60,000 annual operations and currently serves the mid-Atlantic

region. Host to 13 businesses with an employment base of 150, Easton Airport maintains appropriate security levels in keeping with Homeland Security requirements and specifications.

Historic Easton, a nonprofit organization founded in 1974 to preserve the historic sites and monuments of Easton, is currently monitoring a number of historic structure renovation projects which, when complete, will offer mixed-use office and retail space. The historic Tidewater Inn has recently undergone a major restoration and renovation and continues to anchor downtown. The Avalon Foundation and the Academy Art Museum promote cultural and entertainment attractions. The Waterfowl Festival, Inc. stages an annual wildlife arts festival the second full weekend in November, hosting over 400 exhibitors and attracting thousands of visitors.

Talbot County offers an accessible yet secure environment in which to conduct business, and is a remarkable "test bed" for environmental sciences. The Talbot County Office of Economic Development (OED) welcomes the opportunity to discuss the retention or expansion of current businesses, or to discuss relocation of businesses to the region. As the OED states, "Bring Your Science Projects to Our Backyard."

For further information, visit www.talbotcountymd.gov.

Opposite page: Talbot County reports 60 percent of its total land use in agriculture. This page, left to right: Talbot County is host to five incorporated towns, including St. Michaels (shown here), Easton, Oxford, Queen Anne, and Trappe. Easton serves as the commercial, financial, cultural, and medical services hub for the mid-Shore region.

Wicomico County

With its strategic location along the eastern seaboard and at the crossroads of the Delmarva Peninsula, Wicomico County is a center for commerce, industry, health care, education, and transportation. Midway between the Atlantic Ocean and the Chesapeake Bay, Wicomico also offers its citizens a lifestyle second to none, with abundant cultural, recreational, and civic amenities.

Wicomico's economic base is diverse, with agriculture, health care, and education serving as a solid foundation.

As the number-one agricultural producing county in Maryland, Wicomico leads the state in broiler production. Popular crops include corn, soybeans, wheat, and vegetables.

The health care sector is anchored by Peninsula Regional Medical Center (PRMC), a fully Joint Commission–accredited tertiary care facility offering a broad array of specialty and subspecialty services. The hospital employs more than 3,000 associates and offers medical care to nearly 500,000 patients annually. The medical center is in the midst of a $100 million expansion to further enhance services and meet the region's future needs.

The local board of education operates 17 elementary schools, four high schools, five middle schools, and a career and technology center and accommodates more than 14,000 students. Together, Salisbury University, Wor-Wic Community College, and, just 10 miles south, the University of Maryland Eastern Shore employ thousands of people and provide higher education services to more than 14,000 students annually.

In addition to these sectors, Wicomico is home to numerous manufacturers making products used around the world. Selected industries include chemical, printing, electronics, shipbuilding, poultry processing, plastics, fabricated metals, pharmaceuticals, and machinery.

Contributing to Wicomico's amenities and infrastructure are eight incorporated municipalities including Salisbury, Fruitland, Delmar, Pittsville, Hebron, Willards, Sharptown, and Mardela Springs. Salisbury, the county seat, was chosen for the second-consecutive year as one of the "100 Best Communities for Young People" by America's Promise—The Alliance for Youth, and *Inc.* magazine ranked Salisbury the 55th "Hottest Small City."

The transportation of people, goods, and information is critical to Wicomico's economic viability. The Salisbury/Ocean City Wicomico Regional Airport is Maryland's second-largest, with scheduled airline service to and from Philadelphia and Charlotte provided by US Airways Express. The airport is home to numerous corporate clients, a fixed-base operator, an air business center, and a small-business incubator. The Port of Salisbury is Maryland's second-largest port, with over $200 million of products including grain, oil, and building aggregates transported annually along the Wicomico River. Norfolk-Southern provides primary rail services, while broadband access is available throughout the metro core.

Numerous business parks dot the landscape in Wicomico, while primary industrial parks include Northwood, Fruitland, and Westwood Commerce Park. Wicomico's two enterprise zones, offering real property and state income tax credits, encompass the industrial parks and downtown Salisbury.

With a solid economic base, recreational, cultural, and civic amenities abound in Wicomico. Selected attractions include the Delmarva Shorebirds (class-A minor league baseball), the Autumn Wine Festival, Salisbury Zoological Park, Ward Museum of Wildfowl Art, and dozens of parks, marinas, and playing fields. Shopping opportunities are numerous and range from the Centre at Salisbury to unique shops found throughout the county. From the Victorian charm of Newtown to modern condominiums along the Wicomico River, residential options are diverse and plentiful.

Thanks to a stable and friendly business climate, Wicomico's economy is one of balance and diversification. Wicomico's greatest asset, however, is its people, a fact demonstrated through civic pride, terrific corporate citizenship, volunteerism, and community involvement.

For further information, visit www.swed.org.

Both pages, left to right: Pork in the Park, a national barbecue cook-off, is held in Salisbury every April. Historic Pemberton Park is home to the Autumn Wine Festival. Cedar Hill Marina offers boating, crabbing, fishing, waterfowl and wildlife viewing, picnic facilities, basketball, tennis, softball, and many more exciting activities.

Worcester County

Worcester County, on Maryland's Eastern Shore, is bordered by Delaware, the Atlantic Ocean, and Virginia. Its location is an immediate advantage. Situated conveniently in the mid-Atlantic region, Worcester County has the cost advantages of a southeastern community with the market access of a northeastern location; it is readily accessible by road, air, rail, or water to the Philadelphia–Norfolk corridor. Worcester County offers the best of urban and rural living—close to the cultural riches of major cities, yet far enough away to avoid traffic congestion, dangerous crime, and high-cost housing.

The county is home to Ocean City, Maryland's most famous resort, which also offers vacationers year-round pleasures including beach and boardwalk strolls throughout the seasons. Worcester County's economy is driven primarily by tourism. Water-related activities such as fishing and boating occur at the beach and other attractions as well. Pleasures of small-town living can be found in Berlin, Snow Hill, and Pocomoke City. Ocean Pines, the county's largest residential community, offers a full complement of amenities. From an ocean-view condominium to a historic farmhouse, there is something for every lifestyle. Extraordinary waterfront estates, horse farms, and deluxe resort homes on golf courses are also available. Fourteen championship courses provide challenges for golfers.

The county has 18 public boat ramps. Pocomoke River cruises provide leisurely viewing of the area's natural beauty. Other areas with appeal for nature lovers are Pocomoke River State Forest and Park, Assateague State Park, and the Assateague Island National Seashore, where an abundance of wildlife, unspoiled beaches, and the famous Assateague ponies are found. History buffs can browse through the museums including the Costen House, Julia A. Purnell Museum, Calvin B. Taylor Museum, and the Ocean City Life Saving Station Museum. Furnace Town, near Snow Hill, is the 19th-century site of the Nassawango Iron Furnace. Special events include Sunfest, Big Band Dance Series, Pocomoke River Cypress Festival, World Wildfowl Carving Competition, White Marlin and

Tuna Tournament, Springfest, African American Heritage Festival, Delmarva Birding Weekend, Pocomoke River Canoe Challenge, Winterfest of Lights, and more.

Manufacturing in the Pocomoke Industrial Park is growing in square footage and jobs. Armoring-solutions manufacturer Hardwire has completed construction of a new 62,000-square-foot manufacturing building on the Pocomoke River for building composite sheets and parts used in armor on vehicles and buildings for protection against explosives, hurricanes, and tornadoes. The company's sales have exceeded $10 million a month. Mid-Atlantic Institute for Space and Technology has now leased all 42,000 feet of the Pocomoke Flex Building. Among its tenants is the Hawk Institute for Space Sciences, with 30 new aerospace employees located at

the site. Bel-Art Products, a manufacturer of laboratory equipment, has grown to 150 employees and has just made a commitment to another 25 new manufacturing jobs in Pocomoke by early 2009. Royal Plus, a disaster-clean-up company that serves major corporations throughout the country, has made the county seat of Snow Hill the location of its new 112,000-square-foot headquarters. The company rehabilitated an old facility with $5 million invested and now has 110 employees, with 54 hired in 2008.

The Worcester County school system is top notch and offers six elementary schools, three middle/combined schools, and four high schools including a state-of-the-art vocational technical career center, along with nine private schools. All schools are accredited by the Middle States Association of Colleges and Schools. Nearby in neighboring counties are the University of Maryland Eastern Shore, Salisbury University, and Wor-Wic Community College.

Growth of the county's health care industry is largely due to the influx of retirees. Residents receive quality care from Atlantic General Hospital (which now has nearly 700 employees), an orthopedic rehabilitation center, an ever-increasing number of doctor's offices, and other supporting health care businesses.

For further information, visit www.co.worcester.md.us.

Opposite page, clockwise from top: Located on Maryland's Eastern Shore, Worcester County is Maryland's only seaside county, known for Ocean City's clean sandy beaches, outdoor recreation, steamed crabs, and the famous wild pony herd on Assateague State Park and Assateague Island National Seashore. The Worcester County Courthouse in Snow Hill, with classical revival–style architecture that dates back to 1843, stands as an icon in the county's landscape. The scenic Pocomoke River in Snow Hill is ideal for kayaking and canoeing. This page, left to right: The seaside Ocean City boardwalk amusement park offers exciting rides and games. Snow Hill's Furnace Town historical site recalls the 1800s, when ore was gathered, smelted, loaded into barges, and floated down Nassawango Creek.

Southern Maryland

CALVERT, CHARLES, AND ST. MARY'S COUNTIES

The roots of Maryland were planted here in 1634 with the arrival of the colonists aboard the *Ark* and the *Dove* at what is now St. Mary's City. Many areas of Southern Maryland have changed little over the centuries, and historical sights abound. But this is not a region that lives in the past. Traditional industries are adapting to a changing economy. Agriculture has expanded to include agritourism and wineries, while the region's abundant natural resources offer exciting opportunities in renewable and alternative energy. New science and technology parks promise additional growth. Development is tempered by smart growth strategies, ensuring that the region maintains its storied quality of life. As Southern Maryland embraces the future, it does so with a reverence for the past.

CHARLES

● La Plata

CALVERT

● Prince Frederick

ST. MARY'S

Leonardtown
●

0   12.5   25   50   Miles

Calvert County

Calvert County is Maryland's smallest county, but it boasts an enviable reputation for natural beauty, a thriving business climate, and an exceptional quality of life. Great things do indeed come in small packages.

Located 30 miles southeast of Washington, D.C., Calvert County is an environmental jewel bounded on the east by the scenic Chesapeake Bay and on the west by the wide waters of the Patuxent River. This peninsula is ringed by 223 miles of shoreline that make the county a mecca for outdoor enthusiasts. The boating centers of Chesapeake Beach in northern Calvert County and Solomons in the south are home to the region's largest sport-fishing fleet. The area is renowned among mid-Atlantic boaters for its scenic waterways, myriad marinas, and welcoming waterside communities.

Infusing county life is a strong agricultural tradition stretching back over three centuries. Approximately 24 percent of the county's land is currently assessed as farmland. Tobacco, used as currency in colonial times, sustained the county's farm economy until the historic Maryland tobacco buyout program was created in 1999 to remove the crop from production. County farmers are now diversifying their operations to keep farms working. New agricultural pursuits include vineyards and wineries, vegetables, and nursery stock. Local farms are also moving into agritourism ventures through the creation of farm tours, corn mazes, roadside markets, heritage tourism destinations, and other methods aimed at promoting the value of local agriculture.

Geography and history have forged a deep relationship between Calvert County and its natural resources. As a result, strong environmental stewardship has long

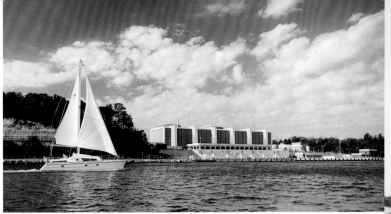

been a county hallmark. Calvert County created the first land preservation program in the state of Maryland, and has set a goal to preserve 40,000 acres of forest and farmland to maintain its rural character. By the end of 2007, the county had permanently preserved in excess of 25,000 acres.

The county has worked to preserve the quality of life for its residents by carefully managing residential growth. Once the fastest-growing county in the state, Calvert County has adopted zoning and land preservation measures to slow growth and limit the total number of households. Residential development is directed to defined regions through the town-center concept. The county's town centers offer attractive, convenient places to live, work, and shop while limiting scattered development and reducing reliance on vehicles.

More than 4,600 acres of parks and open space are set aside for regional recreation. County waterfront and woodland parks offer pristine beauty and wonderful opportunities for fishing, swimming, crabbing, canoeing, biking, camping, and golfing. The county's Chesapeake Bay shoreline is famous among fossil hunters. Waterside cliffs and beaches regularly reveal fossil specimens from the Miocene era of 10 to 20 million years ago when the sea covered southern Maryland.

Calvert County's natural wonders are enhanced by myriad cultural and recreational activities. Residents and visitors are treated to museums, outdoor concerts, theatrical productions, art shows, crafts and antiques fairs, and many other opportunities. Historical buildings and landmarks dot the countryside, and a range of special events and festivals is scheduled throughout the year to highlight the county's diverse and distinctive flavor.

Many families are drawn to Calvert County for its quality public education. The county claims one of the state's highest-ranked public school systems, with an enrollment exceeding 17,000 students. Several private schools also operate in the county along with a campus of the College of Southern Maryland, a two-year institution.

The county's highly educated workforce—nearly 30 percent hold a bachelor's degree or higher—supports a diverse business community. More than 4,000 businesses employ 17,000 workers in the county. Calvert County's largest employers are Calvert Memorial Hospital and Calvert Cliffs Nuclear Power Plant, the state's only nuclear power station. Retail, technology services, energy, manufacturing, and hospitality are among the many industries that thrive in Calvert County. The county is also home to one of the nation's largest liquefied natural gas terminals, which helps stabilize gas prices in the mid-Atlantic.

New businesses are attracted to the county through a variety of incentives, including loan funds, grants, fast-track construction permitting, financing, training, and free business counseling. Located just 30 miles from Washington, D.C., and minutes from the burgeoning Patuxent River Naval Air Station, Calvert County is a prime business location offering proximity to major markets and an unmatched pastoral character.

Calvert County is a study in harmony, a place that has found a fine balance between modern-day enterprise and the ancient rhythms of time and tide. From the bay boardwalks to the bustling town centers, from the rolling farm fields to the sun-dappled forests, residents and visitors alike have come to know Calvert County as the "Charm of the Chesapeake." *For further information, visit www.ecalvert.com.*

Above, left to right: Calvert County's agricultural tradition is evolving as new ventures, such as wine growing, replace tobacco production. The Chesapeake Bay helps define Calvert County's maritime character. The Calvert Cliffs Nuclear Power Plant is one of the county's largest employers and the only nuclear power station in the state. The Calvert Marine Museum features the Drum Point Lighthouse and other exhibits exploring the county's cultural and natural history.

Charles County

Charles County is the best of both worlds. Centrally located in the Baltimore/Washington/Richmond corridor, the community enjoys all of the cultural, entertainment, and economic advantages of a large, urban metro region. At the same time, Charles County is part of Southern Maryland, one of the state's most scenic regions, with hundreds of miles of shoreline, open space, history, and a maritime heritage.

The northern part of Charles County closest to Washington, D.C., is the area where most of the county's growth takes place. More than half of the population—over 80,000 people—live in the unincorporated community of Waldorf. In fact, if Waldorf were incorporated, it would be one of the largest cities in the state. All of the amenities that one would expect in a large suburban center are there. St. Charles Town Center, a regional shopping mall, gets millions of visitors annually. Up and down Route 301, the main road through the county, and all around the mall are popular shopping spots, restaurants, services, and activities.

Beyond the commercial centers, Waldorf's residential communities provide a variety of family-oriented neighborhoods, many within walking or bicycling distance from

local schools. Waldorf is also the home of the state's newest Independent League professional baseball team, the Southern Maryland Blue Crabs.

The county seat of La Plata has a charm of its own. County and town government buildings as well as the Charles County Courthouse anchor the town's walkable commercial center. Historic homes, professional offices, unique restaurants, and specialty shops complete the setting. La Plata is also home to the Port Tobacco Players Theatre, a regionally acclaimed community theater group and one of two such venues in the county.

The other is the Black Box Theater at the Indian Head Center for the Arts in the town of Indian Head, Charles County's other municipality. Indian Head is also the home to a naval installation which hosts several commands, including the Naval Surface Warfare Center. The base is one of the county's leading employers, but proximity to Washington, D.C., is the main attraction for many of the high-tech, professional services companies moving into the county.

Just north of Indian Head in the community of Bryans Road, private developers—in partnership with the county—are building a 260-acre science and technology park for office, research, and manufacturing facilities. This is one of several new business parks that are going up in the county's development district to accommodate the growing demand for business space.

Outside of the cities, Charles County is less "Washington, D.C., metro" in character and more "Southern Maryland" with farms, forests, parks, and over 300 miles of shoreline—most of it on the lower Potomac River. Nature lovers will find miles of hiking trails. Seafood lovers will get their fill. Bird-watchers will find many feathered friends. Fishermen have plenty of options. And historians can connect with the past thanks to the county's rich colonial history dating back to the early 17th century when the first Europeans arrived in what is now Maryland.

With so much to offer—from suburban convenience to nature's bounty—Charles County is the best of both worlds. *For more information, visit www.charlescounty.org.*

Clockwise, from above left: Boating enthusiasts enjoy a delightful day on Charles County's Port Tobacco River. Waldorf is a family-oriented community in a lush, pastoral setting. Employees work in a machine shop at the Naval Surface Warfare Center Indian Head Division, one of Charles County's leading employers.

St. Mary's County

As Maryland's mother county, St. Mary's County is rich in history and recreational opportunities. Surrounded on three sides by the Chesapeake Bay and the Potomac and Patuxent rivers, the county enjoys a relaxed lifestyle and easy access to Washington, D.C., Annapolis, and Baltimore.

This county has many colonial and maritime history sites including St. Clement's Island, site of Maryland's founding, and Historic St. Mary's City, Maryland's first capital and a premier outdoor history museum. The county is home to two of the oldest lighthouses on the Chesapeake: Piney Point Lighthouse and Point Lookout Lighthouse. Other sites include 18th-century Sotterley Plantation and the Patuxent River Naval Air Museum.

More than 50 festivals celebrate the county's way of life and include the summer-time River Concert Series, St. Mary's County Fair, Blessing of the Fleet, Riverside Winefest, Farm-Life Festival, and Oyster Festival and the state's largest Veterans Day parade.

Visitors enjoy panoramic waterfront views and indulge in the freshest seafood at the waterfront eateries dotting the county's shoreline. Some of the finest motor racing in Maryland is available with motocross, IHRA Championship drag-racing, and stock-car racing, all located within minutes of each other. One of the oldest incorporated towns, Leonardtown is graced with one of the few remaining town squares, where quaint shops and

Quality medical services and cutting-edge technology drive the health care options in St. Mary's County. St. Mary's Hospital is a full-service hospital, delivering state-of-the-art emergency, acute inpatient, and outpatient care.

restaurants line the streets and a waterfront park on Breton Bay invites visitors from land and water.

St. Mary's County offers many outdoor recreational activities like golfing, camping, hiking, and biking. Being surrounded by water makes this area perfect for water activities like canoeing, kayaking, sailing and power boating, crabbing, and open-water fishing. Public facilities include 20 public parks, a year-round pool, boat ramps, beaches, fishing piers, tennis courts, BMX bike track, golf courses and sports fields, picnic facilities, playgrounds, and a skate park. The county is family-focused with many youth sports leagues. St. Mary's is also home to four state parks.

St. Mary's County schools include 15 public elementary schools, four middle schools, and three high schools; the James A. Forrest Career and Technology Center; and 11 private schools. The county's public school system is complemented by STEM and Finance academies—academically rigorous programs with a strong emphasis in science, technology, engineering, mathematics, business, and finance.

In higher education, St. Mary's College of Maryland, a nationally ranked, public liberal arts Honors College, is located on the waterfront at Historic St. Mary's City. The College of Southern Maryland fuels a highly skilled workforce and includes a number of online programs as well as a growing number of bachelor's-degree opportunities with partnering universities. The Southern Maryland Higher Education Center houses more than a dozen major colleges and universities providing over 90 academic programs, mostly at the graduate level.

Today's economy is a unique blend of a vibrant high-technology sector alongside rural traditions. St. Mary's County is home to the Naval Air Station (NAS) Patuxent River, the county's largest employer, with over 22,000 workers including military, civilians, and defense contractors. Major tenant commands include the Naval Air Systems Command Headquarters (NAVAIR), and the U.S. Naval Test Pilot School. With over 200 high-tech aerospace and defense contractors supporting the Navy's programs, the county has emerged as a world-class center for maritime research, development, acquisition, testing, and evaluation. Designated a Technology Corridor, the county is home to other top employers—BAE Systems, Boeing, Lockheed Martin, L-3, Northrop Grumman, and Wyle. Nondefense employers include the Paul Hall Center for Maritime Training, St. Mary's Hospital, and St. Mary's College of Maryland. The Lexington Park area, designated a State Enterprise Zone through year 2010, offers a number of incentives for businesses.

There is an array of housing choices in St. Mary's with its waterfront communities, rural towns, and newly constructed subdivisions. From condominiums and apartments to luxury homes, and lots from less than an acre to over 100 acres, there are a house and neighborhood for everyone.

Growth in housing, shopping, restaurants, hotels, the arts, and entertainment attracts new residents and visitors. St. Mary's County cultivates high-tech jobs alongside a traditional lifestyle anchored in the natural bounty of the Tidewater—truly a land of pleasant living. *For further information, visit www.co.saint-marys.md.us.*

Opposite page, clockwise from top left: Four V-22 Osprey aircraft sit along the flight line with rotors turning before test flights at NAS Patuxent River. Historic Leonardtown on Breton Bay is graced with one of the few remaining town squares, where quaint shops and restaurants line the streets. Historic St. Mary's City was the first colony and capital of Maryland and is now one of the nation's most renowned archaeological and outdoor living-history museums. This page, left to right: A blue crab is one of the attractions at the Chesapeake Bay Field Lab, whose tours inspire people to be stewards of the bay. The Oyster Festival National Oyster Cook-off and Shucking Competitions draw tens of thousands of people from across the country.

Western Maryland

ALLEGANY, GARRETT, AND WASHINGTON COUNTIES

Adventure is the byword of this region, be it recreational or entrepreneurial. The trails, lakes, and forests of the Allegheny Mountains offer unlimited activities—from skiing and snowboarding at the state's only ski resort to swimming, fishing, and boating on Maryland's largest lake. Visitors take a journey back in time on the Western Maryland Scenic Railroad or visit the hallowed ground of Antietam Battlefield. Each county boasts a Maryland Arts and Entertainment District with a thriving performing and visual arts scene. With so much to do, Western Maryland presents exciting opportunities for tourism professionals. The region's increasingly diverse economy also includes advanced technology, manufacturing, aerospace and defense, financial services, and health care. Western Maryland is truly a frontier of opportunity.

GARRETT

Oakland

Cumberland

ALLEGANY

WASHINGTON

Hagerstown

0   12.5   25   50   Miles

Allegany County

As one of the state's most mountainous and picturesque counties, Allegany County is bringing a new and exciting community vision to the western region. For incoming companies and relocating residents, the "Mountain Side of Maryland" is a place where quality of life is an integral part of the bottom line.

Allegany County's rich history creates a desirable lifestyle that offers charming neighborhoods, preserved heritage, and 60,000 acres of public recreation lands as a clear alternative to the congested gridlocks of nearby metro areas.

Founded long before the American Revolution, Allegany County prospered during the nation's early years as one of the first gateways west through the Allegheny Mountains. Located near the Eastern Continental Divide, the county was the site of the British outpost at Fort Cumberland and later boomed as a transportation center for railroads, highways, and the C&O Canal. By the mid 20th century, Cumberland was Maryland's second-largest city, and the county was home to seven major manufacturing operations taking advantage of overnight shipment to half of America's population.

Today Allegany County is strategically located to offer a quality of life that can be quite fairly described as the "best of both worlds" for telecommuting, information services, and technology-based manufacturing. With the county only two hours of easy driving from Pittsburgh, Baltimore, and Washington, D.C., local residents enjoy an average commute of only 13 minutes. A population of 69,000 supports two thriving arts and entertainment districts and enjoys an average housing cost that is half the national average.

The recent opening of the Great Allegheny Passage Maryland trail has created a 21-mile ribbon of natural wonder that shares the Western Maryland Scenic Railroad right-of-way between Cumberland and Frostburg. Over 300,000 users

per year enjoy the trail as a destination attraction that connects Georgetown in Washington, D.C., directly to Pittsburgh, Pennsylvania, making it one of the nation's longest continuous trails. Local professionals who live in Cumberland's historic West Side and North End districts use it for pedestrian and bicycling access to the downtown business district—no car needed, no gridlock in sight.

Over half a million people visit Allegany County annually. The smart ones are figuring out a way to stay. Allegany County's appeal for corporate relocation and start-up, however, does not end with a desirable rural, small-town lifestyle.

Local governments have partnered in Allconet, a unique wireless broadband distribution network connected through a proprietary Sonnet Ring system. The wireless network combines with an extensive public high-speed fiber network to provide carrier-class communications for incoming companies and connects major public sector sites including libraries, schools, and government offices.

The Western Maryland Health System serves the community as a locally based nonprofit with more than 2,200 employees. WMHS is completing construction of a new $108 million hospital campus just inside the eastern city limits of Cumberland. A grand opening is set for fall 2009.

Higher education plays a role in the local corporate environment as well. Allegany College of Maryland is unique among Maryland's community colleges for its well-respected technical programs, specializing in the allied health fields. Frostburg State University, part of the University System of Maryland, is developing a reputation for specialties that include green technologies and environmental sciences. The university is also home to a new high-technology business park, Allegany Business Center at Frostburg State University (ABC@FSU). Developed in partnership with economic development agencies, ABC@FSU recently welcomed its first major tenant, InfoSpherics.

Allegany County's Department of Economic Development also provides business space for manufacturing and distribution throughout the county, including the Barton Business Park on Route 220. Companies that have enjoyed success through such arrangements include American Woodmark, Superfos (a Danish plastics manufacturer), and Schroeder Industries. Alliant Techsystems (ATK), a defense contractor located just over the Potomac River, draws heavily from Allegany County's skilled labor force for the design and fabrication of national defense systems.

Allegany County is eager and ready to apply a variety of business incentive programs for qualified corporate relocation prospects and has a long history of successful, incentive-based relationships with employers. Simply put, in the coming years and decades, it is hard to imagine a better place to visit, live, or work than the Mountain Side of Maryland. *For further information, visit www.alleganycountychamber.com.*

Opposite page, clockwise from top left: Rocky Gap Lodge and Golf Resort is located on the shores of Lake Habeeb at Rocky Gap State Park. The atrium at the Compton Science Center at Frostburg State University (FSU) features a Foucault's pendulum. Allegany Business Center is a new high-technology business park at FSU. This page, left to right: Cumberland's Gordon-Roberts House features a museum offering a glimpse into the lifestyle of a Victorian family. The historic town of Cumberland is home to the Western Maryland Scenic Railroad.

Garrett County

Garrett County, Maryland's westernmost county, is known not only as a vacation destination packed with limitless outdoor recreation, but also for its scenic natural beauty. Considered Maryland's "Mountaintop Playground," Garrett County boasts the state's largest man-made lake, Deep Creek Lake, which attracts visitors year-round, and the state's only ski resort, Wisp Resort.

During the winter, visitors to Garrett County may ski or ride on one of Wisp Resort's 32 trails, cross-country ski, go tubing, or head out on a snowmobile tour. During the spring, summer, or fall, they may play the 18-hole golf course, go fly-fishing, or try out the new year-round mountain coaster, a cross between an alpine slide and a roller coaster.

Winter offers not only the activities at Wisp Resort but horse-drawn sleigh rides and dog-sledding. The state parks offer cross-country skiing, snowshoeing, and snowmobiling. Spring, summer, and fall offer not only activities on Deep Creek Lake but also fly-fishing, mountain biking, whitewater rafting, golfing, camping, hiking, and more.

One of the area's newest attractions is the Adventure Sports Center International (ASCI) recirculating whitewater course, located atop Wisp Mountain. The ASCI course offers not only thrills for kayakers and rafters but also stunning views for spectators from a course-spanning bridge. And ASCI course managers can change the intensity of the course from a gentle class 2 for first timers to a thundering class 4

for Olympic-caliber professionals, making it the world's most adjustable man-made whitewater course.

With an average temperature of 66 degrees, the summers offer a welcome respite from the congestion and humidity of the city. The small-town charm and friendliness of this 30,000-person county cannot be beat.

Garrett County has over 76,000 acres of parks, lakes, and publicly accessible forestland. Swallow Falls State Park features virgin forests, scenic trails, and three striking waterfalls, including Maryland's highest, Muddy Creek, at a crashing 53 feet.

Natural history makes a special mark in Garrett County. Hoye Crest on Backbone Mountain is Maryland's highest point, at 3,360 feet. An ice-age relic, the Cranesville Subarctic Swamp is home to prehistoric bogs and forests and is one of the first National Natural Landmarks to be designated by the National Park Service, in 1965. The Casselman River Bridge, once the largest single-span stone arch in the world, is located along the Historic National Road that runs through Garrett County's town of Grantsville. The National Road was built between 1811 and 1818, to carry the traffic and commerce of a growing nation.

Each fall, Garrett County celebrates the spectacular fall foliage of the mountains with its annual Autumn Glory Festival, a five-day celebration of the fall season.

The tremendous tourism appeal of Garrett County offers plentiful opportunities for recreation, retail, and tourism business development. Garrett County is home to over 920 businesses that employ over 10,000 workers. And the growing leisure and retirement market makes Garrett County an especially attractive place to open shop, literally and figuratively. Young professionals are also increasingly moving their families to the area, attracted by the growth and possibilities afforded by new business opportunities and by telecommuting. In addition, Garrett County is just two hours from Pittsburgh and less than three hours from Baltimore and Washington, D.C.

The Garrett Information Enterprise Center has been set up to attract technology-intensive companies, and numerous business parks house everything from manufacturing and financial businesses to educational and health services. Garrett County also participates in the One Maryland Program, which offers significant tax credits for capital investments that create jobs.

For further information, visit www.visitdeepcreek.com.

Opposite page, left to right: Wisp Resort, Maryland's only ski resort, offers 32 trails for skiing and snow-boarding and features one of the most extensive snow-making systems in the East. Deep Creek Lake is Maryland's largest inland body of water, with 65 miles of shoreline, and offers a wide array of water activities. This page, left to right: Bear Claw Snow Tubing at Wisp Resort features two lifts that take tube riders up the hill. At 53 crashing feet, Muddy Creek Falls at Swallow Falls State Park is Maryland's highest waterfall.

Hagerstown-Washington County

Located one hour from the Baltimore-Washington metro area at the strategic intersection of Interstates 70 and 81, Hagerstown is the hub of the regional economy. The county's productive, dedicated, and well-rounded workforce of 400,000 has made this a choice destination for manufacturing, financial service, and logistics companies. Strong industry combined with a public school system ranked among the best in Maryland, a variety of higher education options, and a growing cultural and entertainment district help make Washington County the "Crossroads of Commerce."

The county's pro-business climate continues to be a winning component of its success in landing expansion and relocation projects. As government, business, and community partners help diversify the economy, higher paying jobs are being created in engineering, advanced technology, and the aero-defense sectors.

The area has always been noted for its great transportation infrastructure with easy access to road, rail, and air. The Hagerstown Regional Airport (HGR) has the second-longest runway in Maryland, at 7,000 feet, behind only Baltimore/Washington International Thurgood Marshall Airport (BWI Marshall). HGR has more than 40 defense and aviation firms and 650 employees located on the complex.

Quality of Life

Hagerstown-Washington County is a perfect blend of urban and country life. Its pastoral landscape is filled with rolling hills and country roads as far as the eye can see. Communities date back to the Civil War era, and have historic legacy and quiet charm. Residents enjoy an excellent quality of life—alive with personal, cultural, and intellectual opportunities. Housing options are affordable, crime rates are low, and the education system is world class. In addition, the county is located in close proximity to Baltimore, Maryland, and Washington, D.C., which infuse metropolitan culture and lifestyle into the region.

A revitalized Arts and Entertainment District in downtown Hagerstown complements shopping, historical sites, and museums in Washington County. Residents and visitors enjoy a wonderful collection of beautifully renovated retail shops, restaurants, and condominiums all within walking distance of cultural attractions such as the historic Maryland Theatre, home to the Maryland Symphony Orchestra, as well as the Washington County Museum of Fine Arts. With over 43 parks, including the Antietam National Battlefield, C&O Canal, and Appalachian Trail, the opportunities for hiking, biking, and leisure activities are unlimited in Washington County.

World-class Educational System

The relationship between education and business in the Washington County community is very important. With more than 30 institutions of higher learning within a 70-mile radius of Hagerstown, the area offers an array of educational opportunities. Washington County Public Schools (WCPS) ranks among the top four public school systems in Maryland and continues to deliver world-class education. Most notably, "America's Best High Schools," a report issued by *U.S.News & World Report* analyzing over 18,000 high schools across the country, included six of Washington County's public high schools as among the best. Washington County also has a solid career-and-technology educational model. Washington County Technical High School and Barr Construction Institute are paramount in preparing the county's technology-driven workforce.

Hagerstown Community College (HCC) is the fastest-growing community college in Maryland. HCC offers biotechnology degrees and boasts 4,000 square feet of wet-laboratory space in its Technology Innovation Center (TIC). The TIC, one of the largest business incubators in the state, provides business-development assistance, laboratory, flex space, and offices for technology start-ups, manufacturers, and biotechnology firms.

The University System of Maryland at Hagerstown, located in the heart of downtown, offers more than 30 graduate and undergraduate degree programs through Maryland's five public universities. Kaplan College offers career-focused degree programs, including business, legal studies, technology, and graphic design.

Focusing on the Future

The Hagerstown-Washington County Economic Development Commission will continue to focus on what it does best—assisting new and existing businesses through the process of selecting the best location to relocate or expand. Over the past few years, Washington County has built its reputation as a successful business community and is now being considered for more high-tech, higher-wage projects than ever before. The county's pro-business environment creates opportunities for its citizens, resulting in an excellent quality of life. Hagerstown-Washington County will continue to work with its strategic partners to assist in the growth of the community's existing businesses and aggressively seek new employers to the area that will offer higher paying jobs for its citizens. *For more information, visit www.hagerstownedc.org.*

Both pages, left to right: Downtown Hagerstown Public Square is located in the revitalized Arts and Entertainment District. Park visitors take a walk down Bloody Lane at the Antietam National Battlefield. The Maryland Theatre is the home of the Maryland Symphony Orchestra. The Burnside Bridge over Antietam Creek is one of the most famous stone arch bridges in North America.

PA

RT THREE

CHAMPIONS OF COMMERCE: PROFILES OF COMPANIES AND ORGANIZATIONS

Researcher at The University of Maryland BioPark

PROFILES OF COMPANIES AND ORGANIZATIONS
Biomedical Research Campuses

The University of Maryland BioPark
Baltimore, Maryland

With tenants ranging from early-stage to mature bioscience enterprises, this university-associated research park in Baltimore's thriving Westside downtown district provides a sophisticated office and laboratory environment to support and accelerate the commercialization of innovative biotechnology therapies and simultaneously spurs economic development for the surrounding business and residential community and the region.

Above, both photos: The University of Maryland BioPark is located on the urban campus of the University of Maryland, Baltimore, in the flourishing Westside downtown district.

Taking the discoveries of some of Maryland's top medical researchers and creating partnerships to advance human health was the brainchild of University of Maryland, Baltimore (UMB) President David J. Ramsay, D.M., D.Phil. His vision is now a thriving reality at The University of Maryland BioPark, a downtown Baltimore biomedical research park focused on therapeutic interventions for a variety of medical conditions.

This community of scientists and entrepreneurs is accelerating biotechnology commercialization and economic development in the surrounding community and throughout the region. The partnership of the university with a strong private developer, Wexford Science and Technology, has sped the physical development of the BioPark since its creation in 2004. With two buildings open that house more than a dozen tenants in wet laboratory and office space, and more buildings under way, the BioPark already includes a strong core of companies and academic research centers. The vision for the BioPark at final build-out is 10 buildings totaling 1.8 million square feet set amidst landscaped parks.

In addition to being central to a leading academic medical research institution (the University of Maryland School of Medicine—the oldest public medical school in the nation), the BioPark is also next to a world-class medical center, a world-renowned shock trauma center, and the state's medical center for Veterans Affairs. UMB is also home to professional schools of dentistry, nursing, pharmacy, law, social work, public health, and a multidisciplinary graduate school. University scientists conduct cutting-edge research in areas that include cancer, vaccines, regenerative medicine, genomics, vascular biology, neuroscience, and HIV/AIDS.

New and established research centers at UMB are generating significant discoveries that may ultimately lead to hoped-for preventative treatments, therapeutics, and cures. University of Maryland School of Medicine Professor Robert Gallo, M.D., who directs the Institute for Human Virology (IHV), became world famous in 1984 when he co-discovered that the HIV virus was the cause of AIDS. IHV is the first center in the United States to combine basic research, epidemiology, and clinical research in a concerted effort to speed the discovery of diagnostics and therapeutics for a wide variety of chronic and deadly viral and immune disorders—most notably the HIV virus. Another world-renowned researcher in the School of Medicine, Curt Civin, M.D., director of the Center for Stem Cell Biology and Regenerative Medicine, is manipulating stem cells to allow for immense improvement in transplantation and transfusion therapies.

The Center for Vaccine Development (CVD) is another global leader in research and treatment. Under Myron Levine, M.D., D.T.P.H., the School of Medicine center has earned an international reputation for creating and testing vaccines against cholera, typhoid, malaria, and other infectious diseases, including smallpox, the West Nile virus, and avian flu.

Tenants in the BioPark include emerging drug discovery companies, bioscience service providers that offer important contract research services to support the

development of new drugs, prestigious university research centers, and educational facilities that support workforce training. Among them are:

- **The University of Maryland School of Medicine Institute for Genome Sciences**—Headed by preeminent genome scientist and microbiologist Claire Fraser-Liggett, Ph.D., the institute is dedicated to the application of genome sciences to advance human health. The interdisciplinary, multidepartmental team uses large-scale, cutting-edge experimental and computational tools to better understand gene and genome function in health and disease. Recent breakthroughs at the institute include decoding the genetic blueprint of viruses that cause the common cold, a discovery that could lead to the first effective treatments of the human rhinovirus.

- **SNBL Clinical Pharmacology Center, Inc.**—As the largest new Japanese investment in Maryland in 20 years and the first BioPark tenant, SNBL opened its doors in 2005. With its 96-bed, state-of-the-art Phase I/IIa Clinical Pharmacy Center, SNBL partners with pharmaceutical companies to accelerate drug development from early stage clinical trials. SNBL's parent company, Shin Nippon Biomedical Laboratories, Ltd., maintains branches and subsidiary companies in Japan, the United States, China, and Europe.

- **Alba Therapeutics Corporation**—Relieving the pain of people suffering from autoimmune, immune-mediated, and inflammatory diseases including celiac disease, Crohn's disease, irritable bowel syndrome, and asthma/chronic obstructive pulmonary disease (COPD), or acute lung injury is the mission of the startup company that grew out of research conducted by Alessio Fasano, M.D., medical director of the Center for Celiac Research and director of the Mucosal Biology Research Center at the University of Maryland School of Medicine.

- **Center for Vascular and Inflammatory Diseases (CVID)**—Advancing the understanding of the biological processes that cause a range of life-threatening diseases including stroke, heart attack, hypertension, diabetes, kidney disease, cancer, arthritis, and autoimmune diseases is the mission of the School of Medicine's CVID. Inflammation is emerging as a key contributor to many vascular diseases and plays a major role in autoimmune diseases.

- **Paragon Bioservices, Inc.**—Providing contract research services for pharmaceutical and biotechnology companies as well as for academic laboratories, Paragon identifies, develops, and produces antibodies, proteins, disease markers, vaccines, and reagents for diagnostics. Paragon also provides scale-up production of biopharmaceuticals for research purposes or Phase I/II clinical trials.

Improving human health is the primary focus of the research and work conducted at the BioPark. Beyond the creation of jobs and new capital investment, other positive spin-off effects of the BioPark's construction include workforce development initiatives with a local health science–focused high school, a long-term partnership with Baltimore City Community College for laboratory technician training, and an on-site MBA program with the University of Maryland Robert H. Smith School of Business. In keeping with President Ramsay's initial vision of academic, government, business, and community partnerships, The University of Maryland BioPark has become a permanent anchor in the West Baltimore community of Poppleton and will enrich lives and advance human health throughout the future.

Additional information about The University of Maryland BioPark is available at www.umbiopark.com.

Above left: A researcher conducts an experiment at the Institute for Genome Sciences. Above center: BioPark tenant Alba Therapeutics Corporation is a biopharmaceutical company focused on the discovery, development, and commercialization of therapeutics to treat autoimmune, immune mediated, and inflammatory diseases. Above right: Staff members of the Center for Vascular and Inflammatory Diseases (CVID) at the University of Maryland School of Medicine—David Scott, Ph.D., associate director for graduate education (left); Toni Antalis, Ph.D., associate director for basic research (center); and Dudley Strickland, Ph.D., director of CVID—discuss a project.

PROFILES OF COMPANIES AND ORGANIZATIONS
Biotechnology

Chesapeake Biological Laboratories, Inc.

This contract manufacturer provides pharmaceutical and biotechnology companies worldwide with filling and finishing services—including formulation, testing, clinical-trial and commercial production, and special freeze-drying, inspection, labeling, packaging, and shipping. With a reputation for excellence, it has a significant impact on patient care, helping to bring error-free medications and safety to health care.

Chesapeake Biological Laboratories, Inc. (CBL) is a contract manufacturer that provides filling and finishing services to pharmaceutical and biotechnology companies in the United States and other countries. Offering more than 20 years of experience in its industry, CBL is committed to the highest standards of quality and to industry-standard good manufacturing practices (GMP). The company combines outstanding facilities, equipment, procedures, and personnel to ensure that it consistently delivers quality products to its clients for distribution to patients worldwide.

CBL was founded in 1980 by William P. Tew, Ph.D.; Samuel Cross; and Paul Wilks, entrepreneurial scientists from the Johns Hopkins University School of Medicine. Its first business endeavor, conducted in conjunction with the university, was to provide biochemical analyses of synovial fluid samples from racehorses for hyaluronic acid degradation, to help veterinarians diagnose and manage joint disorders. CBL was then contracted by a renowned pharmaceutical company to provide a commercial hyaluronic acid product for use in ophthalmic treatment. By 1995 CBL had gained a reputation for excellence and began to accept contract work from companies around the world.

Today CBL develops and manufactures injectables for a wide range of pharmaceutical companies, serving as the client's single source of service, from formulation or technical transfer and scale-up to commercial production. The company works in partnership with clients to bring their product to market in the most timely and cost-effective way.

Services and Technologies

From 1990 to 2008, CBL served more than 150 companies and manufactured more than 175 products, maintaining as its core principles high quality project management and client partnership. The company's services include formulation, aseptic filling, assay development, stability testing, clinical-supply production, commercial production, and lyophilization—a process of freeze-drying that is used to preserve temperature-sensitive biologicals and pharmaceuticals. CBL can custom-design GMP processes to handle unique formulations, aseptic filling, and lyophilization processes. It also can custom-tailor inspection, labeling, bulk packaging, and shipping methods for clients.

CBL produces supplies for Phase I, Phase II, and Phase III clinical trials. The company recognizes that clients who have invested in research and development over years-long time spans want to bring their products to clinical trial as quickly as possible. CBL can actively manage the purchase order–to-product process in 120 days using proven components and processes. Equally advantageous are CBL's strong working relationships with the Food and Drug Administration (FDA) and with European authorities, both of which have approved products at CBL facilities.

Superior Facilities

In 1997 CBL relocated its corporate headquarters and manufacturing operations from a 15,000-square-foot facility in northwest Baltimore to its current location at Camden Industrial Park in south Baltimore. The CBL complex includes the 70,000-square-foot main plant, commonly referred to as Building C, and a second smaller plant, Building B, 15,000 square feet of space previously utilized to deliver

drug product to the Strategic National Stockpile. CBL is routinely inspected by the FDA; the Medicines and Healthcare products Regulatory Agency (MHRA) of the United Kingdom (UK); the European Medicines Agency (EMEA) of the European Union, headquartered in the UK; and the Pharmaceuticals and Medical Devices Agency (PMDA) of Japan.

CBL's main plant houses the most advanced equipment and technologies available and meets the international regulations required to serve customers from around the world. The 16 commercial products manufactured by CBL as of 2008 are approved for distribution in the United States, Canada, Europe, and/or Japan.

Building C, consisting of 70,000 square feet, houses corporate headquarters, central commercial manufacturing, three independent Class 100 clean rooms, and two formulation rooms. A multiproduct plant, Building C is dedicated to noninfectious, non-live products. It has the capability of filling and lyophilizing lots in sizes up to approximately 120,000 units of liquid products and up to approximately 82,000 units of lyophilized products.

CBL's parent company is Cangene Corporation, a world leader in the development, manufacture, and commercialization of specialty hyperimmune blood plasma and biotechnology products. Cangene is a leader in striving to reduce infectious diseases such as botulism, hepatitis B, and anthrax and continues to build its success on life-antibody products. A $160 million company, Cangene maintains state-of-the-art research, development, and manufacturing operations in Canada, with headquarters and operations in Winnipeg, Manitoba. Cangene also owns and operates plasma-collection facilities in the United States located in Frederick, Maryland, as well as in California and in Florida.

Growth at CBL

CBL is in the process of a $15 million, two-year expansion of its facilities in south Baltimore. The expanded space will enable the production of new commercial products as they are approved, while also supporting the projected growth of the company's current commercial products. CBL has 110 employees and estimates an approximate 30 percent staff increase within the same time frame.

Throughout CBL's growth, the company has consistently maintained its Baltimore roots. Baltimore and the surrounding areas have provided CBL with the resources to staff its plants for the successful delivery of millions of doses of life-saving and quality-of-life medicines over the years. CBL serves people all around the world who, for the most part, have never even heard of Chesapeake Biological Laboratories, Inc. in Baltimore, Maryland.

The staff of CBL gives back to the community in a variety of ways. It makes canned-food donations to local food banks, contributes new toys to local child care facilities, hosts blood drives on-site with the American Red Cross, and makes contributions to various additional local charities. In 2008 it participated with a National Team in the American Diabetes Association's Step Out: Walk to Fight Diabetes, placing seventh among the corporations that raised the most funds.

Chesapeake Biological Laboratories, Inc. provides additional information about its services on its Web site at www.cblinc.com.

Above left: In a Class 100 clean room in CBL's Building C, an operator checks a plate of syringes after stopper insertion. Above right: In Building B, an operator unloads vials from a 120-square-foot hull lyophilizer.

MedImmune

This company is a global leader in developing novel, proprietary biologics and vaccines. An entrepreneurial, vertically integrated business, it is committed to advancing science to create better technologies and medicines to help people live healthier, longer, and more satisfying lives. It invests in its local communities and provides major support for efforts striving to alleviate infectious diseases worldwide.

Since its founding in 1988 in Gaithersburg, Maryland, MedImmune has distinguished itself as an innovator in developing and commercializing vaccines as well as biologics—agents synthesized from living organisms or their products and used medically as a preventive or therapeutic compound. This company developed and commercialized the first monoclonal antibody for an infectious disease to be approved by the U.S. Food and Drug Administration (FDA), in 1998. MedImmune also developed and commercialized the first and only nasal-spray influenza vaccine approved for use in the United States, representing the first breakthrough in influenza technology in more than 60 years. MedImmune has been the first to achieve other medical advances as well. These included the development of a viruslike particle (VLP) technology that is used in human

papilloma virus (HPV) vaccines to help prevent cervical cancer and the discovery of a treatment for rheumatoid arthritis.

MedImmune was acquired by one of the world's leading pharmaceutical companies, London-based AstraZeneca, in 2007, and has maintained its global headquarters and state-of-the-art research and development (R&D) facilities in Gaithersburg. Next, AstraZeneca brought together all of its biologics activities—including one of its previous acquisitions, the British biopharmaceuticals company Cambridge Antibody Technology—with MedImmune. Today, with some 100 products in its pipeline, MedImmune is leveraging the resources, expertise, and global reach of its parent company while also preserving its original strategy of intelligent entrepreneurship.

Turning raw materials into actual products is the charge of MedImmune's four major manufacturing facilities, which produce antibodies and live viral vaccines. Its Frederick Manufacturing Center, located in Frederick, Maryland, uses an innovative, high-yield technology to produce palivizumab. Its plant in Speke, England, was built specifically to produce its nasal-spray influenza vaccine and enables the company to make up to 50 million monovalent vaccine doses at a time. These are shipped to the United States, where workers at the company's Philadelphia, Pennsylvania, facility blend and package the vaccine. A fourth plant, located in Nijmegen, The Netherlands, makes a drug used to lessen the side effects of chemotherapy and radiation.

With continued growth on the horizon, MedImmune has expanded its European facilities to stay ahead of anticipated demand. It honored its 20th anniversary in 2008 by adding a 92,000-square-foot R&D building in Cambridge, England, in the heart of the bioscience community, and expanding and refurbishing its Nijmegen facility. The new Cambridge building, which was named the Aaron Klug Building after the winner of the 1982 Nobel Prize for Chemistry, comprises two state-of-the-art laboratories that double MedImmune's capacity

for developing new drugs and technologies. The Nijmegen plant has a new clean room designed to facilitate large-scale production of materials for commercial and clinical-trial use. It also has added capacity that enables it to manufacture up to 10 new products per year.

Because a global influenza pandemic is possible today, MedImmune has created a comprehensive strategy and preparation for the rapid development of vaccines. Working in partnership with the National Institutes of Health (NIH), the company has prepared pandemic live, attenuated influenza vaccines (LAIVs) for all subtypes of influenza and is conducting tests to ensure their safety. With the U.S. Department of Health & Human Services*, MedImmune developed the technology to produce pandemic LAIVs in cell culture and the surge capacity to produce these in eggs. To further the development of pandemic vaccines that are being researched globally by other organizations, the company also has made its proprietary reverse-genetics technology available to public and private vaccine manufacturers. Using reverse genetics, influenza vaccines can be generated from DNA segments, alleviating the danger to manufacturers of working directly with the highly infectious viruses.

MedImmune supports a Patient Access Network Foundation that provides millions of dollars in assistance to the underinsured. In addition, MedImmune contributes more than $3 million each year in educational grants and scientific sponsorships, and its employees volunteer to help efforts devoted to advancing health or science education.

MedImmune provides additional information about its products and activities on its Web site at www.medimmune.com.

With its goal of taking six new programs to human clinical trials and identifying seven new drug candidates each year, MedImmune strives to make good on its promise of a healthier life for the world's citizens.

Above left: MedImmune's Gaithersburg headquarters was honored as Best Biotech Office and Best Interiors—Commercial Space in 2004 by the Maryland chapter of the National Association of Industrial and Office Properties, which recognizes superior performance in commercial and industrial real estate. Above right: MedImmune's Maryland locations include the company's biologics facility in Frederick—the Frederick Manufacturing Center. This center highlights MedImmune's leadership in the state's biotechnology industry. Shown here is one of the bioreactors.

* These projects are funded in whole or in part with federal funds from the Office of the Assistant Secretary for Preparedness and Response (ASPR), Biomedical Advanced Research and Development Authority, under Contract Nos. HHSO100200600010C and HHSO100200700036C. The total federal program funding for these contracts is $221,379,570, representing approximately 92 percent of the total amount of the projects. The remaining 8 percent of the total amount for the projects is anticipated to be financed by nongovernmental sources. The content of this publication does not necessarily reflect the views or policies of the Department of Health and Human Services, nor does the mention of trade names, commercial products, or organizations imply endorsement by the U.S. government.

Shimadzu Scientific Instruments, Inc.

The American arm of the rapidly expanding, $2.5 billion Shimadzu Corporation, this Maryland-based maker of high-precision products is committed to contributing to society through pioneering technologies. Today it is using its resources to develop state-of-the-art solutions in the fields of pharmaceuticals and the life sciences, forensics, industry, and the environment, especially focusing on research applications, biotechnology equipment, and environmental protection.

By developing advanced technologies for science, medicine, industry, and the environment, Shimadzu Scientific Instruments, Inc. and its parent company, Shimadzu Corporation, are pioneering discoveries that can improve the quality of life for people throughout the world. Shimadzu Scientific Instruments is an American subsidiary of Shimadzu Corporation, which is headquartered in Kyoto, Japan. Shimadzu Corporation manufactures products in Asia, in Europe, and in the United States in Oregon. It has service and support facilities in Asia, Australia, the Near East, and the Americas, and distributors worldwide.

With a reputation for excellence around the world, Shimadzu Corporation is known for its many inventions, from its creation of the first medical X-ray machine to be used in Japan to its development of the world's fastest DNA sequencer. Shimadzu Corporation was founded in Kyoto in 1875 by Genzo Shimadzu Sr., who started the company to manufacture scientific instruments for education. He began with the belief that Japan should strive to become a leader in science and the goal of making a contribution by spreading scientific knowledge.

In 1877 Shimadzu conducted Japan's first manned balloon flight. Eventually he passed along his talent for technological invention to his eldest son, Genzo Shimadzu Jr., who clearly inherited his father's passion for science and technology. In 1896, two years after his father's untimely death, Genzo Shimadzu Jr., along with Hanichi Muraoka, a professor at the predecessor of Kyoto University, created the first X-ray images made in Japan. By 1909 Shimadzu Corporation had developed Japan's first medical X-ray apparatus. When he died, in 1951, Genzo Shimadzu Jr. had created no fewer than 178 products. He is hailed as one of Japan's 10 greatest inventors.

Carrying on the pioneering spirit of its founding family, Shimadzu Corporation continues to make global contributions in science and technology with the development of numerous product innovations, including photoelectric spectrophotometers, liquid chromatographs, gas chromatograph mass spectrometers, and environmental monitoring analyzers.

Shimadzu Today and Tomorrow

Shimadzu Corporation applies its legacy of scientific invention to the challenges of the 21st century. Its areas of focus include scientific instrumentation, medical systems, aircraft equipment, industrial machinery, and instruments for monitoring the environment. Among its core products are spectrometers, chromatographs, X-ray inspection machines, medical flat-panel detectors, aircraft systems equipment, and environmental-measurement systems. While maintaining its commitment to customers of traditional analytical instruments, Shimadzu Corporation is developing products in the areas of semiconductors, flat-panel displays, environmental monitoring, and the life sciences—areas that it sees as central to its future growth. Initiatives include developing state-of-the-art analytical instruments to conduct increasingly sophisticated genetic and protein analysis, and initiating research into disease biomarker discovery for early disease detection.

Shimadzu Corporation operates as three divisions: Medical Diagnostics, Aerospace/Industrial, and Analytical Instruments. Its Analytical Instruments division is one of the

world's largest manufacturers of measuring-and-analyzing devices and environmental-monitoring equipment. The Analytical Instruments division accounts for approximately 57 percent of Shimadzu Corporation's business, which achieves $2.5 billion in annual sales. The division's American arm, Shimadzu Scientific Instruments (SSI), established in 1975, is headquartered in Columbia, Maryland. SSI provides solutions to laboratories across North America, Central America, and parts of South America for an array of applications in science and industry ranging from drug discovery to biofuel analysis to homeland security. Steady and controlled growth has seen the opening of nine regional offices across the United States; a state-of-the-art Customer Training and Education Center; Shimadzu U.S.A. Manufacturing in Canby, Oregon; and, most recently, Life Science Applications Laboratories in California and Maryland.

The Shimadzu Corporation staff is dedicated to supporting the success of its customers worldwide. Product engineers and applications specialists in Maryland and highly trained field service technicians at more than 50 sites in the Americas are strategically available to provide fast, efficient responses to customers' specific needs. Beyond Japan and the Americas, Shimadzu Corporation maintains headquarters in Europe, China, and other parts of Asia for sales, service, and technical support. The corporation also provides an advanced training and education center in Kyoto for its customers.

SSI Precision Products

SSI products include chromatographs, molecular and elemental spectrometers, balances, and environmental analyzers. Its analytical instruments are used for research and quality control in many endeavors, such as developing new pharmaceuticals and identifying environmental pollutants and food contaminants. For key instruments, including liquid chromatographs and gas chromatograph mass spectrometers, SSI continually builds on its technologies to meet the emerging needs of new research applications. SSI is a leader in products supporting life science research, developing new tools—such as advanced MALDI-TOF mass spectrometers, which support genome and proteome research—by integrating novel chemistry with innovative technology to achieve a unique position as a true provider of solutions for life scientists.

Long before today's global concerns about environmental issues, Shimadzu Corporation was developing environmental-measurement systems to analyze the quality of air, water, and soil. SSI is pushing forward with full-scale promotion of these systems. SSI also offers precision testing and inspection machines that increase production efficiency and help ensure end-product safety and reliability.

Moving Forward

As a global leader in technology solutions for today's world, Shimadzu Corporation maintains research centers in Japan, where it also has established life sciences laboratories for advanced research and development (R&D) of biological instruments and reagents. Among these laboratories is the Mass Spectrometry Research Laboratory in Kyoto, Japan. Headed by Koichi Tanaka, who was awarded the Nobel Prize in Chemistry in 2002, this laboratory conducts research for the development of new mass spectrometry techniques and equipment for analyzing biological macro-molecules such as proteins. In addition, Shimadzu Corporation conducts research jointly with Bristol-Myers Squibb and other research entities in the United States and Europe, universities, and government entities including the National Institutes of Health. By partnering with customers, Shimadzu Corporation will continue to develop instruments that deliver results faster and more efficiently than ever before to meet the needs of researchers, scientists, and manufacturers around the globe.

Shimadzu Scientific Instruments, Inc. provides additional information about its products and activities on its Web site at www.ssi.shimadzu.com.

Above left: Shimadzu Corporation's Prominence Ultrafast Liquid Chromatograph (UFLC) delivers exceptional speed and reproducibility, making it ideal for a variety of laboratories and industries, including pharmaceuticals. Above right: Part of a suite of MALDI-TOF mass spectrometers, the AXIMA Performance TOF/TOF system is ideal for complex biomolecule and polymer characterization.

United Therapeutics Corporation

This biotechnology company develops and commercializes unique products designed to address the unmet medical needs of patients with chronic and life-threatening cardiovascular and infectious diseases and cancer. Its research and development efforts focus on five treatment platforms—prostacyclin analogs, phosphodiesterase 5 inhibitors, glycobiology antiviral agents, monoclonal antibodies, and telemedicine.

United Therapeutics Corporation (United Therapeutics) is a biotechnology company founded in 1996 by Martine Rothblatt, Ph.D., Chairman and CEO. United Therapeutics was formed and continues to be driven by Dr. Rothblatt's desire to save her own child's life by finding a cure for pulmonary arterial hypertension (PAH), a disease that affects the blood vessels between the heart and lungs. United Therapeutics is focused on the development and commercialization of unique products to address the unmet medical needs of patients with chronic and life-threatening cardiovascular diseases, infectious diseases, and cancer. Quality of life is the utmost therapeutic goal for the team at United Therapeutics.

Above: The international headquarters of United Therapeutics Corporation is located in Silver Spring, Maryland.

United Therapeutics is continually researching and developing forward-thinking pharmaceuticals in the spirit of its motto: "Medicines For Life." The company's research and development efforts are actively focused on five treatment platforms: prostacyclin analogs, phosphodiesterase 5 inhibitors, glycobiology antiviral agents, monoclonal antibodies, and telemedicine. One of its goals is to develop and market medications to treat PAH patients across the full spectrum of the disease, with subcutaneous, intravenous, and inhaled prostacyclin therapy, and oral formulations of prostacyclin and tadalafil. The innovative approach that United Therapeutics takes toward business growth generates a rich product pipeline and an excellent return for its investors. The company's revenue has increased from $53.3 million in 2003 to $281.5 million in 2008. It is the only biotech company in the United States to achieve eight consecutive years of more than 30 percent annual revenue growth.

Set on the edge of the urban district of Silver Spring, Maryland, United Therapeutics' ever-expanding campus is also the Company's international headquarters. Remodulin®, the company's parenteral therapy for the treatment of PAH in subcutaneous and intravenous formulations, is manufactured on-site in United Therapeutics' laboratories in Silver Spring.

United Therapeutics also is adding value to the downtown area of Silver Spring by creating exciting and interesting architecture for its offices and laboratory space, including lively public plazas, retail shops, and outdoor gathering space for the community. In accordance with United Therapeutics' initiative to be an environmentally friendly global corporate citizen, all of its new facilities are Leadership in Energy and Environmental Design (LEED)-certified. These sustainable structures use water-efficient systems, capture power from the sun for heat, and harness natural light. United Therapeutics also has offices in North Carolina, Florida, Vermont, Canada, and the United Kingdom.

United Therapeutics, a Delaware corporation, is traded on the Nasdaq Global Select Market under the symbol UTHR. The company provides additional information about its products and activities on its Web site at www.unither.com.

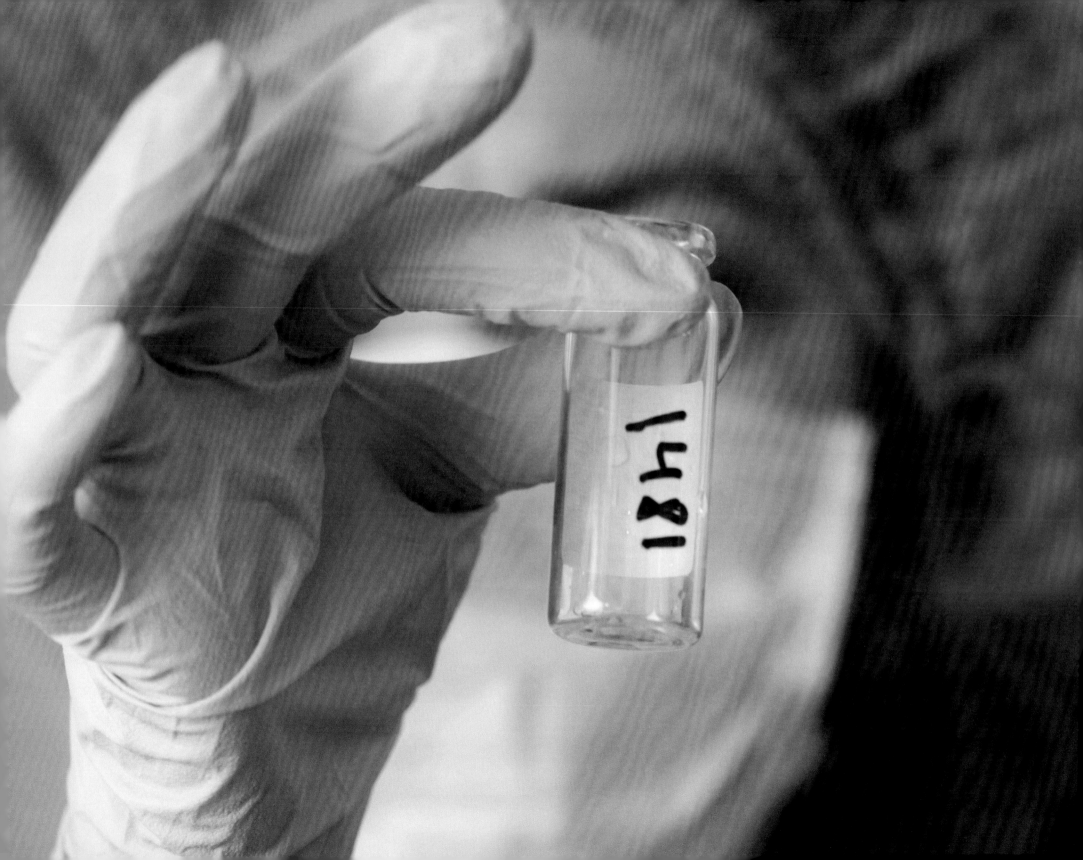

PROFILES OF COMPANIES AND ORGANIZATIONS
Consumer Goods Distribution

Reliable Churchill LLLP

This premier wine and spirits distributor—the largest in Maryland—represents many of the finest suppliers in its industry. A member of The Charmer Sunbelt Group, Reliable Churchill is committed to providing excellent service for its customers and to taking a lead in promoting the responsible sale and consumption of alcoholic beverages in its community.

A Plan for Sustainable Growth

Several milestones mark Reliable Churchill's rich history. In 1988, Churchill became part of Sunbelt Beverage, which in 1994 combined with Charmer Industries to become The Charmer Sunbelt Group (CSG). Then, in 1997, Churchill acquired Quality Brands, moved into a new warehouse, streamlined its business, and increased its operational efficiencies.

The true leap forward for Churchill was its 2002 merger with Reliable Liquors, forming the company that today is known as Reliable Churchill. The combined leadership, resources, and an unrelenting focus on driving business for its key suppliers have propelled the company to achieve strong annual growth. Driving toward even better sales and service, the executive team reinvests that growth in the company: upgrading sales force technology; integrating proprietary sales-analysis tools; implementing Systems Applications and Products (SAP) for wholesale distribution; and expanding warehouse capacity and the distribution fleet to meet anticipated demand. In all, more than $3 million in capital investments were made in the two years from 2006 to 2008.

A Vision Toward the Future

While growth is an important element of the business, Reliable Churchill's vision is to be the "Distributor of Choice" in Maryland. The company accomplishes this goal by providing customers and suppliers with the best possible service, by continually upgrading systems that provide a competitive advantage to business partners, and by creating a business environment that attracts, develops, and retains the highest quality workforce.

Additionally, for Reliable Churchill, being the "Distributor of Choice" means acknowledging and embracing the fact that participation in the beverage alcohol industry is not a right, it is a privilege, and with that privilege comes responsibility. In fact, responsibility is a hallmark of Reliable Churchill that is fully embraced by all associates, from senior executives to warehouse

Above: Reliable Churchill LLLP, based in Baltimore, Maryland, is a premier distributor of wine and spirits, representing many of the industry's finest wine and spirits suppliers.

Reliable Churchill LLLP is a member of The Charmer Sunbelt Group, one of the nation's leading distributors of spirits, fine wines, beers, and bottled water. Reliable Churchill is the critical link between the companies that produce alcoholic beverages and the retail outlets where they are sold or the restaurants and pubs where they are consumed.

Reliable Churchill's roots date back to 1946. Among its 525 associates, there is a nucleus of senior executives who have been with the company for more than 25 years. The company prides itself on strong customer relationships, commitment to training and development, and deployment of industry-leading systems, the combination of which has made them a sales and service leader in Maryland's wine and spirits industry.

personnel to drivers. For Reliable Churchill, this means maintaining a commitment to responsible business practices in dealing with the community, customers, and suppliers, but equally important, assuming responsibility in managing the way products are marketed and sold.

In the community, Reliable Churchill is an active supporter of charities that aid and assist Maryland's children and support the general business climate. Chief among the organizations supported by Reliable Churchill and its associates are the Chesapeake Bay Foundation, with the motto "Save the Bay"; Susan G. Komen for the Cure; the Ray Lewis Foundation; the Downtown Partnership of Baltimore; and the Chesapeake Bay Maritime Museum. Additionally, each year Reliable Churchill associates come together to provide turkey dinners for local families at Thanksgiving, as well as toys for needy children during the holiday season.

A Commitment to Responsible Drinking

In 2003, Reliable Churchill's parent company solidified its commitment to the responsible sales and consumption of alcoholic beverages by investing in a position dedicated solely to working with local community leaders to proactively drive social responsibility in communities and within the industry. Since that time, this collaboration with Maryland officials has positioned Reliable Churchill as an industry leader, widely regarded for partnering with government, legislators,

regulators, suppliers, retailers, and community leaders to heighten awareness and drive the prevention of alcohol abuse and underage drinking.

Reliable Churchill associates and retailers are also actively recruited to support the company's socially responsible initiatives. The company engages with both audiences, including the Maryland Retail Association, to promote responsible server training and education about underage drinking and drunk driving. As a result, Reliable Churchill received a commendation from Maryland Governor Martin O'Malley for "making Maryland a safer place to live."

Recognizing Reliable Churchill as an expert in this area, retailers, including licensees in non-CSG markets, turn to the company for guidance and assistance in providing the tools they need to advance responsible beverage service and lead efforts to fight underage drinking and drunk driving in their communities.

Reliable Churchill LLLP provides additional information about its services and activities on its Web site at www.reliable-churchill.com.

Above left: To achieve its vision of being the "Distributor of Choice" in Maryland, Reliable Churchill continually upgrades the systems that provide a competitive advantage for its business partners. Above right, top and bottom: Reliable Churchill regularly reinvests revenue growth in the company, expanding warehouse capacity and distribution fleet to meet anticipated increases in demand.

PROFILES OF COMPANIES AND ORGANIZATIONS
Defense Technology and Government Services

Alliant Techsystems Inc. (ATK)

This premier advanced weapon and space systems company applies 'rocket science' to ensure mission success in propulsion systems for aerospace, commercial, defense, and space-mission applications. ATK has revenues in excess of $4.5 billion and employs more than 19,000 people in 22 states, with more than 2,200 employees in Maryland.

Above: An aerial view of Alliant Techsystems Inc.'s (ATK's) Elkton Operations in Maryland shows the facility's 550-acre campus, with more than 125 buildings that support the employment of nearly 800 people at ATK Elkton Operations. ATK is a premier defense and aerospace company.

Alliant Techsystems Inc. (ATK), a premier weapons and aerospace company, has locations in 22 states and around the world, and among these facilities it has significant ties to the state of Maryland. A can-do mindset permeates ATK and has helped the company build a reputation for product quality and technical excellence. Formed in 1990, ATK has the combined elements of Honeywell Systems Group, Hercules Aerospace, Thiokol Propulsion, GASL and Micro Craft, Mission Research Corporation, Swales Aerospace, and several smaller aerospace suppliers.

As of April 2009, ATK comprised three groups—Mission, Space, and Armament systems. ATK has more than 19,000 employees and in excess of $4.5 billion in annual revenue and provides market leadership with advanced technology to defend the nation and to support space exploration. The company's products are designed to meet the needs of commercial customers, the U.S. Department of Defense (DoD), and NASA.

ATK is headquartered in Eden Prairie, Minnesota. Its U.S. operations include more than 60 facilities in 22 states and Puerto Rico, and it also has representatives in more than 50 countries throughout the world. ATK's primary operations include the Mission Systems group and Tactical Propulsion and Controls (TPC) division headquarters in Baltimore, Elkton Operations in Elkton, Space Systems in Beltsville, and Integrated Systems in California, Maryland.

Mission Systems

ATK's Mission Systems in Baltimore offers affordable and effective mission-critical solutions with innovative advanced weapon systems and force-protection weapon systems to arm and protect all facets of the military.

Mission Systems is home to a cutting-edge Virtual Engineering Center (VEC)—a multiroom computer simulation and visualization site—designed and equipped to provide enhanced virtual simulation and serve as a state-of-the-art setting for collaborative engineering modeling and evaluation in a secure environment. The VEC system uses advanced three-dimensional visualization and surround-sound technology to provide detailed battlefield simulations (which include weapon systems and command and control) in order to provide the government and other DoD primary contractors with realistic product-performance assessments under simulated battlefield-operations scenarios.

Tactical Propulsion and Controls

Also headquartered in Baltimore is Mission Systems' Tactical Propulsion and Controls division. All of the products of Mission Systems' Tactical Propulsion and Controls division are built with precision as a primary attribute. Many of the products begin on the drawing boards at the Elkton Operations site, where solid rocket motor propulsion systems were pioneered by Thiokol Corporation (now part of ATK).

Elkton Operations

The ATK presence in Maryland is rooted in its Elkton Operations, on 550 acres in Elkton. In early 1948, Thiokol, with just a dozen employees, began to develop composite solid propellants and solid propellant rocket motors. By July of the same year, the first Thiokol-made rocket was static-tested. In 1950, work for the U.S. Army was moved to the Redstone Arsenal in Huntsville, Alabama, but within a year it was reinstated at Elkton to meet the demand from other military services, principally the U.S. Navy. By 1954, the division had more than 50 employees and had established a solid reputation as one of the nation's major suppliers of solid propellant rocket motors.

In 1957, Elkton Operations helped to begin the Space Age, with propulsion that launched NASA's Project Farside deep-space probe. Retro rockets for NASA produced by the division returned Mercury and Gemini astronauts to Earth, and beginning in 1968 Elkton Operations delivered 13 motors for each of NASA's Apollo/Saturn flights.

From the mid 1950s through 2008, more than 2,430 Elkton STAR™ series high-performance upper-stage motors were flown, placing in orbit a variety of communication satellites as well as the Global Positioning System (GPS) constellation while delivering a flight-success rate of better than 99.87 percent. Elkton Operations' solid rocket-propulsion systems supported NASA missions including Moon landings, such as Surveyor in 1966 and the Lunar Prospector in 1999, and Mars landings,

including air bag–inflation gas generators and retro rockets for the Pathfinder, Spirit, and Opportunity rovers. In addition, the division has supported Pioneer and Voyager missions to Venus, Saturn, Pluto, and beyond the solar system.

Elkton Operations also routinely produces booster separation motors for tactical missiles including Harpoon, a U.S. Navy dedicated antiship missile, in addition to boosters for antisubmarine rockets and gas generators to power thrust vector-control nozzles for ballistic missiles—technology that is integral to the U.S. Navy. In early 2008, an ATK-produced third-stage and divert system for a missile defense program performed perfectly in shooting down a disabled U.S. government satellite. During the flight, ATK's SDACS maneuvered to allow the kinetic warhead (KW) to precisely intercept the satellite approximately 153 miles above the Earth—a feat compared to a "bullet hitting a bullet."

Integrated Systems

In 2008, the Integrated Systems division of Mission Systems added a field office in California, Maryland, that supports the division's Advanced Systems and Mission Research Centers in California, its Manufacturing and Development Center in Florida, and its Airborne ISR (Intelligence, Surveillance, and Reconnaissance) Development Center in Texas. ATK Integrated Systems concentrates on the design, development, and production of electronic warfare and defense electronics and special-mission aircraft.

Above, left to right: ATK Elkton's STAR™ motors were used to complete payload separation for United Launch Alliance's successful launch of the Delta II rocket, which carried the NAVSTAR Global Positioning System Block 2R military navigation satellite. Elkton Operations provided 13 motors for Apollo missions. ATK manufactures the two four-segment reusable solid rocket motors for the U.S. Space Shuttle. Elkton Operations produces retro motors and ordnance components that combine with ATK Solid Rocket Motor Upgrade boosters to support Titan space launch vehicle missions.

Alliant Techsystems Inc. (ATK)

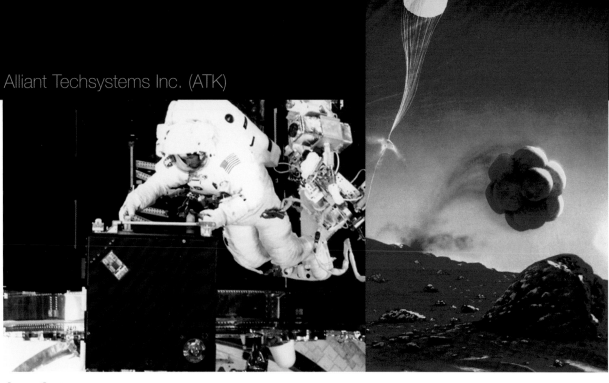

Space Systems

ATK is breaking boundaries in space and its Space Systems is the world's top producer of solid rocket motor propulsion systems. It is also a leading provider of small and microsatellites, satellite components and subsystems, missile defense, and strategic missile propulsion. Additionally, it is a leading producer of lightweight space deployables and solar arrays and a leader in low-cost, quick-to-market launch solutions. In fact, in 2007 Space Systems received a contract for development on NASA's Ares I program, joining a new vision of space exploration.

ATK Space Systems in Maryland began with peanuts—plus about $12,000. In fact, part of the start-up strategy of the engineering-services firm was for the entrepreneurs to buy hot, roasted peanuts from the NASA Goddard Employees Welfare Association and share the peanuts with their NASA Goddard Space Flight Center counterpart engineers. As a start-up group, employees worked from a small office at Goddard as close to the Goddard engineers as possible—and the strategy worked! The small firm was chartered on April 17, 1978, as Swales Aerospace by Tom Swales, chairman, along with Tom Wilson, Ron Luzier, and John Anderes. The founding philosophy was fairly simple—to provide world-class engineering and systems

solutions to enable its customers to succeed. And succeed they did. The firm's simple strategy, combined with advanced technical expertise and unwavering integrity, allowed Swales Aerospace to grow to more than 900 employees. In 1985, it was established at its present location in Beltsville.

In the 1990s, Swales ventured from engineering into manufacturing hardware for satellites and tools for astronauts. This led to designing an instrument package for NASA—far ultraviolet spectroscopic explorer (FUSE)—to explore the universe using the technique of high-resolution spectroscopy in the far-ultraviolet spectral region. Swales went on to become the global leader in the development and manufacture of two-phase thermal technology and solutions for space flight applications—including heat pipe equipment panels; radiators, including deployable radiators; primary structure; and optical benches—equipment that flies on commercial and military communications satellites, NASA missions, and the International Space Station (ISS). Swales—now ATK Space Systems—continues to support the Hubble Space Telescope (HST) through repair missions. A more efficient solar array and a cooling system—near-infrared camera and multi-object spectrometer (NICMOS)—were designed for the HST. NASA's Earth Observing-1 (EO-1), an experimental remote-sensing satellite—for which ATK served as prime contractor, mission integrator, and business developer—was launched in 2000 and remains in service as of 2008.

In 2000, Swales was one of three companies chosen by NASA to develop lightweight spacecraft. Swales was awarded a NASA contract at Langley Research Center and a contract at Goddard Space Flight Center. Swales acquired most of the assets of Dynatherm, a Hunt Valley, Maryland, developer of thermal management systems.

In 2007, ATK, with Swales as prime contractor, delivered the TacSat-3 spacecraft bus to the Air Force Research Laboratory. Swales also was the prime contractor for the spacecraft bus and the satellite dispenser probe carrier for NASA's Time History of Events and Macroscale Interactions (THEMIS), which was successfully launched from Cape Canaveral, Florida. THEMIS consists of five identical satellites designed to fly as a constellation. Its mission is to discover what causes auroras (like the northern lights) in the Earth's atmosphere to change from slow light waves to shifting streaks of color, to determine the cause of global reconfiguration of the Earth's magnetosphere.

Swales Aerospace was acquired by ATK in 2007 and provides a diverse array of engineering, scientific, and technical support to the manned and unmanned NASA/Civil Space community and the DoD. ATK's key capabilities include expertise in mechanical, structural, and thermal design analysis. Additional capabilities include manufacturing, assembly, integration, and test (MAI&T) of space-centric specialty hardware, such as Space Shuttle extravehicular activity (EVA) tools, structures, instruments, optical benches, and mechanisms. ATK also is a leader in building small satellites and microsatellites and continues to make an impact on the small-spacecraft community with its contract awarded in 2008 to co-provide the first operationally responsive spacelift (ORS) satellite.

NASA and branches of the U.S. Armed Forces are the primary customers of ATK. In 2008, 78 percent of ATK's sales, totaling $3.257 billion, were to the U.S. government. The remaining 22 percent of sales were to commercial United States and foreign customers through processes approved by the DoD and the U.S. State Department or the U.S. Commerce Department. ATK products are sold to U.S. allies both directly and through the U.S. government. Major government customers include law enforcement, such as large metropolitan police departments, the Department of Homeland Security, the Federal Bureau of Investigation, and the U.S. Secret Service. Major customers of ATK's commercial products include retailers, such as Wal-Mart, Cabela's, and Gander Mountain, as well as large wholesale distributors.

ATK provides additional information about the company and its activities on its Web site at www.atk.com.

In addition to many employees who work at its facilities in Baltimore, Elkton, and Beltsville, ATK has additional Maryland ties with employees who live in and around Cumberland, Maryland, and work for Tactical Propulsion and Controls at the Allegany Ballistics Laboratory in Rocket Center, West Virginia. Similarly, many ATK personnel live in Maryland and work at the ATK office in Washington, D.C., further reinforcing ATK's ties to the state.

ATK is proud of its technical heritage and its capabilities in solid rocket motor propulsion systems. Its Maryland-based facilities and personnel—including more than 2,200 engineers, scientists, technical program management personnel, support personnel, and technicians—apply "rocket science" to ensure mission success in propulsion systems for aerospace, commercial, defense, and space mission applications.

Above: The International Space Station is equipped with technology solutions developed and manufactured at ATK's Beltsville, Maryland, location.

Northrop Grumman Corporation Electronic Systems

This Maryland company's electronics solutions span the spectrum. It is a leading developer, manufacturer, integrator, and supporter of a variety of advanced electronic and maritime systems for U.S. and international customers for defense and security as well as commercial applications.

Since the 1930s, the Electronic Systems sector of Northrop Grumman Corporation has distinguished itself through engineering innovation, pioneering design, breakthrough thinking, and, above all, achievement. Today Electronic Systems is a global leader in designing and developing advanced solutions for the U.S. Department of Defense and various other U.S. governmental agencies as well as numerous international customers.

Headquartered in Linthicum, Maryland, the Electronic Systems sector's portfolio of defense and commercial electronics and systems includes airborne radar sensors, navigation systems, electronic countermeasures, precision weapons, airspace management systems, communication systems, space sensors, marine and naval systems, and government systems.

The Electronic Systems sector provides some of the most sought-after radar, electronic warfare, and targeting systems in aerospace and defense. The sector's sophisticated technologies form the backbone of today's integrated electronic battlefield—from undersea to outer space and cyberspace. The sector employs approximately 21,000 people worldwide, including about 8,500 employees in Maryland, with major facilities in Linthicum, Annapolis, and Sykesville. The company's annual economic impact in the state is approximately $2 billion.

Northrop Grumman Corporation, with headquarters in Los Angeles, California, is a leading global security company whose 120,000 employees provide innovative systems, products, and solutions in aerospace, electronics, information systems, shipbuilding, and technical services to government and commercial customers worldwide.

Electronic Systems in Maryland

The Electronic Systems sector's Maryland-based products include a wide variety of radar systems for fighter and surveillance aircraft as well as helicopters. These include fire control and navigation radars for the F-16, C-130, B-1B, F-22, and F-35 aircraft as well as other key avionics for the F-16 Block 60 and F-35 aircraft.

Added in 2008 to the company's family of multifunction sensors is the Scalable Agile Beam Radar (SABR) designed for retrofit on F-16 fighters and other platforms. Airborne surveillance radar systems include the heritage Airborne Warning and Control System (AWACS) radar for the Boeing 707 platform, and the Multi-role Electronically Scanned Array (MESA) radar sensor for the Boeing 737 airborne early warning and control aircraft. Northrop Grumman, in a joint venture with Lockheed Martin, also is producing the fire control radar and Longbow Hellfire fire-and-forget missile for the U.S. Army's Apache Longbow helicopter.

Above right: The headquarters facility for Northrop Grumman Corporation's Electronic Systems sector is located in Linthicum, Maryland.

A new Ground/Air Task Oriented Radar (G/ATOR) being developed by Northrop Grumman for the U.S. Marine Corps consolidates the missions of five Marine Corps radars into a single multirole radar system. G/ATOR is a mobile system intended to fully support the Marine Corps's expeditionary warfare requirements and will enable enhanced operational capabilities, thanks to Northrop Grumman's proven Active Electronically Scanned Array (AESA) radar technology.

Over the years, the Electronic Systems sector's Linthicum area operations have supplied the sensors for scores of space-based missions, including NASA's Gemini rendezvous radar; the cloud imager for the U.S. Department of Defense's Defense Meteorological Satellite Program; and other space-based sensors and systems.

Northrop Grumman's Undersea Systems business unit in Annapolis is a leading provider of undersea sensors and systems for a variety of military applications. The Advanced SEAL Delivery System, designed and built in Annapolis, represents the first in a new class of submersibles that will provide greater range, speed, and comfort for Special Operations forces on missions involving high threats.

The Electronic Systems sector also provides nondefense products and services for various U.S. government agencies including postal automation and material-handling systems and biodetection systems for the U.S. Postal Service. Under a contract with the Postal Service, Northrop Grumman is providing 100 Flats Sequencing Systems (FSS) designed to further automate the flats mail stream, which includes large envelopes, catalogues, and magazines. The FSS production units will be installed at Postal Service facilities nationwide.

The corporation, including Electronic Systems, conducts most of its business with the U.S. government, principally the Department of Defense. However, about 20 percent of the Electronic Systems sector's business is with international customers.

Above left: A Northrop Grumman technician checks out an antenna for a ground-based air defense radar system that is in use by customers worldwide. Above right: The Northrop Grumman test bed aircraft shown here is equipped with the Scalable Agile Beam Radar (SABR), newly unveiled in 2008.

Northrop Gruman is the largest industrial employer in Maryland and the largest private employer in Anne Arundel County. About 7,000 employees work in the Linthicum area, with another 500 employees in Annapolis.

A Heritage of Innovation

The Electronic Systems sector was formed in 1996 when Northrop Grumman acquired the Westinghouse Electronic Systems Group. The sector's roots, however, date back to 1938, when the Westinghouse Electric Corporation's radio division moved its operations from Chicopee Falls, Massachusetts, to a new facility on Wilkens Avenue in southwest Baltimore.

The following year, Westinghouse more than doubled the size of its Baltimore manufacturing facility to accommodate production of the then–highly secret SCR-270 aircraft warning radar. On December 7, 1941, having just recently been deployed, the SCR-270 detected a number of unidentified aircraft heading toward Pearl Harbor. As history well knows, however, the radar's warnings went unheeded, leading to a disastrous result.

Throughout World War II, the company continued to develop key defense technologies, resulting in numerous new products—the majority of which were radio components that played an integral role in defeating Nazi Germany.

Production later shifted to radar sensors—a field that Electronic Systems still dominates today.

Northrop Grumman's Electronic Systems sector has been situated in Linthicum since 1952. The move of the company's aerospace-related business from its original site in Baltimore to the Linthicum area was part of a business expansion and was also designed to be in close proximity to Friendship Airport—now Baltimore/Washington International Thurgood Marshall Airport (BWI Marshall Airport), which was also being constructed during this same time period.

Northrop Grumman's location of its expansive engineering and manufacturing complex to Linthicum, adjacent to the airport, enables convenient, direct access of company test-bed aircraft to airport runways. Today the company maintains two hangar facilities that house several test-bed aircraft used to flight-test new radar sensors, as well as other avionic systems under development at the sector. Electronic Systems' location in the Baltimore–Washington, D.C., high-technology corridor also provides convenient access to its U.S. Department of Defense and other government agency customers in the Washington, D.C., vicinity.

A five-story, 160,000-square-foot office building under construction adjacent to the Electronic Systems headquarters in Linthicum, projected for completion in

Above right: The company maintains a fleet of seven specially equipped aircraft at its facility adjacent to BWI Marshall Airport.

late 2009, will enable consolidation within the headquarters campus of a variety of existing business activities previously housed in several nearby leased and company-owned facilities, resulting in improved operational efficiencies and effectiveness. The energy-efficient office facility will also enable optimum use of space by incorporating flexible office-design concepts. The majority of the new building will be occupied by several hundred employees of Northrop Grumman's Advanced Concepts and Technology Division who are primarily involved in research and development work.

Northrop Grumman in the Community

Northrop Grumman has a rich history of community involvement, with the emphasis on support for education, health and welfare, and arts and cultural activities, especially in those communities where the company maintains plants and offices. Employees also are very generous in their support for local charities. Each year, Northrop Grumman employees in the Baltimore area contribute more than $1 million in payroll deductions to various charities.

However, support for educational initiatives, in particular, programs that encourage young people to consider careers in engineering-related fields, is a cornerstone of the company's community outreach efforts. Through such company-sponsored programs as WORTHY, Discover "E," and the annual Northrop Grumman Engineering Scholars program, the company is helping to encourage students with an interest in science, technology, engineering, and mathematics (STEM) education to consider pursuing engineering and science-related degree fields in college.

In collaboration with the Maryland State Department of Education, Northrop Grumman introduced the Teachers and Engineers for Academic Achievement (TEAACH) internship program to integrate engineering concepts into school curriculums.

Electronic Systems also has teamed with the Maryland State Department of Education, The Johns Hopkins University, and Project Lead the Way in support of the Retirees and Engineers for Academic Achievement (REAACH) outreach program. The program regularly brings engineers to the classroom to provide teachers and students with practical STEM insight. The engineers participate in

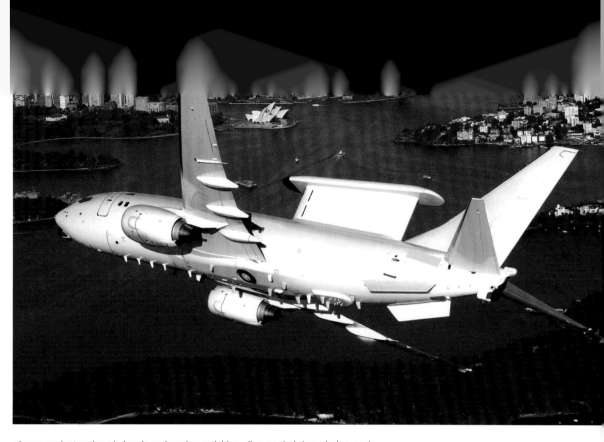

classroom instruction via hands-on learning activities, discuss their knowledge, and share their industry experience.

The company's longtime educational outreach partnership with the Maryland State Department of Education earned both of these organizations the prestigious Innovator of the Year Award for 2008 from *The Daily Record* newspaper.

Also, Northrop Grumman Electronic Systems has been selected for the third-consecutive time as one of the Best Places to Work in the Baltimore area by *Baltimore* magazine based on an in-depth biannual survey of the top employers in the region.

Northrop Grumman Corporation Electronic Systems provides additional information about its products and activities on its Web site at www.es.northropgrumman.com.

Above: Northrop Grumman produces the Multi-role Electronically Scanned Array (MESA) radar for the Boeing 737 airborne early warning and control aircraft.

Middle River Aircraft Systems

This GE subsidiary company develops complex aerostructure systems for today's aerospace needs and tomorrow's air-travel visions while maintaining its industry reputation for delivering the highest quality products and serving the industry's specialized needs.

Above: Middle River Aircraft Systems' (MRAS) one million-square-foot facility is situated on the bank of Maryland's largest body of water, the Chesapeake Bay.

Glenn L. Martin, former Wright brothers partner and aviation pioneer, purchased 1,260 acres of farmland in 1929 on which to build an aircraft manufacturing plant—the site where Middle River Aircraft Systems (MRAS) is located today. Martin quickly emerged as a leader in the aviation industry by becoming one of the world's leading suppliers of military aircraft during World War II, as well as developing and launching the *China Clipper* seaplane, legendary for completing the world's first commercial flight across the Pacific. Eighty years later, MRAS, a wholly owned subsidiary of the General Electric Company (GE), continues Martin's tradition of

innovation and excellence through its design, manufacture, and service of complex aerostructures for both commercial and military aircraft.

MRAS is headquartered in eastern Baltimore County and is situated directly on the bank of the Chesapeake Bay. The one million-square-foot facility contains manufacturing, laboratory, and office space designed specifically for the fabrication of aerospace hardware, and employs approximately 1,000 of Baltimore's most dedicated employees.

MRAS operates in three areas of business, specializing in nacelle and thrust reverser systems. A nacelle system is a streamlined enclosure for an engine on an aircraft—composed of an engine inlet, fan cowl, aft cowl, and thrust reverser. The thrust reverser is a key component of the nacelle system, acting as the brakes of a jet. MRAS is the fourth-largest supplier of nacelle components in the commercial sector and has more than three decades of experience in designing and manufacturing nacelle systems. It is recognized as a GE Nacelle Center of Excellence.

MRAS also conducts business in complex aerostructure design, development, and manufacturing, specializing in composite and metallic structures. Additionally, MRAS concentrates on outstanding aftermarket support, providing technical, logistics, and field support to its global customer base. MRAS is a supplier to companies worldwide, including GE, Pratt & Whitney, Lockheed Martin, Boeing, Airbus, Bell Helicopter, the United States Navy, and more than 150 commercial airlines.

MRAS has always been dedicated to establishing itself as a leader in the aerospace industry. Carried from its conception by a self-taught engineer through mergers with the American-Marietta Company in 1961, Lockheed in 1995, and GE in 1997, MRAS prides itself on being a local business that caters to a global market. When GE acquired the business from Lockheed Martin, it set up MRAS as a separate entity. GE—the brainchild of Thomas Edison—retains its innovative spirit and strong sense of integrity, which shine through in all GE divisions and are mirrored in the everyday operations of MRAS.

In 1941, 19 women were hired to work on the factory floor at the Glenn L. Martin Company, founding the "Rosie the Riveter" movement during World War II. Following Martin's lead, MRAS keeps the interests of the community, as well as the health and safety of employees, in mind. From development to customer support, safety is of utmost importance. Close attention is paid to design and manufacturing with an emphasis on ergonomics. Additionally, MRAS has taken efforts to reduce its environmental impact. MRAS has increased efforts to reduce energy use and cost, as well as carbon dioxide (CO_2) emissions, through lean processes coined by GE. In 2007 GE named MRAS an eCO_2 Star–certified site for reducing greenhouse-gas emissions by 5 percent or more from 2004 to 2006.

MRAS, one of the largest suppliers of composite nacelle systems and composite airframe structures for commercial and military aircraft markets, provides a lightweight, quiet, and energy-efficient structure, resulting in reduced fuel usage and carbon emissions. MRAS has manufactured composite structures for more than 30 years, starting with the composite transcowl for the CF6-80C, which is the best-selling engine and nacelle for large, wide-body aircraft worldwide. Its 3,800th unit was shipped in 2008, placing it as the largest revenue generator of MRAS products to date. MRAS is working to improve existing nacelle technologies by developing a lighter, integrated structure, as well as developing an E-Nacelle through the replacement of hydraulic and pneumatic systems with highly reliable and lightweight electrically powered actuation and anti-icing systems. Continually striving to develop simplified processes and integrate automation into the design and manufacturing of nacelles and aerostructures, MRAS is able to deliver products that are weight-efficient, energy-efficient, and cost-efficient.

MRAS provides additional information about the company and its products and services on its Web site at www.mras-usa.com.

MRAS aims to continue to expand in the nacelle market and adjacent markets with global partners to offer the best technology at the best price. MRAS has a high export volume, supplying companies such as Airbus France and Embraer Brazil with a variety of products and support. MRAS also works with its engineering branches in Poland and India, as well as with GE's Global Research Center. It has further partnerships within the community including the University of Maryland and the University of Delaware. With its clear vision of growth, MRAS will continue Martin's tradition of aerospace excellence for years to come.

Above left: MRAS developed a lightweight, all-composite, acoustically friendly thrust reverser system for the Boeing 747-8 aircraft.

AAI Corporation

Founded in 1950 and headquartered in Hunt Valley, Maryland, AAI Corporation creates innovative products and services for America's warfighters on land, in the air, and at sea. The company provides unmanned aircraft systems; training and simulation systems; automated aerospace test and maintenance equipment; armament systems; aviation ground support equipment; and logistical, engineering, and supply chain services.

Above left: Headquarters for AAI Corporation is conveniently located in Hunt Valley, in northern Baltimore County, Maryland. Above right: AAI uses cutting-edge technology, as well as lean-manufacturing and Six Sigma continuous improvement methodologies, in its operations areas. Shown here, employees work on AAI's Shadow® unmanned aircraft, in service with the U.S. Army, the U.S. Army National Guard, and the U.S. Marine Corps.

Aircraft Armaments Inc. was founded in 1950 by five entrepreneurs and veterans of the defense industry who raised $1,000 in capital among them. Later renamed AAI Corporation to more accurately reflect its broad range of products and services, the company moved to its northern Baltimore County headquarters in 1954. Today, AAI's more than 2,600 employees work at corporate locations worldwide totaling 1.1 million square feet.

About AAI

AAI is a global provider of innovative aerospace and defense products and services including unmanned aircraft systems (UAS), training and simulation systems, automated aerospace test and maintenance equipment, armament systems, aviation ground support equipment, and logistical, engineering, and supply chain services. In 2007, AAI became an operating unit of Textron Systems, a Textron Inc. company. United Industrial Corporation, AAI's parent company, was publicly traded on the New York Stock Exchange until its acquisition by Textron.

The company's business units are subsidiary AAI Services Corporation, Advanced Systems, Test and Training Systems, and UAS. AAI also has acquired Australian UAS manufacturer Aerosonde Pty Ltd.; United Kingdom–based electronic warfare test and simulation product provider ESL Defence Ltd.; and Austin, Texas–based Symtx Inc., a manufacturer of functional test systems.

AAI at Work

Innovation is central to AAI's success. AAI employees share the drive to create and use the latest technologies to improve the business, as well as its products and services. This drive supports AAI's mission—providing the highest quality and most technologically advanced products and services to support and safeguard America's warfighters.

Continuous improvement goes hand in hand with this mission. As part of the Textron family of businesses, AAI participates in the robust Textron Six Sigma program. Through advanced training in lean-manufacturing and Six Sigma method-ologies, employees take an active role in creating processes and procedures and in improving upon them.

AAI's Shadow® UAS received an experimental airworthiness certification from the Federal Aviation Administration (FAA)—the first permitting an unmanned aircraft to operate at a public-use airport serving general aviation. This was granted to AAI based on its policies and procedures for building, maintaining, and supporting its aircraft and training its people. These robust processes also were honored by the global growth consulting company Frost & Sullivan, which presented AAI with its Award for Technology Innovation for industry-leading unmanned aircraft technologies in 2007 and 2008.

The company's operational excellence initiatives make AAI recognized in the industry. In fact, AAI received the 2007 Presidential Award for Commitment and Excellence by the Baltimore Chapter of the Association for Operations Management. AAI also is working toward an overall Capability Maturity Model Integration Level 3 appraisal. The company's Charleston, South Carolina, opera-tion achieved this goal in February 2008, and AAI's software group has achieved and maintains its Level 5 certification. The Defense Security Service has recog-nized the company with its highest rating for security processes, procedures, and enforcement.

AAI in the Community

AAI prides itself on corporate citizenship. With its long history in Baltimore County, the company reaches out to the community in many ways. During the holidays, AAI employees donate toys to children locally through the Villa Maria Continuum. In addition, employees support Villa Maria through mentorships throughout the year and with an annual "Day of Caring," during which AAI employees volunteer

their services to help the community in countless ways, including gardening and repairing bicycles.

AAI is a member of the board of directors of the American Red Cross of Central Maryland, and has supported the organization for many years through monthly blood drives.

AAI also is the largest sponsor of the Dulaney High School REX 1727 FIRST (For Inspiration and Recognition of Science and Technology) Robotics Competition team. Participating students benefit from the mentorship of AAI employees, who attend team events and teach classes on subjects including systems engineering and program management.

Employees also support their ultimate customers, America's warfighters, by sending them comforts from home throughout the year, such as stationery and snacks.

AAI—Past, Present, Future

Employees are the heart of AAI's business. They bring dedication to innovation and to the company's mission, as well as care for each other and their community. In fact, AAI has been named one of *Baltimore Business Journal*'s "Best Places to Work" for three years running—in 2006, 2007, and 2008. With these core values, the robustness of its products and services, and the strength of its Textron family of businesses, AAI is well positioned to continue its long, flourishing history as one of Maryland's most prominent companies.

AAI provides additional information about the company and its products and services on its Web site at www.aaicorp.com.

Above: AAI products, such as its Joint Service Electronic Combat Systems Tester (JSECST), shown here, provide confidence for warfighters that the systems they will be relying on are mission ready.

Thales Communications, Inc.

This Clarksburg, Maryland–based company is a worldwide leader in battle-proven, tactical radio equipment and solutions, enabling America's warfighters and first responders to accomplish their mission more safely and more effectively through the application of visionary technology.

of the most reliable, trusted equipment in the field today—equipment with technology that will serve far into the future.

Thales Communications, Inc. is a global leader in the development and manufacture of innovative tactical communications and information systems for warfighters and first responders. The company serves the ground, naval, airborne, and homeland security domains, developing products and solutions that address the technological and environmental challenges—especially those with size, weight, and power constraints—presented in real-world situations.

Thales Communications pioneered software-defined radio technology, which essentially converts the functions provided in hardware in legacy radio systems to software, resulting in equipment that is smaller, lighter, and more flexible. For the user, whether a soldier on the battlefield, a firefighter in the wilderness, or a sailor on a naval vessel, software-defined radio technology brings extreme reductions in the size and weight of equipment and increases in power, interoperability, capability, and overall performance. The company is a leader in its industry, providing some

Highly Regarded Products

Thales Communications is a trusted partner of the United States government, participating in formal government programs and specialized initiatives. The company serves the U.S. Department of Defense, U.S. civilian agencies, and allied and coalition forces worldwide.

A U.S. proxy company, Thales Communications is part of the Thales Group, a leading international electronics and systems group that serves defense, aerospace, and security customers worldwide. The Thales Group employs 68,000 people in 50 countries.

Thales Communications, which was originally incorporated as Racal Communications, has been in existence since the mid 1960s and has always been located in Montgomery County, Maryland. After a few mergers, acquisitions, and name changes, it became known as Thales Communications in 2001. Since that time, the company

Above left: Thales Communications, Inc. headquarters is located in Clarksburg, Maryland. Above right: A Thales Communications handheld radio is in use on the battlefield.

has expanded from one to four facilities in Montgomery County, with locations both in Clarksburg, where it is headquartered, and in Germantown. In addition to its four Maryland locations, Thales Communications has established repair and maintenance facilities in Iraq, Kuwait, and Afghanistan, bringing its support close to the warfighters in combat who depend on the company's products and services.

Thales Communications has received much recognition over the years for its industry leadership, technology innovation, and role in the Maryland economic and technology communities. Formal recognition has included the Frost & Sullivan Growth Strategy Leadership Award; the U.S. Senate Productivity Award; the Montgomery County Department of Economic Development Workforce & Economic Development Employer of the Year Award; the Maryland International Business Leadership Award from the World Trade Center Institute and the Maryland Department of Business & Economic Development; and the Non-Residential Excellence in Recycling Award for Montgomery County Division of Solid Waste Services, as well as the Technology Council of Maryland's Information Technology Product of the Year Award, which the company has received twice.

Charitable Contributions

Thales Communications is a supporter of many charities—local, national, and global. In addition to the company's corporate participation, its employees are active in philanthropic and volunteer activities. Some of the organizations and events sponsored by Thales Communications include the American Heart Association, the Association of the U.S. Army Annual Ten-Miler, the Avon Walk for Breast Cancer, the Clarksburg Civic Association, Fisher House Foundation, the Frederick Marathon, Frederick Mission of Mercy's Frederick Food Bank, Montgomery Hospice, the Special Operations Warrior Foundation, the UNICEF Tsunami Disaster Relief Initiative, the Leukemia & Lymphoma Society, the National Multiple Sclerosis Society, and the Salvation Army. Additionally, in 2004 the company created its own Scholarship Award Program, through which it

annually presents scholarships for undergraduate education to select children of company employees on the basis of academic record, demonstrated leadership and participation in school and community activities, honors received, work experience, goals and aspirations, and unusual personal or family situations.

Lives Depend on Its Products

Committed to best practices and an ongoing focus on quality, Thales Communications has earned both ISO 9001:2000 certification and the Carnegie Mellon Software Engineering Institute's Capability Maturity Model Integration (CMMI) Level 3 rating. The company's products are made in the United States—developed and manufactured in its Clarksburg and Germantown plants. Thales Communications is a net exporter, providing strong support to both the local and U.S. economies.

Thales Communications is committed to delivering the most capable, innovative, and reliable tactical electronics products and to earning every day the World Class rating it received from a third-party, independent customer survey company for effective and responsive customer service.

With strong financial performance based on technology success, Thales Communications is structured for sustained growth, and continues to execute a proven strategy based on leveraging core technology to meet the ongoing challenges and requirements of its government customers.

The company plays an important role in the global war on terror, developing technology to help warfighters and first responders execute their missions successfully and return home safely. Thales Communications, Inc. recognizes that lives depend on its products, and the company takes that responsibility very seriously.

Thales Communications provides additional information about its products and activities on its Web site at www.thalescomminc.com.

Above left: Employees assemble tactical radios at Thales Communications. Above right: The manufacturing facility at Thales Communications produces state-of-the-art communications systems.

Annapolis Micro Systems, Inc.

Based in Annapolis, this electronic product and design company is a leader in the emerging field of reconfigurable computing. It designs and builds high-performance commercial off-the-shelf (COTS) computers and is known for its engineering excellence and dedication to quality. It provides a full line of standard product solutions to high-bandwidth, computationally intensive problems, as well as application expertise and support.

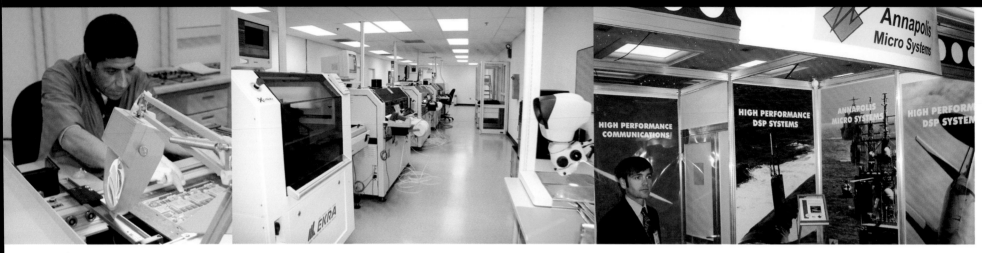

Long known for its engineering excellence, dedication to quality, and commitment to its customers, Annapolis Micro Systems, Inc. designs and builds high-performance computers. The company is a leader in field programmable gate array (FPGA)–based performance and targets high input/output (I/O) bandwidth, computationally intensive problems.

Starting in 1982 as a woman-owned small custom-engineering house, Annapolis has performed electronic design services for a large number of companies, including Fortune 500 corporations such as Intel and Schlumberger, and a small local firm that designed sensors for race cars. Privileged to work with IBM Fellow Evon Greanias and his research team for 12 years beginning in 1983, Annapolis developed concepts and prototypes, and assisted IBM in securing a number of patents in the field of touch technology. Working as a product-development house through the 1980s and mid 1990s, Annapolis established a top-notch team with the skills and equipment necessary to design electronic products, including hardware and software design and implementation; printed circuit board layout; digital and analog

application-specific, integrated circuit (ASIC) design; and surface-mount product manufacturing. Annapolis developed, among other products, appliances for local area networks, an emulator for the Intel 8096 microprocessor, and medical instruments, and it served as an ASIC design center for Atmel. In 1994 Annapolis took part in the National Security Agency Technical Transfer Program's first official transfer, licensing the design for SPLASH 2, then a radical new parallel-processing machine, using FPGAs as the processing elements. In 1995 Annapolis transitioned from a services provider to a product house, and in 2008 it started shipping WILDSTAR™ 5 —the 11th generation of its Xilinx FPGA-based processing products.

Annapolis is the world leader in commercial off-the-shelf (COTS) FPGA-based high-performance-processing products, leading the industry in sheer I/O capacity and processing performance, the dollar volume of FPGA boards sold, and the number of types of boards sold. Typical processing-intensive applications for this kind of board include radar, sonar, signal intelligence (SIGINT), electronic intelligence (ELINT), digital signal processing (DSP), FFTs, communications, software radio, encryption,

Above left: Detailed product inspection is performed at Annapolis Micro Systems, Inc. as part of the company's dedication to quality.
Above center: Shown here is part of the company's manufacturing line.
Above right: At an industry exhibition, Annapolis promotes its capabilities in high-performance computing.

image processing, text processing, pattern matching, gas and oil exploration, financial algorithms, and genomic algorithms.

In a board-for-board comparison, the adaptive/reconfigurable computing power of FPGA-based processing outperforms conventional processors, resulting in significant improvements in processing speed, size, weight, power, and cost. An FPGA design is a custom-made, downloadable parallel-processing design that is specifically crafted for a particular application. It accelerates the application so that it will operate in hardware at hardware speeds—far faster than could be achieved with software on a generic processor. Data is processed in real time on-site, saving the time and money involved in data collection and off-site processing. Processing can be modified by reconfiguring the chip (downloading a different FPGA file in real time) to fix bugs, adapting to a new set of interface requirements, or modifying the processing in response to information found in the data itself. New applications can be delivered in place, without human on-site intervention, by any means of file transfer, including network, hard drive storage, smart card, or wireless modem.

Launched in 2008, Annapolis's WILDSTAR 5 for IBM blade chassis, delivers impressive interconnectivity and configurability, with six pluggable processing and memory modules and up to four pluggable analog-to-digital (A/D), digital-to-analog (D/A), or high-speed communication I/O cards. Current processing/memory modules have Xilinx Virtex 5 FPGAs. Annapolis will deliver modules with Tilera multicore processor chips and modules with Xilinx Virtex 6 FPGAs in 2009. Annapolis also supports other form factors, including virtual memory extension (VME/VXS), XMC, and peripheral component interconnect express (PCIe) solutions.

The Annapolis CoreFire™ FPGA Application Builder, with 2,000-plus modules, including FFTs and FIR filters, transforms the FPGA development process, making it possible for theoreticians to easily and quickly build and test their algorithms on the real hardware that will be used in the field. The combination of Annapolis

COTS hardware and CoreFire allows customers to make massive improvements in processing speed while also achieving significant savings in equipment size, weight, and power; person hours; cost; and calendar time to deployment.

Annapolis is famous for the high quality of its products and for its unparalleled dedication to ensuring that its customers' applications succeed. Annapolis offers training and exceptional support for the development of special applications, as well as more conventional support. Annapolis customers include government agencies, the U.S. military, government research facilities, prime contractors, large corporations, small companies, and universities in the United States and abroad.

In 2005 Annapolis opened a wholly owned subsidiary, Annapolis Micro Systems AB, in Stockholm, Sweden, to position a sales and customer support force in Europe to better serve its growing body of customers in the European Union.

Still a Woman-owned Small Business, now with 56 employees, Annapolis was listed among the 2007 *Inc.* magazine 5000 Fastest Growing Companies. All of the company's products are designed and manufactured in the United States. Its 33,000-square-foot Maryland facility has multiple cleared areas and a surface-mount manufacturing line where employees assemble and test all the products. In 2009 Annapolis extended its surface-mount manufacturing line with the purchase of a third pick-and-place machine, nearly doubling its capacity for board throughput.

Annapolis Micro Systems, Inc. provides additional information about its products and services on its Web site at www.annapmicro.com.

Above left: In December 2008 the Annapolis team celebrated the company's first delivery of WILDSTAR™ 5 for IBM blade chassis. Above center: Shown here is an Annapolis Micro Systems full chassis. Above right: Assembled boards await testing.

PROTEUS Technologies, LLC

This growing company is an innovative, leading-edge software and systems engineering firm working with the intelligence community, federal executive departments, and commercial industries, providing software development, knowledge and language, database, and network and systems engineering solutions.

Transformation, innovation, and agility are pillars of any successful information technology (IT) company expected to grow, prosper, and endure. Upon its formation in 1999, PROTEUS Technologies, LLC was aptly named after the ancient Greek sea god. It was transformed in 2001 under the leadership of a new CEO, and today, innovative and agile, it is one of the National Intelligence Community's most highly respected software engineering firms. PROTEUS specializes in developing solutions within the U.S. Department of Defense (DoD) arena of signals intelligence and cyber- and net-centric information operations. It works with clients locally in Maryland and Virginia, as well as globally throughout the extended DoD enterprise, to protect national security interests.

PROTEUS strives to be each client's preferred partner by owning that client's mission, objectives, problems, and needs. Corporate commitment to engineering excellence drives the delivery of results that have immediate impact and long-term significance to the nation. Lauded by clients for innovation, effectiveness, and high performance, PROTEUS solution offerings include software development, database, knowledge and language, and network and systems engineering. Many of its applications are deployed worldwide and actively collect, filter, store, correlate, and mine intelligence knowledge for analysts. Several of the company's innovative software solutions have been directly briefed to DoD directors and the U.S. president and vice president.

PROTEUS today, with more than 140 employees and revenue projections exceeding $30 million for 2009, continually receives accolades from distinguished national and Maryland organizations. The company has been honored for growth and technical innovation by a number of organizations including Deloitte & Touche, the Maryland Technology Council, the *Baltimore Business Journal*, the *Washington Business Journal*, *SmartCEO* magazine, and the Small and Emerging Contractors Advisory Forum.

Recognizing that the success of PROTEUS heavily relies on its employees' passion for advanced technology, the company emphasizes recruitment and retention of superior engineers and support staff members from the finest colleges and universities in the United States. PROTEUS maintains an impressive corporate résumé with more than 75 percent of its staff members holding advanced degrees, as alumni of prestigious engineering institutions such as the University of Maryland, Johns Hopkins University, Stanford University, the Massachusetts Institute of Technology, Carnegie Mellon University, Lehigh University, the University of Pennsylvania, the University of California, and many others. Employees are encouraged to seek new and rewarding opportunities to pursue their career dreams through a host of continuing educational and professional-development activities. Fostering agility in the response of PROTEUS to its clients' needs, the company's Technicare programs span peer networking and formal mentor-protégé programs, special interest groups, and other support for educational pursuits, as well as traditional professional development and training programs. PROTEUS reinvests earnings in its employees and their future, and as a result PROTEUS employees find themselves among peers who include dedicated, highly educated engineers and world-renowned authors.

Above right: The PROTEUS headquarters in Annapolis Junction offers more than 26,000 square feet of office space, with professional offices, video conferencing, flexible engineering-development areas, a training center, a fitness center, and a fully accredited secure laboratory. Another 8,000-square-foot engineering facility is located nearby in Columbia. Inset: Teresa M. Taylor serves as President and CEO of PROTEUS.

All photos: © 2009 segamiMedia

While honing its technical solutions, nurturing industry partnerships, and advancing employees' careers, PROTEUS actively pursues a strategy for the company's long-term growth, sustained profitability, and corporate endurance. A key component of this strategy is the development of a solid physical infrastructure, including cutting-edge facilities. In 2008 PROTEUS expanded its headquarters facility in Annapolis Junction, Maryland, to more than 26,000 square feet to house its corporate, engineering, and fitness facilities. These facilities, equipped with a gigabit IT backbone, include flexible engineering-development areas, IT laboratory space, a technical library, videoconferencing, a training center, and a fitness facility furnished with a full array of cardiovascular equipment, free weights, and strength-training circuit equipment. The company also maintains an 8,000-square-foot facility for PROTEUS Engineering Services in Columbia, Maryland, which houses a 3,000-square-foot custom-designed and DoD–accredited information facility. Further expansion into Boston, Massachusetts, and Garland, Texas, is imminent as the company continues to grow.

PROTEUS strongly believes in giving back to the communities in which its employees live and work. PROTEUS employees are encouraged to extend themselves,

PROTEUS Honors Include:

- **Deloitte & Touche Fast 50 Award** (three-year winner; the company ranked first in Maryland in 2005)
- **Deloitte & Touche Business Diversity Award** (in 2008)
- **SmartCEO magazine Future 50 Award** (for three consecutive years, from 2005 to 2008)
- **Maryland Technology Council Government Contracting Firm of the Year finalist** (in 2007 and 2008)
- **Chesapeake Regional Technology Council Tech Company of the Year finalist** (in 2007)
- **SmartCEO magazine "Resilience Award" winner** (in 2006)

demonstrate teamwork, and provide voluntary leadership for "passionate causes" and those in need. PROTEUS community outreach programs include support for pediatric cancer research, East Stroudsburg University Richard Prince Memorial Fund Computer Science scholarships, the Boys & Girls Clubs of Annapolis and Anne Arundel County, the ALS Association–DC/MD/VA Chapter, Treats for Troops, the Animal Welfare Society of Howard County, the Armed Forces Communications and Electronics Association (AFCEA), and local and world Little League Baseball. The company is proud of its employees' generosity and dedication to supporting organizations that are making a difference in people's lives—and making Maryland and communities around the world stronger.

Inspired by the mythology of its namesake, PROTEUS Technologies stands tall on the pillars of transformation, innovation, and agility to create new ways forward through the IT challenges of today and the complexities of tomorrow. PROTEUS provides additional information about the company and its services on its Web site at www.proteus-technologies.com.

Clockwise, from top left: Charles T. Taylor, Ph.D., is the Founder and Executive Vice President of PROTEUS. PROTEUS develops software that provides analysts with highly intuitive applications and tools for making critical decisions of importance to national security. PROTEUS sponsors, and its employees participate in, the annual Walk to Defeat ALS (Lou Gehrig's disease). PROTEUS headquarters is home to a state-of-the-art PROTEUS fitness center.

Exceptional Software Strategies, Inc.

This provider of information technology solutions and services continues to grow as it supports clients including the U.S. government, educational institutions, and private industry. The company focuses on business-process management, geographic information system (GIS) solutions, Web portal development, learning solutions, and creative multimedia solutions.

Above: Exceptional Software Strategies, Inc. is headquartered in Linthicum, Maryland.

Exceptional Software Strategies, Inc. was founded in 1996 by Raymond Bowen III and Paul Stasko. As information technology (IT) consultants looking in at enterprises from the outside, Bowen and Stasko became disillusioned with the way they saw employees being treated in the world of government IT. To them, the best company would be a company whose owners treated their employees the way they themselves would want to be treated. So, in 1996 Bowen and Stasko incorporated a business under the name Exceptional Software Strategies in order to do just that. Today, after more than 13 years of success, Bowen and Stasko are determined to maintain Exceptional Software as a privately owned company. They insist that the company be operated by its founders.

Over a decade since its humble beginnings, Exceptional Software is a leading minority-owned business with more than 120 employees on-site at its Linthicum, Maryland, headquarters and off-site in the surrounding areas.

Bowen and Stasko have always approached problems by using their engineering backgrounds as a first foothold. Logical steps and strategic planning were Bowen and Stasko's trademarks as they worked to build their business and establish that business in the competitive industry of government IT contracting. Even as the demands of business management grow with the company, Bowen and Stasko continue to participate in some engineering activities. Their reasons: they were engineers first and that knowledge is what has allowed them to succeed.

Bowen and Stasko firmly believe in using strategic partnerships to develop solutions. With many multiyear contracts in operation, their strategy of thinking outside the box continues to bring them success. Bowen and Stasko's approach has allowed Exceptional Software to gain a reputation in its industry that has earned it key contracts for future growth.

An Exceptional Outlook

The company's mission is to provide innovative IT experts who solve business problems by working in partnership with clients. Exceptional Software leverages knowledge of management, business, and IT to ensure the success of every client and every employee. In order to accomplish their austere undertaking, the company offers a variety of innovative product solutions and services including, but not limited to: geographic information systems (GIS) tools, learning solutions, information security services, enterprise systems management, and software and systems engineering services.

Over the company's history, Exceptional Software has branched from software engineering services to information-security services and systems engineering and technical assistance (SETA) services. Within the past few years alone, Exceptional Software has entered the GIS and computer-security markets, and in 2000 focused on the rapidly evolving Internet and multimedia market. This has allowed Exceptional Software to enter a full range of multimedia markets, from video transcription to multimedia presentations, portal technologies, online training classes, and Web portal development. These products make it easier for clients to integrate and exploit media and video elements.

Exceptional Software's offerings earned it *Washington SmartCEO* magazine's Future 50 Award for three consecutive years, an honor bestowed upon 50 companies in the greater Baltimore area that have experienced the fastest growth. Other recognition received by Exceptional Software includes identification by the *Baltimore Business Journal Book of Lists* among the Baltimore area's Largest Network System Integrators, Largest IT Consulting Firms, and Largest Minority-Owned Businesses.

Giving Back to Employees and the Community

Exceptional Software employees are a group of talented professionals who maintain products and services of the highest quality for their clients. In return for their

valuable work, the company offers award-winning benefits. In 2007 *Corridor Magazine* named Exceptional Software one of Baltimore's "Greatest Places to Work" and in 2008 the *Baltimore Business Journal* named the company among the "Best Places to Work" in Baltimore. Employee benefits include family health and dental insurance with premiums paid, tuition assistance, and paid time off for holidays, vacation, bereavement, and maternity leave. In addition, employees enjoy events each year such as a holiday party, a company picnic, and golf outings.

The company's generosity extends beyond its employees. Exceptional Software's founders have supported numerous charitable organizations in Maryland, including the Baltimore School of Arts, the Fellowship of Christian Athletes, local schools, and local churches. The company has supported employees' charitable initiatives ranging from Girl Scouts of the U.S.A. to missionary work. Cofounder Bowen serves on the boards of directors of several nonprofit organizations that deal with issues such as youth outreach, special concerns for women, public safety, education, children with learning disabilities, and others.

Especially unique to Exceptional Software's vision, however, is employee-initiated support for a large number of charitable events. The company has sponsored Walk MS for multiple-sclerosis research, Breast Cancer Awareness Marathons, Girl Scout activities, and numerous other events that employees have personally brought to the attention of Bowen and Stasko for support.

No matter what IT consulting a business needs, Exceptional Software Strategies can provide it. The company provides detailed information, contact information, and additional information about the services it offers on its Web site at www.exceptionalsoftware.com.

Above left: Exceptional Software Strategies is a growing business with more than 120 employees. Above right: To assist clients in meeting some of today's toughest business challenges, Exceptional Software has created a variety of innovative information technology products and solutions.

Camber Corporation

This professional technical services defense contractor offers creative solutions, responsive engineering services, and technical support to customers around the world through its aerospace defense, national security, and training, technology, and systems groups. Camber Corporation recognizes that its employees are its greatest asset and that customer-focused efforts are the primary reason for its success.

Above, all photos: Camber Corporation's Chem-Bio Division (CBD) trains individual operators, maintenance technicians, and entire installations through full-scale chemical, biological, radiological, nuclear, and explosive (CBRNE) exercises. CBD supports the research and quality-control aspects of the detection of biological warfare agents through the Critical Reagents Program.

Since its founding in 1990, Camber Corporation has grown to over 28 offices and 54 on-site locations providing responsive support to customers across the United States. With more than 1,880 employees, Camber completed approximately $310 million of business in 2009. Camber provides professional technical services to the U.S. Department of Defense and other government agencies at over 100 locations worldwide. Key focus areas include information technology, homeland security, chemical and biological support, training and education, decision support systems, modeling and simulation, systems engineering, and software engineering. Camber's service network touches important defense interests in every Unified Combatant Command; over 150 U.S. Army, Air Force, and Navy programs; U.S. National Guard headquarters in every state and territory; and more than 25 North Atlantic Treaty Organization (NATO) or coalition countries in Europe, Asia, and Africa.

Camber Corporation is a major services supplier for the aerospace, defense, and technology industry of Maryland. Camber has three divisions serving the "Old Line State" covering the central, capital, and southern regions of Maryland and providing chemical, biological, radiological, nuclear, and explosives (CBRNE); naval systems; and intelligence and security expertise.

Headquartered just outside of the Aberdeen Proving Ground–Edgewood Area in Abingdon, Maryland—and with an office, repair facilities, and warehouse operations in Frederick, Maryland—Camber's **Chemical Biological Division** began providing local support in Maryland in 1999. Camber offers cradle to grave services, supplying subject matter expertise to a variety of programs, installations, and military units. Camber supports all branches of the U.S. Department of Defense, the U.S. Department of Homeland Security, and state and local governments. Camber's experience and expertise support its customers' requirements throughout the system lifecycle, from initial concept and design to engineering and manufacturing process creation to operational and sustainment support and demilitarization of chemical, biological, and radiological equipment. Additionally, Camber provides 24-hours-per-day, seven-days-per-week operational security and support to key infrastructure locations. Camber is renowned for providing trusted scientists and specialists in the conduct of independent technical reviews and evaluations of nonmedical CBRNE defense systems and medical diagnosis equipment.

Beginning in 1992, with offices on the shores of Southern Maryland, Camber's **Naval Systems Division** supports the Naval Aviation Systems Command (NAVAIR) at

Patuxent River Naval Air Station; NAVSEA in Newport News, Virginia; and the Navy Recruit Training Center in Great Lakes, Michigan. Camber delivers technical, logistics, and engineering services to a variety of Naval service programs such as the Joint Strike Fighter, Super Sea Stallion Helicopters, the Marine Corps V-22 Osprey, and CVN-78 Aircraft Carrier. Camber applies the latest in technology, interdisciplinary knowledge, and innovative solutions to the Navy customer and is recognized as a leader in acquisition program support, cost analysis, test and evaluation, and all aspects of sustainment technology to include condition-based maintenance. Camber is constantly finding new ways to better support the government program teams that bring the best possible products and weapons to the marines and sailors who defend the United States of America.

Camber's **Intelligence and Security Division** supports several initiatives within Maryland. Camber offers intelligence analysis and information assurance services, specializing in operating within classified environments for the U.S. Department of Defense and the Intelligence community. Additionally, Camber provides regional support to the state of Maryland through contracts such as Maryland's Consulting and Technical Services (CATSII).

Camber's initiatives in information security are the keystones of the Camber Cyber Program. In support of its customers, Camber has developed proven computer security tools that are used for test and validation of computer security postures and content validation to prevent unintended information leakage. These tools have become standards

within the Intelligence community and are also used within other federal organizations. Camber also provides advanced technical and strategic support in computer network operations to include policy development, certification and accreditation, vulnerability testing, and computer network defense. Collectively, these efforts provide a "defense in depth" approach to address the challenging nature of today's cyber threat.

Camber is an active corporate citizen, supporting its local communities through such diverse activities as hosting annual charity golf tournaments for the Johns Hopkins Children's Center for Cancer and the Maryland Special Olympics. Camber also contributes financial support for organizations and events such as the Boys and Girls Clubs, the annual Harford County Run for Shelter, and the St. Mary's River Concert Series. Camber ardently supports the military—in Maryland and overseas—through its Blue and Gold membership in the U.S. Navy League.

Camber knows that to continually provide exceptional customer service, the attitudes and values held by its employees and promoted overall by Camber must focus consistently and continuously on making customers successful. Camber is very proud of its reputation for providing superior service, highly skilled employees, and best value to its customers. Camber is "Customer Focused, Employee Driven."

Additional information about Camber Corporation and its services is available on the company's Web site at www.camber.com.

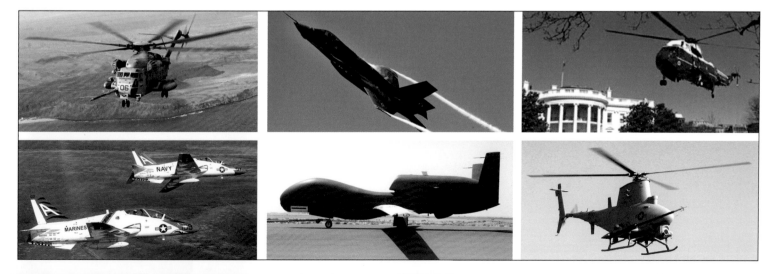

Top, all photos: Camber's trusted team of experts in its Intelligence and Security Division develop security-testing tools, validate system security postures, and assist in developing security policies for some of the most sensitive and safeguarded national assets. Bottom, all photos: Through its Patuxent River, Maryland, office, Camber's Naval Systems Division (NSD) provides technical support for all pictured U.S. Navy and Marine Corps aircraft (top row, from left): CH-53E Sea Stallion, F-35 Joint Strike Fighter, and VH-3D Presidential Helicopter; and (bottom row, from left): T-45 Aviation Training Systems, Global Hawk Unmanned Aerial Vehicle (UAV), and Fire Scout UAV.

Sabre Systems, Inc.

This firm designs innovative technology solutions that enable its government and commercial clients to solve problems, work more efficiently, and maintain their competitive advantage. The company's clients—located throughout the United States and in 14 foreign countries—include the Naval Air Station Patuxent River, the U.S. Naval Academy in Annapolis, U.S. Army Aberdeen Proving Ground, and the U.S. Census Bureau in Suitland.

across the globe—many in harm's way—are equipped with the very best and most capable aircraft, weapons, and support systems to ensure their safety and their ability to protect and defend the freedom and security of the United States of America.

For the U.S. Naval Academy, Sabre supports functions such as Web hosting and portal design, staffing the help desk, and providing midshipmen with state-of-the-art computer and information processing technologies. The company considers it a privilege to support future generations of naval leaders through education and training programs.

Sabre recently established an office in Aberdeen to support the U.S. Army's Command, Control, Communications, Computers, Intelligence, Surveillance, and Reconnaissance (C4ISR) mission, which is moving from Fort Monmouth, New Jersey, to Maryland. Sabre provides communication engineering, information assurance, and program management support to many of the Army's acquisition programs.

At the U.S. Census Bureau, over 90 Sabre employees support the Geography and Population divisions. The company's software developers ensure the quality of Census data collected in preparation for the 2010 Census. The valuable information gathered will enable the government to make important decisions regarding the distribution of $300 billion in federal funds to local, state, and tribal governments each year.

Sabre is also committed to giving back to the communities where its associates live and work. From sponsoring national programs at the local level, such as the American Red Cross, Big Brothers Big Sisters, the Lions Club, and the U.S. Marine Corps Toys for Tots, to supporting cultural programs such as the St. Mary's River Concert Series and Chamber Orchestra of Southern Maryland in Concert, the company is actively involved in nonprofits, charitable giving, volunteerism, and other community service projects. More information is available on the company's Web site at www.sabresystems.com.

Sabre Systems, Inc., founded in 1989, is a privately held information technology and professional engineering solutions provider. Above: The company serves clients around the world, including the U.S. Naval Academy in Annapolis (graduation shown at left), the Naval Air Station Patuxent River (RQ-8 Fire Scout unmanned air vehicle landing on USS *Nashville* off the Maryland coast shown at center), and the U.S. Census Bureau in Suitland (right). Below right: Sabre employees participate in many philanthropic efforts, such as the Run for Hospice in Leonardtown.

Sabre Systems, Inc. is a quality-driven professional services company that specializes in providing technology, scientific, and management solutions to government and commercial clients. The company's core capabilities are information technology, professional engineering, program management, training and logistics, and software development solutions. Committed to customer satisfaction, Sabre takes pride in providing clients with experienced professionals who are highly skilled, trained, and educated.

More than half of the company's workforce supports the U.S. Department of Defense and other large federal agencies throughout the state of Maryland. Government client locations include the U.S. Naval Academy, the Naval Air Station, U.S. Army Aberdeen Proving Ground, and the U.S. Census Bureau.

Sabre has over 280 dedicated professionals supporting the nation's largest, busiest, and most complex Acquisition, Research, Development, Test, and Evaluation Centers of Excellence—Naval Air Station (NAS) Patuxent River. These professionals work across numerous major acquisition programs and engineering and support competencies of the Naval Air Systems Command and Naval Air Warfare Center Aircraft Division, providing critical support across the spectrum of key disciplines to include program management, engineering, software development, and information technology. Their unique skills, capabilities, and uncompromising commitment to excellence help ensure that the young men and women serving in the Armed Forces

K&L Microwave

Dedicated to producing high quality, cost-effective solutions, this designer and manufacturer of radio frequency and microwave technology combines technical expertise, manufacturing savvy, sales innovation, and high quality standards to create outstanding products for military and commercial markets.

K&L Microwave, an innovative designer and manufacturer of radio frequency and microwave filters, components, and integrated assemblies, is continually setting the technological pace for the industry. Recognized as a world leader by top-tier defense contractors and wireless infrastructure providers throughout the world, K&L has facilities in the United States, China, the Dominican Republic, and the United Kingdom.

Above: K&L Microwave is headquartered in Salisbury, Maryland.

The company's headquarters and three facilities totaling 170,000 square feet are located in Salisbury, Maryland. These facilities, as well as the ones overseas, enable K&L to supply both military and commercial customers with many superior products such as microwave filters, duplexers, and subassemblies. Among the industries that rely on K&L technology are satellite and radio communications, radar, fire control radars, telemetry applications, missile guidance systems, mobile radio base stations, and air traffic control and communications.

K&L is committed to achieving excellence through aggressive investment in research and development, capital investments in manufacturing technology, and the implementation of proven and innovative designs. Design and applications engineers have access to an extensive design library and a variety of cutting-edge software tools; manufacturing and testing equipment is state-of-the-art; and knowledgeable sales people work with engineers to provide customers with the best products for their evolving needs.

K&L has earned a reputation for high quality products and superior customer satisfaction since the company was founded in 1971. Soldering and workmanship practices conform to standards set by customers and the military, the American National Standards Institute (ANSI), and the Institute for Interconnecting and Packaging Electronic Circuits, including IPC J-STD-001 and IPC-A-610. Throughout the company's operations preventive- and corrective-action software and automated testing software contribute to the K&L philosophy of continuous improvement.

In addition to having a Quality Management System and an Environmental Management System, K&L exceeds Occupational Safety and Health Administration (OSHA) standards. The company is committed to increasing environmental awareness and activism; protecting the health, safety, and wellness of employees; and supporting the community. In 2009 K&L was named Employer of the Year for the private sector by Maryland Works, Inc., in recognition of outstanding leadership and a commitment to employing people with disabilities.

Additional information is available on K&L's Web site at www.klmicrowave.com.

Left: Innovative designs
created by staff engineers
make K&L Microwave
a leader in custom-
designed filters.

PROFILES OF COMPANIES AND ORGANIZATIONS

Development, Construction, and Real Estate

Development Design Group, Inc.

From Middle America to the Middle East and across the world are dynamic and creative mixed-use centers, waterfront developments, and residential communities that are the work of this award-winning, Baltimore-headquartered design group, consisting of top-notch architects and designers from around the globe who practice in multicultural collaboration.

Above: Designed by Development Design Group, Inc. (DDG), the Easton Town Center in Columbus, Ohio, is a mixed-use town center integrating shopping with offices, entertainment, and more. Building styles from different periods create the impression of a town that has evolved over time.

For innovative planning, architecture, graphics and design services, domestic and international clients turn to Development Design Group, Inc. (DDG), an award-winning company that specializes in creating memorable destinations with a multidiscipline approach. DDG is a Baltimore-based firm that offers extensive experience in every aspect of property development as well as a reputation for superior work. The company's diverse portfolio includes retail and entertainment venues; first-class hotel, leisure, and resort facilities; unique office and residential designs; town-and-leisure centers; and large-scale mixed-use projects.

A recognized industry leader, DDG has won more than 90 national and international design awards since it was established in 1979, including top honors from the Urban Land Institute, the Pacific Coast Builders Conference, as well as the U.S. and European branches of the International Council of Shopping Centers. Among the firm's award-winning projects in the United States are Town Square in Las Vegas, Nevada; National Harbor in Prince George's County, Maryland;

The Market Place at The Woodlands, Houston, Texas; and several Muvico Theater complexes.

Forward-Thinking Firsts

DDG's portfolio is proof of the firm's consistent ability to position itself in the forefront of retail design trends. Notable projects include the often-emulated Easton Town Center in Columbus, Ohio, and the first American-style shopping malls in the Middle East and Indonesia—BurJuman Centre in Dubai, United Arab Emirates, and Pondok Indah Mall in Jakarta, Indonesia. These venues set examples with their creative design and have undergone successful expansions to keep up with their increasing popularity with visitors.

Equally innovative is Expo Xplore in Durban, South Africa, the first branded extreme sports venue that integrates a variety of board sports within a retail setting. This complex offers an energy-filled experience: inside, it features basketball and rock climbing, bold graphics, and a programmed light and sound show. Outside is a Tony Hawk–designed skate park, an off-road 4x4 course, and a standing-wave surfing pool. On American soil, DDG has masterminded Westgate City Center in Glendale, Arizona, which includes a town center, an outdoor events plaza, residential lofts, hotels, town-homes, retail space, and more than two million square feet of class-A office space.

The firm offers architectural planning, design, and master planning for mixed-use, retail, entertainment, residential, hospitality, and town centers and also provides graphics and model-fabrication services. The graphics department offers full-service environmental graphics, logos, and production materials, while the model division creates intricate, remarkably detailed scale models that are a vital and distinctive part of the firm's marketing and design services.

Creating Iconic Destinations

DDG credits a flexible corporate culture and a willingness to listen carefully to the client's vision for its far-reaching success. DDG employees come from all over the

globe and approach foreign cultures with an open mind rather than bringing their preconceived notions into a setting. They see their role as one of turning the client's vision into reality—an approach that is valued in every culture from Middle America to the Middle East and beyond.

"Creative Pragmatism"—DDG's idea that creativity must be balanced with professionalism, consistency, and accountability—has long been a guiding principle of the firm. Its associates are encouraged to address the unique culture, physical and natural environment, financing, commercial necessities, and intended use of a project instead of conforming to a particular architectural style. By striving to approach their work creatively, focus on the importance of ambiance, and generate projects that harness positive experiences, DDG's talented staff demonstrates to the world a difference between a place and a destination.

Building Relationships

From its headquarters in Baltimore, DDG operates as a global firm that fills a highly specialized niche. The company has established working relationships with architects and designers around the world, and these serve as the foundation for delivering its design services to a broad range of clients. Many business contacts introduce DDG to new clients and collaborate on subsequent projects. The firm has designed a broad range of spaces from art-house theaters and small restaurants to large, master-planned residential and mixed-use projects covering thousands of acres or hectares.

Building relationships with new talent is seen as an investment in the future—an excellent way to maintain the company's diversity. DDG works in partnership with the University of Cincinnati to provide an internship program; offers scholarship funds and internships to aspiring South African designers and architects; and hosts interns from the Institut Teknologi Bandung in Bandung, Indonesia; Alexandria University in Alexandria, Egypt; and a premier architectural firm in Shanghai, China.

With combined fluency in more than 23 languages, the company's design specialists blend their knowledge, expertise, and international perspectives, resulting in destinations that are harmonious with their surroundings and culturally refined to suit the lifestyles of their clients. Whether creating a mixed-use project in China or an open-air market in the United States, a stimulating exchange of cultural perspectives and ideas is a critical component of what has brought Development Design Group success worldwide and industrywide.

Development Design Group, Inc. provides additional information about its services on its Web site at www.ddg-usa.com.

Above left: The Westgate City Center in Glendale, Arizona, is designed in the "Arizona Deco" style, including southwestern coloring, stucco, and metal and masonry elements. Center top: Istinye Park in Istanbul, Turkey, is designed with a circular arrival plaza set between an open-air "lifestyle center" and a glass-roofed retail area. Center bottom: The standing-wave surfing pool is one of the exciting features offered to shoppers at Expo Xplore in Durban, South Africa. Above right: Zonk'izizwe in Midrand, South Africa, is a mixed-use master plan integrating retail, residential, and office space and mass transit.

Bragunier Masonry Contractors, Inc.

Proud of its Clear Spring roots, this award-winning full-service masonry contractor specializes in block, brick, and stone work, passing on low-cost savings to customers, taking pride in practicing outstanding safety, and staying connected to the community by providing local job opportunities and supporting youth organizations.

Four Decades of Excellence

One of Maryland's largest masonry contractors, Bragunier Masonry is a family-owned and -operated business based in Clear Spring. The company was established in 1962 by owner and president Donald L. Bragunier, who founded the business with his wife, Charlene (who acted as the administrative assistant), employing one laborer, a single mixer, and a truck. In the beginning, the company provided masonry contracting services for residential housing in the Washington County area.

The company's reputation for fair prices and outstanding work resulted in a large volume of projects coming from the Washington metropolitan area. Bragunier Masonry eventually expanded into industrial and commercial work, including office buildings, churches, hospitals, nursing homes, apartment buildings, warehouses, motels, schools, and prisons. The skill of the company's crew has led to jobs as far north as Fishkill, New York, and as far south as Charlottesville, Virginia.

Throughout the northeastern United States stand buildings distinguished by the outstanding block, brick, and stone work of Bragunier Masonry Contractors, Inc., a full-service masonry contractor serving Maryland, Pennsylvania, Virginia, West Virginia, and Washington, D.C. The company's work runs the gamut, from basic foundations to multimillion-dollar projects and from private sector jobs to contracts for local, state, and federal government.

Projects that bear the Bragunier Masonry stamp of excellence include the Food and Drug Administration in Silver Spring, Maryland; the Maryland State House in Annapolis; the Verizon Center in Washington, D.C.; the Alexandria Courthouse in Alexandria, Virginia; several Jessup Correctional Institute facilities; and many schools and colleges throughout the company's territory. Even the White House and the Pentagon have been enhanced by the work of this award-winning contractor.

Today Bragunier Masonry employs 150 workers from the tristate area, many of whom have served the company for 30 years or more. The company's foremen have more than 400 years combined experience between them. These loyal employees, dedicated to the company for over two decades, take pride in their work and truly care about the company and its customers. They realize that when they shine, the company also shines.

Deeply connected to the Clear Spring community, Bragunier Masonry employs local high school students during summer break and supports several local youth organizations and charities, including school athletic, cheerleading, and band activities; Future Farmers of America; and 4-H members in Washington County, Maryland, and West Virginia.

A Common Sense Approach

Bragunier Masonry is proud of its rural location in a small converted farmhouse on the outskirts of town, where fields of Black Angus cattle surround the company's property. As part of its strategy to keep overhead low, Bragunier Masonry has kept its headquarters in the original Clear Spring location, enabling the company to offer lower bids than the competition, resulting in savings for the customer. Bragunier Trucking Company, a subsidiary, was formed in 1980 to transport building materials from suppliers to project sites, eliminating the middleman and further reducing costs.

Donald Bragunier's common sense approach to business and his penchant for delivering excellent work at a fair price keeps his workers busy and his desk full of blueprints. The company usually has a hand in at least 50 projects at a time, such as the new Regional Medical Center in Hagerstown; housing units at the Maryland Correctional Training Center in Hagerstown; Linganore High School in Frederick; the Twinbrook Station in Rockville; and the C-5 Flight Simulation Facility for the West Virginia Air National Guard in Martinsburg, West Virginia.

Bragunier Masonry's accomplishments and its employees have received many honors throughout the years. For its work at the Catholic University Columbus School of Law in Washington, D.C., the company received honors from the Washington Building Congress, which praised Bragunier Masonry for superb coordination of complicated patterns. The company also received the 1991 Greater Washington, D.C., Entrepreneur of the Year Award from Ernst & Young. In recognition of excellence and outstanding contributions to the success of Harkins Builders, Bragunier Masonry was chosen as one of the top 25 subcontractors by the firm, which honored the company's contributions from 1965 through 1990.

Committed to safety, Bragunier Masonry is equally proud to have achieved the Platinum Level in the Safety Training Evaluation Program (STEP) offered by Associated Builders and Contractors, Inc. and to have an associate, Alex Martinez, receive a certificate of commendation for outstanding contributions to project safety in the Pentagon Wedge 1 Renovation Program, presented by AMEC Construction Management, Inc. More information about Bragunier Masonry Contractors is available on the company's Web site at www.bragunier.com.

This page, both photos: Bragunier Masonry performed all masonry work for Canton Square in Baltimore (left) and Rockville's Grosvenor House condominiums (right).

Price Modern LLC

Originally established in Baltimore over a century ago, Price Modern has become a leader in providing workspace solutions able to support the ever-changing, complex needs of the modern office environment. The company, whose employees are seasoned professionals with vast national experience, is known for its creative solutions and distinctive products.

Above left: Co-owners Robert S. Carpenter (left), president and chief operating officer, and Milford Marchant (right), chairman and CEO, are at the helm of Price Modern LLC. Above right: Price Modern employees are key team members, providing expertise, creative solutions, and excellent follow-through.

Established in 1904 as a printer and stationer under the name The Price Company, Price Modern LLC has evolved into a trusted provider of furnishings for commercial, health care, institutional, educational, and government facilities throughout the mid-Atlantic region. In the early 1970s, The Price Company merged with two regional office-products firms, the Modern Stationery Company and the H. L. Marchant Company, to form Price Modern. Office collaboration, computer technology, and the need for increased worker productivity propelled the need for an entirely new way to furnish an office. At that point, an industry and a company came together. In 1981 Price Modern formed a strategic alliance with Haworth, a Michigan-based manufacturer of innovative office-interior products and now a leader in the development of sustainable workspaces. Today Haworth and Price Modern are recognized by Fortune 1000 companies as premier suppliers of products and service solutions.

Price Modern also attributes its success to hardworking, dedicated employees who know how to develop and maintain customer relationships. Companies and institutions like CareFirst BlueCross BlueShield, T. Rowe Price, Watson Wyatt Worldwide, Northrop Grumman, the National Institutes of Health, and Johns Hopkins Hospital have relied on Price Modern for decades to help with their facilities' needs as they have changed and grown. Creating, implementing, and managing workplace solutions are the focus of Price Modern employees and have provided the foundation for the company's success.

"First We Listen..."

With over 200 leading national and global manufacturers represented, Price Modern has a motto: "First we listen..." The company listens to clients in order to understand their business, their people, their culture, their history, and their future.

Furnishing a better way of life.

Only then do the Price Modern design and sales consultants make sound and knowledgeable recommendations to accurately guide businesses through the furnishings selection process. From order placement to delivery and installation, every detail is expertly managed by a team of trained, experienced, and accredited professionals. The team oversees that the project management, logistics, delivery, installation, and warehousing are all coordinated to result in a project that is on time and on budget. On-site product training, ongoing product maintenance, and repair services continue as client needs change.

Environmental Responsibility

Price Modern and Haworth realize that achieving sustainable harmony with the environment is one of the most important long-term challenges facing the human race in this century. Price Modern has made a commitment to sustainability by offering Leadership in Energy and Environmental Design (LEED™) workshops, having LEED Accredited Professionals on staff, and relocating its Washington, D.C., showroom to a LEED Certified space. Haworth has also made a commitment toward becoming a sustainable corporation; a large part of that commitment is developing and manufacturing products that have minimal impact on the environment. For businesses seeking products that will contribute to LEED Certification points, Price Modern offers the expertise of professionals who will specify products that meet or exceed the requirements of the LEED Green Building Rating System.

In the Community

Price Modern believes in supporting the community and giving back. The year 2008 marked the 11th time that Price Modern was the flagship sponsor for the Lacrosse for Leukemia Fall Invitational Tournament, which is a fund-raising event for the Leukemia & Lymphoma Society Maryland Chapter. In addition, the company sponsors events that support the Alzheimer's Association of Maryland. Also in 2008, the employees gathered at their holiday party to build bicycles that were then donated to the Boys & Girls Club of Annapolis. The company consistently sponsors and is actively involved in several industry-related nonprofit organizations on the local and national levels, including the International Interior Design Association (IIDA), the U.S. Green Building Council (USGBC), the International Facility Managers Association (IFMA), and the American Institute of Architects (AIA).

For over a century, Price Modern has been customizing workplace solutions to meet the needs of businesses—large or small; start-ups or well-established companies; local, national, or global. Being a part of the community and giving back to the community is part of being a leader in the community. Additional information is available on the company's Web site at www.pricemodern.com.

Above left: From order placement through project completion, an entire team of professionals works behind the scenes and on-site to ensure that each Price Modern project is completed on time and on budget. Above right: Price Modern provides innovative, environmentally friendly solutions for customized work spaces that provide the best possible atmosphere for businesses.

The Banneker Group, LLC

This diverse company provides general contracting and facilities maintenance for public and private sector clients, delivering services of superior quality on time and on budget, with a flexible workforce that is experienced in design-build and maintenance work. It also helps in the renovation of schools and recreation centers in support of the community.

Both pages: Pinnacles of The Banneker Group, LLC's portfolio include the Pienza Italian Market restaurant (above) and Old Hickory Steakhouse (opposite page), both located at the Gaylord National Resort and Convention Center in National Harbor, Maryland.

From the Pienza Italian Market restaurant and Old Hickory Steakhouse at the Gaylord National Resort and Convention Center in National Harbor, Maryland, to the Washington Monument in Washington, D.C., and the Pentagon in Arlington, Virginia, the professionals at The Banneker Group, LLC, bring successful solutions to design-build projects. Established as a facilities-maintenance firm in 1998, the company, based in Laurel, Maryland, has grown to offer a wide range of services—including general contracting; cost estimating, scheduling, and engineering; construction management; and facilities maintenance—for public and private enterprises.

General contracting services include traditional competitive bidding, performance-based contracts, construction oversight, and design-build services. Within its services, The Banneker Group provides contract negotiation and administration; estimating, including total project-cost projections, and value engineering; construction scheduling, critical path method analysis, and cost loading

information; resource allocation; and a level of quality control and quality assurance that is designed to ensure client satisfaction for every job.

The company's roots in facilities maintenance remain an integral part of the business. Contract clients receive comprehensive operations and maintenance services including installation and preventative maintenance for mechanical, electrical, and plumbing systems; landscaping, groundskeeping, and pest control; and janitorial services. The Banneker Group provides comprehensive project management and work-control management and enforces high standards of quality control. The Banneker Group provides additional information about all of its services on its Web site at www.thebannekergroup.com.

In 2008 The Banneker Group established its own educational facility—TBG University—which offers construction-education programs at the company's offices in Laurel. The Construction Management program prepares students for business and management operations while giving them the knowledge of procedures related to up-to-date construction technologies. Topics covered include building materials, codes and regulations, types of fabrication, estimating, and construction accounting and financing. Among the classes offered are Construction Print Reading, Construction Accounting, and Construction Estimating I and credits are transferable to Prince George's Community College.

In addition to working on many of the area's well-known landmarks, The Banneker Group provides critical assistance to the community. For the District of Columbia Center for Therapeutic Recreation, the company provided general cleanup, new landscaping, and repair of the perimeter fencing. For eight public schools in the nation's capital, the company performed renovations and improvements as part of the Washington, D.C., metropolitan area's Buff and Scrub initiative. The Banneker Group also participated in upgrades and beautification projects, such as picking up litter, spreading mulch, and painting for the Vansville Neighborhood Recreation Center in Beltsville, Maryland.

Tricon Chemical Corporation

Headquartered in Forestville, this service-oriented company manufactures and distributes water treatment chemicals and installs and services efficient water treatment programs. Solutions and products are customized to prevent problems such as expensive equipment replacement, mechanical breakdowns, tenant complaints, and health hazards.

No challenge is beyond Tricon's expertise. Among the company's highly satisfied customers are schools, libraries, banks, apartment buildings, restaurants, office buildings, large metropolitan wastewater plants, and many other establishments that could not operate without successful water treatment systems. These organizations turn to Tricon with a variety of water problems: boiler scale and corrosion, water fountains plagued by slime and algae, lime accumulation in a water distribution plant, inconsistent hot water supply, the odor and health hazards of a clogged drain, and floor damage from excessive condensation in and blockage of a drainage system.

Customer service is as important to Tricon as solving problems and blending chemicals. The skill and talent of the company's associates is considered its greatest strength. Customer service representatives work with on-site engineers to provide monthly service and maintain effective chemical and mechanical programs. Support is also given in the form of continuing education and training programs for clients. Close management, constant attention to quality control, and a rigorous training process have ensured a steady stream of happy clients and customer referrals.

Tricon Chemical Corporation is an expert at tackling the unseen problems that arise wherever water flows—in boilers, heating and cooling systems, fountains, pools, sewers, and drains. As a solutions provider, a service company, and a manufacturer, distributor, and seller of water treatment compounds, Tricon eliminates rust, corrosion, scale, algae, and microbicides before they emerge, solves the problems they cause if they are already on-site, and brings its clients peace of mind.

Tricon is a water chemicals expert. The company manufactures and blends industrial water treatment compounds and specialty chemicals and sells and distributes industrial chemicals. The chemical and sales department directs the formulation and manufacturing of chemical treatments and provides trained chemical technicians and service personnel. Chemical mixers blend industrial water treatment compounds and specialty chemicals while group leaders supervise tracking, delivery, and on-site chemical storage.

Tricon's chemical compounds are sold locally, regionally, and nationally. The company's industrial chemicals are classified as specialty, inorganic, and organic. A few examples are water treatment compounds, detergents and antifreeze, sludge remover for diesel and jet engine fuel, heavy equipment industrial cleaners, wastewater polymers, caustic soda, and bulk liquid chlorine. Tricon also distributes the products of reputable Fortune 500 manufacturers such as Cargill, Incorporated; Dow Chemical Company; BASF Wyandotte Corporation; Monsanto Company; Buckman Laboratories; and Union Carbide Corporation.

Additional information about Tricon Chemical Corporation can be found on the company's Web site at www.tricon.com.

Above, both images: Tricon Chemical Corporation fixes or prevents problems wherever water flows, providing customized, safe, and cost-effective chemical treatment and water cleaning programs.

NAI The Michael Companies, Inc.

Providing commercial real estate services around the globe, with a focus on the greater suburban Maryland region, including Maryland, Virginia, and Washington, D.C., this full-service company offers creative and successful solutions to real estate sales, leasing, development, and property management by combining years of real estate experience with dedicated teamwork.

Above: The Brick Yard Business Park is one of the many projects of NAI The Michael Companies, Inc. The property is a 65-acre development that will feature more than 650,000 square feet of office, warehouse, and flexible space in a professional campus setting in Beltsville and Laurel, Maryland.

A leading full-service commercial real estate organization based in Lanham, Maryland, NAI The Michael Companies, Inc. successfully serves clients in the greater Washington, D.C., metropolitan region and supports its employees by upholding a philosophy of professionalism, integrity, and service excellence. Enhancing these values are the company's quality operations, cost-effective systems, and solid teamwork, all of which enable it to achieve its mission—successfully meet the needs of clients by continually providing excellent performance and services, locally and internationally.

NAI Michael is the exclusive representative in suburban Maryland for New America International (NAI) Global, a premier network of independent commercial real estate firms and one of the largest commercial real estate service providers worldwide. NAI Global manages a network of 5,000 professionals and 325 offices in 55 countries around the globe. NAI Global's widespread professional resources enable NAI Michael to offer clients fast and efficient acquisition, leasing, and disposition of commercial real estate and to leverage its services to companies and investors looking to expand their holdings nationwide.

NAI Michael offers a variety of services ranging from the development of government facilities, corporate office buildings, and industrial warehouses to sales and leasing for restaurants, retail centers, residential communities, and churches. The company also sells investment properties and unimproved properties, consults with landowners and builders regarding property development, and offers property-management services. NAI Michael manages more than seven million square feet of office, industrial, high-tech, and retail space.

NAI Michael was built on the premise that a spirit of teamwork combined with a skilled management team would result in a premier organization devoted to consistently delivering value-added services to its clients. Today the NAI Michael staff of 50 has earned a reputation for excellence in all commercial real estate sectors.

As a leader in its industry, NAI Michael invests in technology advances. Among these is REALTrac Online, which enables associates to maintain real estate listings, update market information, identify potential clients, and provide financial analyses as needed. To effectively advise clients throughout the decision-making process, the NAI Michael research division finds and disseminates timely leads, comparable properties, and other information critical to the company's recommendations to clients. The professionals at NAI Michael also are active in many local and national organizations that promote civic, political, business, and economic development.

NAI The Michael Companies, Inc. provides additional information about its services on its Web site at www.naimichael.com.

PROFILES OF COMPANIES AND ORGANIZATIONS
Education

Salisbury University

Located on the scenic and historic Eastern Shore, only 30 miles from its famed Atlantic beaches and 20 miles from the beautiful Chesapeake Bay, Salisbury University is a Maryland campus on the move. Nationally recognized for its exceptional academic programs, the university encourages students to become involved in international study, research projects, internships with professional organizations, and community outreach.

Above: Salisbury University (SU) President Janet Dudley-Eshbach talks with students and faculty on the Eastern Shore campus, where personal connections are valued. SU is a proud member of the University System of Maryland.

Historical Growth

Home to more than 7,800 students from some 30 states and 62 nations, Salisbury University (SU) offers a creative curriculum that emphasizes undergraduate research, study abroad, professional internships, and civic engagement.

Having evolved from a normal school to a public comprehensive university with a private school atmosphere, SU now offers 42 undergraduate majors and 13 graduate programs in the liberal arts, sciences, and professions including business and education. All four of its schools are endowed—a rarity among public institutions nationwide.

"These are exciting times at Salisbury University," says President Janet Dudley-Eshbach, Ph.D. "Our reputation as 'A Maryland University of National Distinction' is growing." Dudley-Eshbach is leading the way, ushering in a new era with significant campus transformations.

Cutting-Edge Facilities

Building for a better tomorrow, in fall 2008, SU opened the $65 million, 165,000-square-foot Teacher Education and Technology Center, a showcase building for education in the mid-Atlantic region. It features $5.3 million in technology, including SMART classrooms, a digital photography lab, and one of the few campus-based, high-definition digital video production studios in the nation.

A new home for the Franklin P. Perdue School of Business and a 600-bed residence hall and retail complex are scheduled to open in 2011. Building purchases and other construction are also developing and expanding the SU campus, starting with a four-level, 850-space parking garage. Dedicated to environmental sustainability, SU is pursuing the U.S. Green Building Council's LEED certification for these new projects.

National Acclaim

SU ranks among the nation's Top 100 and Top 50 "Best Value" public colleges, according to *Kiplinger's Personal Finance* and *The Princeton Review*, respectively. SU also is consistently one of *U.S. News & World Report*'s Top Public Universities in the North and is the highest-placing public master's-level university in Maryland. Such accolades are a testament to the university's excellent yet affordable education.

Faculty include distinguished Fulbright scholars and the Eastern Shore's first Maryland Professor of the Year, selected by the Carnegie Foundation for the Advancement of Teaching and the Council for Advancement and Support of Education. Since 2003, 14 SU professors have received the Regents Award for Excellence, the University System of Maryland's highest faculty honor.

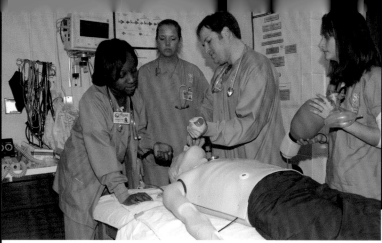

A national leader in student-centered research, SU is the only comprehensive university in the country that has hosted the National Conference on Undergraduate Research (NCUR) twice. SU also is the only Maryland campus to host NCUR.

On the playing field, SU scholar-athletes have earned distinction in one of the top NCAA Division III programs in the United States, with nine national championships in men's lacrosse and field hockey in the past decade.

Distinct Programs

Helping to meet workforce demands and alleviate critical shortages, SU is one of the state's largest educators of future teachers. Its nursing students have the highest pass rate of all baccalaureate programs in Maryland on the National Council Licensure Examination.

In addition, SU's nationally accredited baccalaureate degree in respiratory therapy, the only one in Maryland, is taught on campus and through the Universities at Shady Grove. A growing satellite program in social work reaches students at three distance-learning sites statewide.

The Center for International Education, established by Dudley-Eshbach, allows students to combine service with travel: Business students study global economics in China, education majors teach children in New Zealand, and nursing students provide aid in Africa. The Center for Conflict Resolution is one of only two in the nation to offer bachelor's and master's degrees. In the fine arts, SU offers the state's only collegiate glass-blowing program.

Community Outreach

Campus organizations such as the Small Business Development Center and Healthy U of Delmarva are invaluable resources for the region. The Institute for Public Affairs and Civic Engagement (PACE) places students in public service internships in local, state, and national government.

SU is home to the Salisbury Symphony Orchestra and the Nabb Research Center for Delmarva History and Culture, a repository for some of the nation's oldest records and artifacts. Its Ward Museum of Wildfowl Art is one of *USA Today*'s "10 Great Places to See American Folk Art." The Sea Gull Century bike ride attracts some 6,000 people annually and is Wicomico County's largest one-day tourism event.

SU students are nationally recognized for their volunteerism in such programs as the American Cancer Society's Relay For Life. More than 35,000 alumni, including Perdue Farms CEO Jim Perdue, Baltimore Ravens owner Steve Bisciotti, and Broadway actress Jennifer Hope Wills, also make their mark nationwide.

With an established reputation for excellence, Salisbury University is poised to play an increasingly prominent role in higher education and economic development across Maryland, the mid-Atlantic region, and the nation. Additional information is available on SU's Web site at www.salisbury.edu.

Above left: Holloway Hall is the oldest building on SU's beautiful 182-acre campus, which has national arboretum status and a growing reputation as a Maryland university on the move. Above right: SU respiratory therapy students work in laboratories on campus and at health facilities across the state. SU's nationally accredited respiratory therapy baccalaureate is one of some 50 nationwide and is the only one in Maryland.

Towson University

This university offers more than 100 bachelor's, master's, and doctoral degrees and other programs for its diverse student body. Its well-developed array of opportunities also includes athletics; arts, entertainment, and social events; and venues for valuable community service—forming a quality environment in which students can prepare to become contributing leaders and citizens of today's complex global society.

Founded in 1866, Towson University is recognized among the nation's best regional public universities, offering more than 100 bachelor's, master's, and doctoral degree programs in the liberal arts and sciences and applied professional fields. Towson is known for its excellent programs in business, computer science, health professions, fine arts, communications, and the arts and sciences.

Located in suburban Towson, eight miles north of Baltimore, the university's beautifully landscaped, 328-acre setting offers a pleasant environment for study and a diverse campus life, as well as easy access to a wealth of university and community resources.

With more than 21,000 students, Towson is the second-largest public university in Maryland and is distinguished as Maryland's metropolitan university. Towson combines research-based learning with practical application through its eight colleges and its many interdisciplinary initiatives. Partnerships with public and private organizations throughout Maryland provide further opportunities for research, internships, and jobs.

The resources of a large university and the personal attention of a small college make Towson a unique place in which to study and learn. Most classes have an enrollment of fewer than 25 students, and a student-faculty ratio of just 18 to one ensures that every student's voice can be heard. Students work closely with their professors and take part in engaging classroom discussions. On-campus facilities such as Towson's state-of-the-art library, music and art studios, and science laboratories provide tools for students of all disciplines.

Towson students choose from programs of study in the College of Business and Economics, the College of Education, the College of Fine Arts and Communication, the College of Health Professions, the College of Liberal Arts, and the Jess and Mildred Fisher College of Science and Mathematics. Top undergraduate students are distinguished as members of Towson's Honors College. The College of Graduate Studies and Research offers graduate education at the master's and doctoral levels.

Towson's wide range of undergraduate and graduate programs are designed to prepare students for success in today's rapidly changing workplace. A strong liberal arts foundation anchors a Towson undergraduate education and emphasizes service learning, civic engagement, internships, and study abroad. Many graduate programs that serve working professionals have been developed and expanded to respond to workforce trends.

Above right: Towson University's 328-acre, well-landscaped campus offers traditional and modern architecture combined with plentiful open space and nature's woods and streams.

Towson is serving regional needs and demands by developing many basic and applied research programs that involve not only students and professors but also the community, government, and the private sector. To continue its long-standing commitment to the region, Towson formed the Division of Economic and Community Outreach (DECO) in 2004. Today DECO brings together innovative, forward-thinking individuals from a variety of disciplines both on and off campus to address educational, economic, intellectual, and social issues as they relate to Marylanders. DECO's units include the Center for Homeland Security, Economic and Workforce Development, the Center for Geographic Information Systems, and the Regional Economic Studies Institute, among others.

Towson's campus community is strong. Students build lifelong relationships through fraternity and sorority life, volunteer for service initiatives such as Habitat for Humanity and the American Red Cross Corps, represent their classmates through the Student Government Association, compete in club and intramural sports, and write articles for the award-winning student newspaper *The Towerlight*. All told, there are more than 150 active student clubs and organizations at Towson, with more added every year.

Intercollegiate athletics are also an important part of life at Towson for players and fans alike. As Towson enters its 30th year of NCAA Division I competition, the Tiger athletics program sponsors 20 teams—13 women's and seven men's. Students cheer Tiger football, lacrosse, and track teams from the stands of Johnny Unitas Stadium, the third-largest stadium in Baltimore. The university's 5,000-seat Towson Center arena is home to Tiger basketball, gymnastics, and volleyball.

Student life at Towson also includes a full complement of arts and entertainment—from jazz to chamber music, drama to musicals, and art exhibits to dance. Each year more than 80,000 people attend some 200 performances, exhibitions, films, and lectures at Towson's Center for the Arts and other campus venues. Big-name bands perform at Tigerfest, an annual spring festival that draws crowds of up to 10,000 enthusiasts. The Asian Arts and Culture Center presents a full calendar of events designed to promote the visual and performing arts of Asia. Family entertainment and children's arts programs are offered throughout the year.

From its humble beginnings more than 140 years ago, Towson University has grown to become the largest comprehensive university in the Baltimore area. With each graduating class, the university continues to prove that public higher education pays untold dividends in the well-being of individual students, their families, and their communities. It is a legacy that Towson will continue to preserve for many years to come.

Towson provides additional information about the university on its Web site at www.towson.edu.

Top left: Towson provides state-of-the-art science laboratories for its students. Top center: Tigers fans enjoy watching football and other sports at Johnny Unitas Stadium. Top right: Typically small class sizes—fewer than 25 students per class—help to ensure that Towson students can fully engage in classroom discussions. Above left: Towson students build lifelong friendships through the more than 150 student clubs and organizations at the university.

The Community Colleges of Maryland

Maryland's public community colleges are distinguished as comprehensive, open-admission institutions with affordable tuition. By providing academic opportunities such as transfer degrees, workforce training, and lifelong learning, these community colleges encourage new and existing business development and create long-term economic growth.

education. Many students attend community colleges in order to upgrade their skills to meet changing employment trends and to learn new technologies.

Building Maryland's Workforce

Maryland residents are turning to their local community colleges to earn a degree or certificate, to build a career, and to receive custom-designed training classes in a variety of fields: technology, health care, manufacturing, business, education, and the arts, to name a few. In turn, Maryland businesses depend on their local community colleges for training that will upgrade employee skills

Maryland's community colleges—16 in all—play an important role in the lives of students, in the business community's need for a trained and educated workforce, and in creating a healthy state economy. Students benefit from their increased earnings and improved lifestyles. Taxpayers benefit from an expanded economy and low social costs. And the whole community benefits from more job opportunities, higher business revenues, and greater availability of public funds. It is a win-win-win alliance.

With half a million credit and noncredit students attending Maryland's community colleges each year, the colleges are committed to offering a variety of quality programs and services that satisfy the community's needs. Among them are core academic education, transfer education, job training, workforce skills and certification, developmental education, adult basic education, and continuing

and help them—both the employees and the businesses—maintain a competitive advantage in the marketplace.

Maryland's community colleges have a significant positive impact on the state's workforce: 80 percent of the state's employment growth is in job skills that can be mastered at community colleges; 94 percent of community college students stay in Maryland to enter or re-enter the workforce; and associate degree graduates earn 39 percent more per year than high school graduates and students who earn a one-year certificate earn 17 percent more.

The well-being of Maryland residents is also in very capable hands considering the colleges' commitment to occupational health and safety training. The state's community colleges train 80 percent of first responders, including police officers,

firefighters, and emergency medical technicians. They also educate more than 60 percent of the state's health care workers in more than 50 allied health career programs. And these colleges are the leading providers of the state's registered nurses, licensed practical nurses, and nursing assistants.

Opening Doors to Higher Education

Without affordable community colleges, many individuals would not have access to post-secondary education. Tuition and fees for Maryland's community colleges are about half that of public four-year colleges and universities. Community colleges enroll more than half of all Maryland residents attending college in the state, transferring 8,500 students and awarding more than 12,000 associate degrees and certificates a year.

Through articulation agreements and partnerships with Maryland's four-year colleges and universities, Maryland's community colleges offer seamless transfer and scholarship opportunities for students pursuing bachelor and advanced degrees.

Maryland's community colleges also provide local youth with a jump start on their college education. About 4,000 Maryland high school students are dually enrolled in a community college. Many of these students attend their local community college on scholarship and earn enough college credit to begin college with sophomore-level status. Six out of 10 high school graduates who remain in Maryland to attend college go to their local community college. Maryland's Association of Community Colleges provides additional information about the colleges on its Web site at www.mdacc.org.

Community colleges serve a growing and diverse population, continually adapting to the needs of their communities while remaining affordable and accessible. In addition to offering convenient access to learning at campuses throughout the state, Maryland's community colleges offer courses at area high schools, community centers, local business sites, and online. These colleges are successfully fulfilling their motto: "Where You Need Us. When You Need Us."

Above left: Each year, nearly 500,000 Marylanders attend one of Maryland's community colleges, which offer degree and transfer programs as well as career training and personal enrichment classes.
Top right: The 16 community colleges offer courses in the health care field such as medical assisting, nuclear medicine, and nursing assistant training.
Bottom right: Students have access to diverse learning resources, including state-of-the-art computer laboratories, smart classrooms, academic advising, career counseling, and other dedicated student services.

Roland Park Country School

A college preparatory school for girls from kindergarten through grade 12, Roland Park Country School has educated women of intelligence, creativity, integrity, and vision for more than a century—learning together under one roof. The school is committed to providing students with a top-notch education and the tools necessary to pursue their passions with confidence, responsibility, and an understanding of the world around them.

Set in northern Baltimore City, Roland Park Country School (RPCS) has educated girls and young women for more than a century. RPCS is an independent, college preparatory school dedicated to the intellectual, aesthetic, physical, and moral development of its students. An esteemed faculty works to nourish not only each student's mind but also her sense of self. Rigorous academic programs and a strong, varied curriculum combined with integrated technology, arts, and athletics characterize the rich history of excellence evident at Roland Park Country School.

Rich History

The school was established in 1894 and officially became Roland Park Country School in 1901. It earned the distinction of being the first fully accredited independent school for girls in Baltimore City. RPCS suffered two devastating fires but the community's resilient spirit did not waver, and RPCS found its new home on the current campus, known as Chestnutwood, in 1980. In 2008, with the construction of an environmentally responsible "green" Athletic Complex, RPCS completed the third and final phase of its Campus Master Plan, which began in 1994. Phase One consisted of an arts center and a library. Phase Two consisted of a science wing, technology center, dining hall, middle school, and another library. RPCS was the first girls' school in Maryland to be awarded a Cum Laude Chapter, and the first independent school in Baltimore City to be named a Maryland Green School. While RPCS has maintained its focus on educating young women throughout its history, boys were originally admitted through the third grade. Today there are

700 girls and young women in kindergarten through grade 12.

Tenacity of Purpose

The mission of RPCS is to maintain high academic standards while encouraging self-discipline, independence of thought, tenacity of purpose, creativity, and spiritual well-being. The school strives to instill in its students a lifelong love of learning as well as the motivation to look within and beyond themselves in order that they become responsible, contributing members of college and community life. The goal of the school is threefold: to cultivate the intellect, develop strong character, and build vital young women.

Above left: Middle School students at Roland Park Country School (RPCS) face engineering challenges in each grade, which emphasize cooperative, experiential learning. Above right: Shown here is the Dorothy Mears Ward House on the Chestnutwood campus of Roland Park Country School.

Southern Maryland Higher Education Center

This outstanding center for higher education offers graduate and upper-division professional degree programs to the professional workforce of the tri-county region through its affiliation with nine distinguished university partners. The center also serves as a training, conferencing, and meeting facility for the U.S. Navy; state, county, and local governments; technology trainers; and public schools and organizations.

Above, all photos: Southern Maryland Higher Education Center, a regional state facility with state-of-the-art technology, serves the university and professional training needs of the Southern Maryland region, including training for members of the U.S. Navy.

Established by the State of Maryland to serve the university and professional training needs of Calvert, Charles, and St. Mary's counties, the Southern Maryland Higher Education Center (SMHEC) presents almost 90 academic programs, including 42 master's degrees and five doctorate degrees through nine universities and colleges. A regional facility with state-of-the-art technology, the Center is located on 24 acres in the Wildewood Professional and Technology Park in California, Maryland, where 35 high-technology classrooms and laboratories and several multipurpose conference rooms serve a growing community of professionals.

SMHEC has required ongoing expansion and growth to fulfill its mission—which is to accommodate the region's need for higher education—including providing graduate education and professional training and development for the Naval Air Station at Patuxent River, meeting the critical need for qualified teachers in Southern Maryland's public schools, and supporting the instruction of high-technology workers in the tri-county region. The state of Maryland and its political leaders believe that a successful economy today and in the future will depend on effectively blending technology and higher education.

SMHEC successfully meets the needs of the area's 30,000-strong high-technology civilian and military workforce by providing a range of engineering, applied sciences, and management graduate degree programs. The center offers 33 degrees in engineering and technology including three doctorates; 34 graduate education programs including two doctorates; and programs in business administration, management, social services, community and clinical counseling, information assurance, executive leadership, and nursing.

Before the SMHEC was established in 1994, individuals in Southern Maryland seeking advanced degrees and other educational opportunities had to travel long distances to reach universities in the Washington-Baltimore region. Today university-level programs are conveniently available to a population of more than 300,000. In addition to 42 master's and five doctorate degrees, the center also offers 13 bachelor completion programs, 16 graduate certificates, and 13 education certification programs. Approximately 3,000 class enrollments are recorded at SMHEC each year.

The universities offering degree programs at SMHEC are The Johns Hopkins University, the University of Maryland College Park, the University of Maryland University College, George Washington University, The Catholic University, Towson University, the College of Notre Dame of Maryland, Gratz College, and Capitol College. Additional information is available on SMHEC's Web site at www.smhec.org.

PROFILES OF COMPANIES AND ORGANIZATIONS

Environmental Engineering and Services

HAZMED, Inc.

This award-winning Maryland-based firm offers environmental engineering and consulting, as well as information technology and records management expertise, providing government and commercial clients with professional support to perform some of their most challenging objectives. The company has generated a track record of technical accomplishment, client success, and growth.

The company offers solutions to some of the most challenging situations in four core business areas: environmental engineering and consulting, homeland security, information technology, and records management and document conversion. HAZMED provides additional information about its services, projects, and activities on its Web site at www.hazmed.com.

Experienced Leadership

At the helm of this results-oriented company is entrepreneur Jacqueline W. Sales, company owner, president, and CEO. With a master's degree in environmental engineering from Howard University, Sales gained professional experience with the EPA Office of Solid Waste and Emergency Response and also the Department of Energy's Office of Environmental Guidance (now the Office of Environmental Policy and Assistance).

Sales's expertise includes developing and implementing federal regulations, policies, and strategies for the management of hazardous, radioactive, and medical wastes; guiding the cleanup of contaminated sites; working with federal, state, and local agencies and congressional subcommittees, as well as private industry; and chairing national and regional waste forums.

An Award-Winning Enterprise

HAZMED and Sales have received numerous awards for performance. HAZMED received the U.S. Small Business Administration (SBA), Region III, Small Business of the Year 2000 Award for its work and dedication to providing quality technical services to U.S. government agencies and its dedication in fostering growth and prosperity for minority businesses. HAZMED was honored with the Outstanding Minority Business Award by the National Minority Business Council in 2000, which cited the company's growth and success in the environmental field. Accolades also came from the Prince George's County Chamber of Commerce in 2000, which presented the Small Business of the Year award to HAZMED based on outstanding business practices and community commitment.

Throughout the nation, government agencies and private companies rely on HAZMED, Inc. and its environmental engineers and scientists, regulatory and policy analysts, attorneys, and computer specialists to provide them with tailored solutions for projects related to environmental compliance, waste management, and homeland security. The company has successfully completed technically demanding projects for a wide range of government and commercial clients, including the U.S. Department of Energy, the U.S. Environmental Protection Agency (EPA), the U.S. Department of Defense, and the U.S. Department of Homeland Security. HAZMED also has provided services for major commercial firms including Science Applications International Corporation (SAIC), ICF International (ICF), and Computer Sciences Corporation (CSC). HAZMED is a protégé of The Boeing Company.

HAZMED was founded in 1988. Its success stems from a corporate culture that demands quality, rewards excellence, and promotes teamwork and has produced a track record of technical accomplishment, client success, and business growth.

Above left: Jacqueline W. Sales is the owner of HAZMED, Inc. Above right: The company's corporate headquarters is located in Prince George's County, in Lanham, Maryland.

Representative HAZMED Services and Projects

HAZMED operates as four core business areas, focusing on environmental engineering and consulting plus homeland security, accompanied by expert assistance in information technology and records management and document conversion.

Environmental Engineering and Consulting Services provided by HAZMED include

- Environmental management—waste management and environmental restoration, site assessment, land acquisition, and assistance with environmental justice and tribal issues
- Regulatory compliance—activities within the Resource Conservation and Recovery Act (RCRA); the National Environmental Policy Act (NEPA); and the Comprehensive Environmental Response Compensation and Liability Act (CERCLA)
- Oversight services—construction management, project direction, quality assurance, cost estimating, and on-site surveillance
- Risk management—project planning for toxic-spill sites and removal, sampling, and analysis; occupational safety and health services; pollution prevention and recycling; and analytical testing and evaluation

Engineering and Consulting Projects of HAZMED include

- Radioactive-waste management—technical and management support for the U.S. Department of Energy Radioactive Waste Acceptance Program at a Nevada Test Site
- Chemical pharmacy—operation of the HazMart facility for the U.S. Army Research Laboratory in Aberdeen Proving Ground, Maryland
- Environmental impact statements (EIS)—preparation of EIS for firing range–clearing activities at Fort Stewart, Georgia

- Compliance with the U.S. Department of Labor's Occupational Safety and Health Administration (OSHA)—respirator protection for radionuclides in support of a dosimeter program for more than 200 technicians at the U.S. Army Research Laboratory in Aberdeen Proving Ground, Maryland
- Engineering and construction management support—oversight of environmental remediation activities for the U.S. Army Corps of Engineers at Fort Campbell, Kentucky; St. Louis, Missouri; and Camp Bullis, Texas

Homeland Security Services provided by HAZMED include

- Border security management—provision of subject-matter expertise, command, and control; hot-site management; geospatial architecture and design; and Web portal design, development, and hosting
- Emergency preparedness and response—counter-terrorism planning; consequence management; planning, training, and exercises; and threat and vulnerability assessment
- Critical-infrastructure protection—construction management oversight and electronic records management and conversion

Homeland Security Projects of HAZMED include

- Construction management services—gates and barrier program for the U.S. Army Corps of Engineers at Fort Campbell
- Counter-terrorism exercise—Trans-Alaska Pipeline System

(TAPS) counter-terrorism exercise for NASA

- Operational readiness—aid for the Emergency Operations Center and the Emergency Broadcasting System at NASA Langley Research Center in Norfolk, Virginia
- Command control—Intelligent Computer-Aided Detection (ICAD) system integration into border-sensor technology; Web-based, nationwide real-time reviews; and geospatial event sharing for the Customs and Border Protection office of the U.S. Department of Homeland Security
- Records management—enterprise-wide records management systems for the Federal Emergency Management Agency (FEMA) Mitigation Directorate

---

Sales was voted one of the Top 100 Women in Maryland by *The Daily Record of Baltimore* in 1999, 2003, and 2007 and was inducted in the Circle of Excellence upon receiving this recognition three times. McDonald's Corporation recognized Sales in 2004 as a history maker in the field of science. In addition, she was a 1999 finalist for the Maryland Ernst & Young Entrepreneur of the Year in Science and Technology. While working at the EPA, Sales received a Bronze Medal in 1988 for her efforts in establishing regulations for disposal of hazardous waste. Sales also was

recognized by the EPA in 1988 as one of the outstanding Women in Science and Engineering.

HAZMED is headquartered in Prince George's County, in Lanham, Maryland, and maintains a staff of 100 people at its field and project sites in Aberdeen Proving Ground, Maryland; Burlington, Vermont; Fort Campbell and Fort Knox, Kentucky; Wright-Patterson Air Force Base, Ohio; San Antonio, Texas; Rock Island Arsenal and Scott Air Force Base, Illinois; and Crystal City, Virginia.

Above: HAZMED engineers perform compliance inspection at the U.S. Army Reserve Center at Camp Bullis, Texas.

PROFILES OF COMPANIES AND ORGANIZATIONS

Financial Services

NBRS Financial Bank

The oldest locally owned and managed independent commercial bank operating in Harford and Cecil counties, this renowned financial institution is dedicated to providing its customers with the highest quality service through local management, advanced technology, and a wide array of electronic financial services. A valued member of the community, it contributes to the economic strength and health of its region.

The oldest locally owned and managed commercial bank operating in Harford and Cecil counties, Maryland, NBRS Financial Bank is well equipped to meet the banking and financial needs of the communities in which it operates. Living and working in the communities they serve, members of the bank's board of directors, management, and staff gain local market knowledge and understanding that enables them to base financial decisions on what is best for their community and market and to provide an unmatched level of personal service and responsiveness.

The bank was founded in 1873 by two prominent local businessmen, Jesse Wood and James M. Evans, as The Evans and Wood Bank. In 1880 it became The National Bank of Rising Sun, located in the town of Rising Sun, Maryland, and in 2002 its name became NBRS Financial Bank with the adoption of a state banking charter.

In 2000 the bank opened its first branch office in the city of Havre de Grace, Maryland. Since then the bank has continued to open new branch offices, including its ninth location, which was opened in 2008 in Port Deposit, Maryland.

Today the bank operates branch offices in Harford and Cecil counties, Maryland, as well as southern Lancaster County, Pennsylvania. The local board and management of this growing institution is committed to safeguarding the strength, reliability, and safety that have been a hallmark of the bank for more than 125 years.

Personal Service and Convenience

As a community bank, NBRS Financial Bank takes pride in the level of service and responsiveness it is able to provide its clientele. It is attentive to its customers, many of whom are known by name at their branch, and provides excellent service and convenient access as it strives to meet the needs and expectations of its customers.

NBRS Financial Bank offers a broad range of financial services to individual and business customers. These services combine with the bank's modern technology to provide customers with convenience, improved customer support services, increased security and privacy, in addition to competitive rates. In 2008 NBRS Financial Bank introduced Rewards Checking, a program that rewards customers with higher than average interest rates for using the bank's service charge free electronic banking services. Jacob H. "Jack" Goldstein, chairman, president, and CEO of NBRS Financial Bank, says, "We want our customers to experience the superior financial services and products that are available to them without sacrificing the quality, friendly service they are accustomed to at NBRS Financial Bank."

NBRS Financial Bank uses state-of-the-art technology to provide its customers with efficient services and convenient banking access. Its senior management team remains current with electronic advancements created for the financial services industry to ensure that its customers have access to the most up-to-date banking services. Convenient service is delivered by NBRS Financial Bank through its growing

network of branch offices, telephone banking, a network of ATMs, debit cards, and Internet banking; additionally mobile banking is planned for the near future. NBRS Financial Bank provides additional information about all of its products and services on its Web site at www.nbrs.com.

An Invested Community Partner

NBRS Financial Bank has experienced significant growth in the 21st century. Its assets have reached $250 million, and since 2003 its employment has grown by 46 percent, which translates to a contribution of more than $4 million into the local economy. With increased assets and employment, NBRS Financial Bank is better able to serve its communities with more deposit and credit services, which contribute to a healthy local economy.

NBRS Financial Bank also contributes to its communities' economic vitality to assist with improvements for their quality of life. For example, when evaluating loan requests for real estate development, NBRS Financial Bank considers the potential environmental impact the project will have on the area. Furthermore, NBRS Financial Bank reinvests its deposits locally, which contribute toward a healthy local economy.

NBRS Financial Bank is an active participant in community organizations and cultural and social activities. Members of its board of directors and management team serve in leadership positions in many community organizations, including the Career Technology and Education Council for Harford County, Presbyterian Homes of Maryland, and the Triangle Health Alliance. The bank also invests in many local nonprofit organizations. Working in partnership with local schools, including those situated in economically distressed areas, NBRS Financial Bank participates in mentoring programs that teach basic financial literacy skills to students of all ages from elementary school through high school. The bank has been recognized by the Maryland Bankers Association for its financial education of school-age children.

In 2006 NBRS Financial Bank received the Harford Award—sponsored by the Harford County Chamber of Commerce—as retail business of the year, based on growth, creative strategies, support for education, environmental sensitivity, community service, and enhancement of the county's business climate.

Commenting on the bank's focus of helping its communities and its customers, Goldstein says, "Our mission is to continually seek a win-win situation. I enjoy helping our customers solve problems and become even more successful."

As a locally owned and managed independent commercial bank, NBRS Financial Bank distinguishes itself as an institution that invests locally to assist in the economic success of the communities in which it operates.

Above left: The main office of NBRS Financial Bank is located in Rising Sun, Maryland. Above right: Among the bank's directors and management team are, from left, seated, Joseph Snee Jr., director; Sharon C. Walla, director; Teresa Greider, executive vice president and chief financial officer; and Lowell W. McCoy, director; and standing, Jacob H. "Jack" Goldstein, chairman, president, and CEO; Robert Dael, senior vice president; Jesse Wood, director; John S. "Jay" Tosh Jr., director; James A. Crothers II, director; and Robert E. Shallcross, chairman of Rising Sun Bancorp, a one-bank holding company of NBRS Financial Bank.

SECU Credit Union

Maryland's largest state-chartered credit union has provided members with quality financial services for nearly six decades. Today it remains committed to meeting the needs and expectation of its membership—nearly a quarter of a million Marylanders—offering comprehensive financial products and services.

SECU began humbly in October 1951 when a group of volunteers started operating a credit union from a borrowed desk and chair in an office-building hallway in downtown Baltimore. Its first member was Theodore R. McKeldin, then-governor of Maryland. Within one month SECU had enrolled 33 members and had accumulated $3,487 in assets. A few months later, in January 1952 it made its first loan—of $180— and the credit union continued to grow during the following decades, gaining an expanding membership and network of branch offices.

SECU began introducing new products and services throughout the 1980s, offering IRAs and credit cards and providing ATM access. In the 1990s, SECU's convenient services grew to include expanded office hours, additional ATMs, and Expressline, a 24-hour telephone account-access system. Throughout its nearly 60-year history, SECU has demonstrated its commitment to serving its members with modern conveniences and excellent products.

SECU is committed to providing comprehensive, fairly priced, first-rate products and services. It offers a variety of borrowing options with competitive loan rates, along with tools to help its members manage their credit. Offering a full line of credit cards, SECU delivers numerous credit options to meet the individual needs of its members through practical credit limits and competitive interest rates. SECU's savings and checking accounts are tailored to its members' needs, and it also offers reasonably priced insurance products. Its business services are designed to serve the unique needs of owners of smaller businesses.

The Credit Union Advantage

As a credit union, SECU is able to provide its members with significant benefits not available through a bank. As nonprofit, cooperative organizations, credit unions return their profits to their members through better rates and lower or nonexistent fees. National studies have shown that credit unions are consistently able to offer rates that are more competitive and to provide superior customer service compared with many other financial institutions. Remembering that

Above: SECU Credit Union provides members with 16 convenient branch offices throughout Maryland. This one is located in Pasadena.

SECU Credit Union is a full-service credit union in Maryland dedicated to helping its members achieve their financial goals and dreams. Members enjoy a wide array of financial products and services. The largest state-chartered credit union, SECU serves some 247,000 members through 16 community branch offices. With 2007 total assets of $1.7 billion, SECU was ranked among the top 75 credit unions in the country in the *2007 Credit Union Directory*.

its members are its owners, SECU follows this credit union tradition by focusing on its members, helping them to meet their goals.

Financial Security

SECU has observed many changes in the economy throughout its long history and has developed safe and sound practices that are focused on providing value to its members while not putting the institution as a whole at risk. It exercises prudent lending practices that do not include subprime mortgage loans, and it is regularly audited by state and federal regulators as well as its own Supervisory Committee, which consists of member-volunteers. Its deposits and IRAs are insured up to $250,000 by the National Credit Union Administration, a government agency.

SECU's investments are with U.S. government agencies that have high financial ratings and are backed by the federal government. It maintains a conservative investment policy with no financial relationships to the brokerage community.

SECU provides additional information about its services and products on its Web site at www.secumd.org.

In the Community

SECU was started by a team of volunteers. That spirit has continued as its employees volunteer time and money to improve Maryland communities. SECU strives to improve its communities by fulfilling its mission of helping its members achieve their financial goals. It does so by supporting financial education and contributing to financial and social causes.

Since 2006 SECU has collected school supplies for underprivileged children returning to school. In 2007 it launched a youth-oriented financial education program that holds monthly classes at its headquarters in Linthicum; donated $22,500 to help Marylanders of all ages begin savings plans; and provided funding for flu shots for Maryland state employees. That same year, its employees contributed more than $25,000 to United Way during the SECU United Way campaign.

In 2008 SECU provided job-shadowing opportunities for students from a local high school; sponsored two initiatives that focused on raising awareness of personal finances and promoting savings among youth; and supported Money Power Day at Baltimore Polytechnic Institute to encourage financial responsibility. Additionally, it regularly holds on-site American Red Cross blood drives; sends children to Junior Achievement's BizTown, which offers an interactive, real-world financial learning experience; and funds the SECU State Scholarship for State Employees.

SECU remains committed to providing excellent financial services and products to its member-owners. Combining financially sound practices with its focus on meeting its members' needs, SECU has become an important, contributing member of the Maryland community.

Above: SECU's headquarters and operations center is located in Linthicum, Maryland.

Legg Mason, Inc.

Headquartered in Baltimore, Maryland, Legg Mason, Inc. is one of the 10 largest asset management firms in the world, serving individual and institutional investors in 190 countries on six continents. Dedicated to creating value for its clients, shareholders, business partners, and employees, Legg Mason sets a standard of excellence in the financial services sector.

Right: Legg Mason's new headquarters building—shown in its final stages of construction before its mid-2009 opening—is located in Baltimore, Maryland. Legg Mason has evolved from a regional securities brokerage into a global asset management firm, serving individual and institutional investors in 190 countries on six continents.

Legg Mason, Inc. is a diversified group of global asset management firms, or "affiliates," who are recognized for their proven investment expertise and long-term performance. With unique investment approaches that have been developed over decades, the Legg Mason affiliates provide clients with a broad spectrum of equity, fixed income, liquidity, and alternative investment solutions, from mutual funds to college savings plans to variable annuities to separately managed accounts. The specialized expertise of each Legg Mason affiliate allows the company to serve many of the most sophisticated investors in the world.

Mission

Legg Mason's mission is "best-in-class" global asset management, measured both by performance and by the trust and loyalty of clients and partners. The company has served investors since its founding in Baltimore in 1899—for much of its history as a brokerage firm, later as a capital markets business, and today as a pure global asset manager. Through this rich history and evolution, Legg Mason has developed a strong culture and sense of purpose that has guided generations of employees and helped the company to succeed across market cycles. While its business has changed form, Legg Mason has always focused its mission on being a preferred choice for clients and setting a standard of excellence in financial services.

As the global markets become more interdependent, Legg Mason is able to meet the changing needs of investors anywhere through its on-the-ground presence in major financial capitals and its network of distribution partners, including major banks, brokerages, insurance companies, and investment consultants. Through its global reach, Legg Mason can deliver investment excellence to clients anywhere in the world.

Corporate Citizenship

Legg Mason is committed to being a responsible global corporate citizen and views that commitment both as a strategic priority and as an ethical mandate.

The company supports philanthropic and community initiatives, values diversity in its thinking and workforce, and has a strong culture of honor and integrity.

- **Philanthropy**—Legg Mason has a long history of supporting community efforts philanthropically through the Legg Mason Charitable Foundation, and the firm believes that investing in communities is an important part of its corporate responsibility. Through charitable giving, the firm invests in areas that promote community well-being, from reducing poverty and providing food and shelter to improving education, encouraging the arts, and more.
- **Environment**—As a global asset manager, Legg Mason is committed to being a responsible corporate citizen and has a strong focus on sustainability and the environment. Climate change is one of the most challenging issues in the world, and protecting and preserving the environment is of paramount importance to Legg Mason as well as to many of its shareholders, clients, business partners, and employees. Legg Mason's new corporate headquarters in Baltimore, opened in summer 2009, was built to achieve LEED (Leadership in Energy Efficiency and Design) certification.

- **Volunteerism**—Legg Mason strives to enrich the communities in which its employees live and work through employee volunteerism and community engagement. It actively encourages associates to lend their time and talent to organizations across global communities, and its employees play an active role in helping to make the firm's philanthropic interests and community outreach successful and sustainable.
- **Diversity**—Legg Mason believes that diversity is essential to its success as an organization since its business benefits from sharing different perspectives, a breadth of experience, and a constantly renewable source of energy and ideas.

A Tradition of Excellence

Legg Mason's transformation from a regional, diversified financial firm to a leader in global asset management is testament to its ability to adapt and to grow. In this era of globalization, where change is a constant, Legg Mason is committed to pursue growth on a global scale and to deploy its capabilities across markets, creating value for its clients, shareholders, business partners, and employees. And as a proud citizen of Baltimore for over a century, Legg Mason is committed to supporting the city and the Maryland community and to helping represent this beautiful and vibrant region to the world.

Additional information about Legg Mason is available on the company's Web site at www.leggmason.com.

Above left: Legg Mason's executive management team includes (from left to right): Ronald R. Dewhurst, David R. Odenath, Jeffrey A. Nattans, Charles J. "C. J." Daley Jr., Mark R. Fetting, and Joseph A. Sullivan. Above right: Legg Mason employees lend a hand to clean up Baltimore's harbor with the Baltimore Harbor Watershed Association and the Living Classrooms Foundation.

MECU of Baltimore, Inc. is the third-largest credit union in the state of Maryland. Founded in 1936 to serve Baltimore City employees who were being taken advantage of by loan sharks, MECU has expanded to serve anyone who lives, works, worships, or attends school in Baltimore. Service to members was at MECU's core when it was founded and remains its guiding principle today.

Foundation

The first offices of MECU were in the guard station of City Hall. By the end of its first year, MECU had assets worth more than $10,000, and by the end of its first decade, it had assets close to a quarter of a million dollars with no losses. Today MECU serves more than 90,000 members, and its assets total more than $870 million.

Growth

Over the years, MECU has added products and services to better provide financial opportunities to its members. Personal loans have expanded to include vehicle loans as well as a full line of mortgage and home equity products. Basic share savings have become a full range of money market accounts and investment-grade certificates of deposit.

Some of its products are unique to MECU, such as its Buy in Baltimore mortgage, which lowers interest rates by 25 basis points for any member buying a home in Baltimore City. Members choose between MECU's fixed rate and variable rate mortgages, and the rate is lowered on whichever one a member chooses.

Because credit unions are financial cooperatives, MECU has worked to provide its members with excellent prices on loans and high interest rates on deposit products. MECU is especially proud of having returned a cash bonus to its members every year since 1981 in the form of an extraordinary dividend and a loan interest rebate.

Above right: In 2007 MECU of Baltimore, Inc. opened its new headquarters branch in a restored 1920s-era bank. The branch was officially opened by, from left, Michael V. Beall, president, Maryland and District of Columbia Credit Union Association; E. Jay Brodie, president, Baltimore Development Corporation; Herman Williams Jr., chairman of the board, MECU; Otis Rolley, member, MECU board of directors; and Bert J. Hash Jr., president and CEO, MECU.

MECU Today

Today MECU has eight branch offices in Baltimore City and nearby Baltimore County to serve its members. Its headquarters operations center and branch office is located on Redwood Street in the heart of Baltimore's financial district.

MECU members can take advantage of the lowest rates on loans and the highest rates on deposits available every day. To give its members access to their funds nationwide, MECU put together a network of more than 58,000 accessible ATMs, larger than the networks of the largest national banks.

MECU now offers business services for members who operate small businesses in the area. Among its many services, MECU provides access to business checking without the high fees that many other financial institutions charge, enabling members to put more into expanding their businesses.

MECU provides additional information about its products and services on its Web site at www.mecu.com.

Commitment to Community

As Baltimore's credit union, MECU is committed to serving the entire community of Baltimore. In addition to making financial services products affordable for anyone wishing to establish a banking relationship, MECU reaches out to assist community organizations in helping the least advantaged of Baltimore. In fact, MECU ranked fourth in the region for charitable contributions, based on total assets and number of employees.

In addition, MECU's dedicated Outreach Committee has established ongoing volunteer relationships with a number of community organizations, including Sandtown Habitat for Humanity, Our Daily Bread, and Meals On Wheels.

MECU's branch offices have established partnerships with six elementary schools in the city, and every year MECU hosts a book drive to collect enough books so that all students in these six schools are able to select a book for themselves at the end of the school year.

In 2005 MECU held its first annual Charity Cup Golf Tournament to raise funds to expand its outreach into the community. With the funds generated through this event, MECU is able to present its partnership schools with

checks for supplies and also provides 10 scholarships for Baltimore City high school students through the CollegeBound Foundation.

Moving Forward

As MECU plans its future, service to members is central in the process. MECU is investing in new technology to ensure fast, accurate, and secure transactions for members, as well as to provide new financial products and tools to serve a changing financial environment.

Significantly, MECU is also investing in the youth in its community—its future members. Working with the CollegeBound Foundation and with schools in Baltimore City, MECU is teaching young people how to manage their money and understand credit. MECU took working with students to another level when it opened its first student-run credit union at the Academy of Finance at Digital Harbor High School. The student-tellers received two weeks of training just as MECU's regular tellers do. Three days a week the student-tellers will be able to open accounts and perform transactions for students and faculty members.

MECU of Baltimore, Inc. has a bright future, and its commitment to youth today will pay off with strong leadership tomorrow.

Above left: MECU staff members are involved in reaching out to serve the community. Shown here, staffers pack bags with small presents to be given to residents of a nursing home in the area. Above right: MECU restored a 1920s-era bank as its new headquarters. The original bank vault evokes a sense of strength and security, such as that which MECU provides to its members.

T. Rowe Price Associates, Inc.

Founded in 1937, this Baltimore-based firm provides individuals and institutions around the world with a collaborative approach to investment management excellence. Its commitment to "putting the client first" is grounded in principles established by its founder, who said, "I believed that if I worked conscientiously for my clients and succeeded in doing a good job for them, my compensation would follow and be on a sounder and more enduring basis."

prosper only if his clients prospered. His namesake firm still operates today under the same fundamental principle.

Over the years, Price became an investing legend and an early pioneer with his "growth-stock" theory of investing. This unknown and untested investment philosophy was based on his visionary idea that companies, like people, have life cycles of growth, maturity, and decline. He believed that it was possible to earn superior returns by investing for the long term in well-managed companies whose earnings and dividends could be expected to grow faster than inflation and the overall economy.

Investment Philosophy

The T. Rowe Price investment philosophy has been refined over seven decades, yet the basic principles have remained unchanged, consistently demonstrating the difference between T. Rowe Price and its competitors:

- Proprietary Research—a team of in-house investment analysts collaborates across time zones and international borders to deliver fundamental, bottom-up research
- Attention to Risk—the firm seeks to provide a careful balance between risk and potential reward throughout market cycles
- Experienced Investment Team—tenured fund managers are focused on seeking investments that deliver superior long-term performance to clients, rather than on chasing market fads
- Style Consistency—fund managers set clear expectations around risks and potential rewards, and strictly adhere to each fund's investment charter

Recognized in 2008 by independent investment research provider Morningstar, Inc. as a "proven center of investing excellence," T. Rowe Price has grown to become a major global investment manager.* In 1986 T. Rowe Price Group became a publicly traded company (NASDAQ (GS): TROW). Through its subsidiaries, it

Above: T. Rowe Price Associates, Inc. is headquartered in Baltimore, Maryland, and maintains offices across the United States, as well as locations in Canada, South America, Asia, Australia, and Europe.

More than 70 years ago, Thomas Rowe Price Jr., a chemist by training whose true passion lay in analyzing investments rather than formulas, was determined to leave his career in the brokerage business for a relatively new profession— investment counseling. Rather than continue in brokerage, where he could earn commissions on customer trades regardless of whether the customer made money, he yearned for a profession where his own interests and his clients' interests would be aligned. In the investment counseling business, his fees would be based on a percentage of his client's assets. Therefore, Price would

*Source: www.Morningstar.com, October 14, 2008

manages assets on behalf of individual investors and many of the world's leading corporations, public retirement plans, foundations, endowments, financial intermediaries, and sovereign entities.

In addition to its Baltimore headquarters, T. Rowe Price has offices throughout the United States, as well as locations in Canada, South America, Asia, Australia, and Europe, which deliver in-depth local knowledge and focused investment solutions. It is one of the few independent investment management firms included in the S&P 500 Index, widely regarded as the best measure of the broader U.S. stock market.

T. Rowe Price offers a full range of investment strategies across multiple asset classes, capitalizations, sectors, and styles. Investment vehicles include separately managed portfolios, subadvised portfolios, trusts, mutual funds, and commingled vehicles.

Ultimately, what matters most to clients is T. Rowe Price's ability to create value for them over the long term. This value may come in the form of investment strategies that seek to outperform those of their competitors. It may come from the superior service their firm's associates provide or from intangible elements, such as the T. Rowe Price culture, which inspires investor confidence. The culture includes

• a collaborative approach to investment management excellence,
• a focus on disciplined processes,
• ongoing dialogue with clients, and
• applying multiple perspectives to new challenges.

Around the world, T. Rowe Price associates share a collective commitment to helping their clients achieve their financial goals. The firm's leaders form a Management Committee whose members average more than 25 years tenure

with T. Rowe Price—helping to ensure continuity in the firm's business practices and a core commitment to client success. Experience has taught them that the best way to create success is by integrating talented people and creating a collaborative culture with proven processes to create value for clients.

Responsibility to Clients and the Community

This same approach is used for T. Rowe Price's community involvement. More than 40 percent of the firm's associates participate annually, dedicating their time and talents through volunteer work, board service, and financial contributions. Each year, this commitment to service, to giving back, and to investing in a shared future continues to grow.

The firm's strong sense of fiduciary responsibility and commitment to its institutional and individual investors drive the organization. The end result is a culture of believing in the firm's own growth and that profits should follow primarily from the success created for clients.

For additional information about T. Rowe Price and its investment solutions, visit www.troweprice.com.

Above: The firm's associates are involved in serving the diverse communities where they live and work, helping to solve real needs by donating their time, expertise, and financial support.

Cedar Point Federal Credit Union

Consistently maintaining earnings and increasing capital while reaching more than $280 million in assets, this credit union, a nonprofit financial cooperative, provides the opportunity for members to save and to borrow money at fair and reasonable rates of interest and offers other cost-effective financial services to meet the special needs of its 30,000 members—personnel at the Patuxent River Naval Air Station and residents of the surrounding community.

Above: Cedar Point Federal Credit Union (CPFCU), a member-owned, not-for-profit financial cooperative, is based in Lexington Park, Maryland.

Cedar Point Federal Credit Union (CPFCU) was founded in St. Mary's County in 1945 aboard the Patuxent River Naval Air Station located on Chesapeake Bay near the mouth of the Patuxent River. As the air station rapidly grew in response to World War II, the credit union grew as well, continually adding services that matched the needs of its members. Established as a cooperative effort of "people helping people," CPFCU's purpose at the outset was to promote the financial health of its members—an ideal that remains central to its mission more than 60 years later.

Today the CPFCU operates five offices; owns 21 ATMs, 10 of which are on board the Naval Air Station; and operates a mobile ATM service that travels throughout the community to various events to serve members attending the events.

There also is an ATM in the Charlotte Hall Veterans Home to accommodate the home's residents and employees. The credit union's experienced professionals, managers, and board members are committed to serving all members, both on and off the base, and strive to make CPFCU members' primary financial institution of choice.

Committed to Communication and Education

Delivering outstanding service and information is key to the credit union's success. Members are kept up-to-date via a monthly newsletter and other materials concerning rate changes; loans, which include personal, vehicle, property, construction, and mortgages; and new products and services. The CPFCU actively participates in Business Showcases, Members Luncheons, Legislative Breakfasts, and State of the County Luncheons and other functions throughout the county.

Cedar Point Financial Services, Inc. (CPFS) is the credit union service organization (CUSO) that offers many vital services to CPFCU members, such as assisting them with investment and insurance products, making financial decisions that affect their Thrift Savings Plan, and funding construction loans for nonmembers. In addition, CPFS offers educational seminars on first-time homeownership, estate planning, financial planning, retirement planning, investments, pension plans, long-term care, college funding, and related financial topics. To additionally serve the community, the credit union holds safety programs each year that include a fingerprint kit and photograph that parents could use if a child were missing.

For its excellence in educating members the CUSO received a Certificate of Recognition from the U.S. Department of the Treasury for noteworthy contributions in promoting financial education among members. Its "Retirement . . . Do You Have A Plan?" program was recognized as being highly effective. The credit union's list of awards and honors also includes receiving the St. Mary's County Chamber of Commerce's 2006 Lighthouse Award for demonstrated revenue growth and job creation and involvement in the community.

Children Saving Money

CPFCU believes in educating children about the importance of saving money, beginning with the Looney Tunes Club for young children, and then at age 14 with the YOUth Savings Club. The 3,000 accounts in the YOUth Savings Club hold savings of more than $1 million, which pay annual dividends. CPFCU's "A"chievement program gives YOUth Savings Club members one dollar for each "A" on the child's report card in five specified key subjects. Children on the "A" Honor Roll are enrolled in a drawing for $100 cash. For college students, there is a student MasterCard.

A One-Stop Financial Center

CPFCU provides members with online Internet access to their accounts via the Personal Credit Union (PCU), enabling them to transfer funds, pay bills, view and print copies of checks and statements, place a stop payment, or apply for a loan. The credit union also offers Teller24, enabling account access and transactions by telephone. It also provides foreign currency exchange to accommodate its many on-base members traveling throughout the world. Foreign currency may be purchased in person at the CPFCU Headquarters Office in Lexington Park, Maryland, or may be ordered online—and CPFCU will exchange foreign currency into U.S. dollars when the member returns home. CPFCU provides additional information about its services and products on its Web site at www.cpfcu.com.

CPFCU makes itself available to its members when they need assistance, whether for a routine transaction or for an emergency. The credit union recognizes the importance of creating an organization that not only is financially strong and stable but also is a positive and supportive environment for credit union members and employees. Built on the traditional values of commitment to service, integrity, ethics, cooperation, and team spirit, the Cedar Point Federal Credit Union takes pride in making its day-to-day decisions based on the best interests of its members and looks forward to continued growth and service.

Above: CPFCU provides a wide range of convenient, low-cost financial services to its members. Excellent customer service is a priority at CPFCU, both at the branches and online.

Bank of America

Defining success by helping its customers realize their goals, this longstanding financial institution strives to create opportunities for the people it serves. Providing innovative services, a complete range of financial products, and convenient neighborhood locations as well as online access, Bank of America is a global leader in its industry.

Above: In partnership with Harford Habitat for Humanity and Harford Technical High School, Bank of America provided volunteer and financial support for this green, modular home.

Bank of America is one of the world's largest financial institutions, serving individual consumers, small- and middle-market businesses, and large corporations with a full range of banking, investing, asset management, and other financial and risk-management products and services. The company provides unmatched convenience in the United States, serving approximately 55 million consumer and small business relationships with more than 6,100 retail banking offices, more than 18,500 ATMs, and award-winning online banking with nearly 30 million active users. Bank of America is among the world's leading wealth management companies and is a

global leader in corporate and investment banking and trading across a broad range of asset classes serving corporations, governments, institutions, and individuals around the world. Bank of America offers industry-leading support to more than four million small business owners through a suite of innovative, easy-to-use online products and services. The company serves clients in more than 150 countries.

Bank of America's Commitment to Communities

Bank of America understands that the success of its business is intrinsically linked to the health and vitality of its communities, and the company believes it has both an opportunity and an obligation to find effective ways to help the economy and the nation prosper. In Maryland, that commitment extends to everything from affordable housing, workforce development, and economic development programs to financial literacy, volunteer efforts, and cultural endeavors.

"Our commitment to improving communities and neighborhoods is based in our desire to give every individual a better place to live and do business," says William Couper, mid-Atlantic president. "By leveraging our resources effectively to meet the needs of our communities, we are contributing to the long-term economic and social health of Maryland."

By partnering with local community leaders, Bank of America invests its philanthropic resources to address the critical needs of the communities it serves. Through a signature philanthropic program, the Neighborhood Excellence Initiative®, Bank of America recognizes, nurtures, and rewards nonprofit organizations, local heroes, and high school students working to improve the community. By strengthening the capacity of nonprofits and developing the next generation of community leaders, the company is contributing to the long-term success of its community.

Additional information about Bank of America's products and services is available on the company's Web site at www.bankofamerica.com.

Sandy Spring Bank

Performing commercial banking operations, mortgage banking, and other related financial activities, this community bank is built on a philosophy of service and a long-standing tradition of enriching the lives of clients, employees, and shareholders. It is driven to be a successful, independent financial services company that creates rewarding experiences for customers.

Sandy Spring Bank is a neighborhood banking institution with a long-standing reputation for outstanding client service and a steadfast commitment to the community. The bank's roots date back to 1868, when a group of farmers created The Savings Institution of Sandy Spring, which used most of its deposits to provide home loans for residents of the community. Today Olney-based Sandy Spring Bank is the largest publicly traded bank headquartered in Maryland and the oldest banking institution in the region.

Sandy Spring Bank offers a full line of financial services for individuals and businesses through its network of 42 community offices in the greater Baltimore–Washington, D.C., metropolitan area. Services include telephone banking; sophisticated online banking products for individuals and businesses; as well as free ATM access at more than 37,000 locations nationwide. FInancial services include commercial banking, retail banking, commercial real estate, treasury management, investment management and fiduciary services, mortgage lending, and investment services. Three subsidiaries owned by Sandy Spring Bank enable the company to offer an enhanced array of financial products and services.

- West Financial Services offers comprehensive financial planning, wealth management, and asset management for high-net-worth individuals, businesses, and associations.
- The Equipment Leasing Company offers leasing options to businesses that need to acquire capital equipment.

• Sandy Spring Insurance Corporation offers commercial and personal lines of insurance as well as surety bonds, workers' compensation, and professional liability protection.

Sandy Spring Bank believes that businesses should be integral contributors to their communities' growth and spirit by investing in organizations, programs, and initiatives that contribute to the area's strength and vitality. Since its founding, the bank has enthusiastically supported events designed to raise money for charity; for community celebrations held to rebuild homes for low-income residents; for in-school banks set up to teach children about the value of saving money; and for programs created to make the community a better place in which to live, work, and raise a family.

Sandy Spring Bank provides additional information about its services, products, and activities on its Web site at www.sandyspringbank.com.

In addition to placing a high value on its role in the community, the bank values its relationships with clients and employees by establishing trust and operating with integrity—which it considers to be a key factor in its success. Equally important is teamwork, in order to achieve the common goal of serving clients; and celebrating the diversity of people, client needs, and the bank's business markets. Finally, the bank is performance driven, which it defines as committed to continually growing, evolving, and identifying new financial solutions to earn and retain the loyalty of its clients—today and in the future.

Above: Since its founding more than 140 years ago, Sandy Spring Bank has been an active and enthusiastic supporter of the communities it serves.

to change and expand. Today any employee or retiree of an employer located within 20 miles of one of PBCU's branches can join the credit union. PBCU's more than 47,000 members are served by 100 PBCU employees at the credit union's three branch offices, including Golden Ring, located in Baltimore; Hunt Valley; and Bel Air.

PBCU shares the cooperative values that characterize credit unions, which are democratically governed, member-owned, nonprofit, cooperative financial institutions. PBCU offers economic opportunity and financial security for its members, who benefit when the credit union's profits are returned to them through advantageous rates and services. More than 600 employer groups in greater Baltimore offer free credit union membership through PBCU as a benefit for employees.

PBCU offers an array of products and services for businesses and individuals and serves business-to-business financial transaction needs. It provides checking accounts, direct deposit, payroll deduction, free telephone service around the clock, e-statements, mobile banking, high-interest savings accounts, certificates of deposit, IRAs, auto loans, mortgages, and more. PBCU delivers numerous business banking products and services designed to help its business members develop a flexible banking program designed to save money. The credit union's business checking accounts are set up to meet the unique day-to-day banking needs of businesses. It also offers business savings accounts and certificates of deposit, as well as Simplified Employee Pension plans (SEPs) for small-business owners and the self-employed. Other products and services include small-business-oriented credit and check cards, a variety of business loans to help start or expand businesses, and conveniences that save time and money, such as payroll services and merchant services.

Since its founding in 1935, Point Breeze Credit Union has remained committed to providing its members with professional financial services of high quality. PBCU provides additional information about its products and services on its Web site at www.pbcu.com.

Above: Point Breeze Credit Union has three branch offices in the greater Baltimore area to serve its members. Clockwise, from left, are the Hunt Valley branch; the Golden Ring branch, located in Baltimore; and the Bel Air branch.

Point Breeze Credit Union (PBCU) was established in 1935 by a small group of employees at the Western Electric Company plant near Baltimore. When the credit union opened, it had 419 members—all Western Electric employees—and it placed an emphasis on high quality service. With its 75-year anniversary in 2010, the nonprofit financial institution continues to honor this tradition. Its mission is to meet its members' financial needs by providing competitive financial services and products, superior service to members, and state-of-the-art technology.

In 1983 PBCU began offering membership to employees beyond Western Electric. Striving to meet the changing needs of its community, the credit union has continued

Point Breeze Credit Union

PROFILES OF COMPANIES AND ORGANIZATIONS
Health Care, Pharmaceuticals, and Medical Devices

Johns Hopkins Medicine

This renowned medical institution makes it its mission to improve the health of the greater community and the world by setting standards of excellence in clinical care, medical education, and research. Diverse and inclusive, it provides the most advanced patient-centered medicine to diagnose, treat, and prevent human illness and foster health.

Right: This landmark dome tops one of the world's best known and widely praised hospitals, The Johns Hopkins Hospital. It is not only a superb national and international reputation that counts—the hospital has consistently received the Consumer Choice Award for the Baltimore region from the National Research Corporation (NRC), a firm specializing in health care performance measurement. NRC annually honors the hospitals that local customers rate for quality and image, based on a survey of more than 200,000 households in 48 states and the District of Columbia. Johns Hopkins has been one of only a few hospitals nationwide to earn top-choice status in a multimarket region.

A Tiny Sampling of Achievements by Physician-Scientists at Johns Hopkins

- Ushered in modern heart surgery by developing the blue baby operation to correct a congenital defect that starves the blood of oxygen
- Discovered restriction enzymes, the "biochemical scissors" that gave birth to genetic engineering, winning the Nobel Prize in Medicine
- Identified aquaporin, the protein that controls the body's ability to release water, winning the Nobel Prize in Chemistry
- Helped to develop the first effective treatment for sickle cell anemia
- Co-discovered human embryonic stem cells, which can develop into nearly any type of cell in the adult body

If there is a single word that draws people to Johns Hopkins Medicine, it is *hope*. Whether they have a well-known but no less frightening condition such as heart disease or cancer, or an illness so rare that few physicians ever see it, people come to Johns Hopkins—not only from Maryland but from across the country and around the globe—seeking treatments that may be offered nowhere else.

In fact, much of what is taken for granted in medicine today—from the rigorous training of physicians and nurses to the emphasis on research and the rapid application of that research to patient care—emerged from innovations made more than a century ago at a brand new medical center in Baltimore, The Johns Hopkins Hospital.

In the late 1800s, hospitals took care of patients but did not extend their work to finding the next treatments, the next cures. From the moment its doors opened in 1889, however, Johns Hopkins aimed to not merely practice medicine but also transform it. The physicians who launched The Johns Hopkins Hospital and the Johns Hopkins University School of Medicine were guided by the pathbreaking vision of grounding health care in discovery. And so it has remained.

Anchored in Baltimore, Reaching the World

Today one overarching name—Johns Hopkins Medicine—identifies the virtual organization that unites faculty physicians of the Johns Hopkins University School of Medicine with the health care professionals and facilities that make up the broad Johns Hopkins Health System. Together these institutions are an integral part of Maryland's largest private employer.

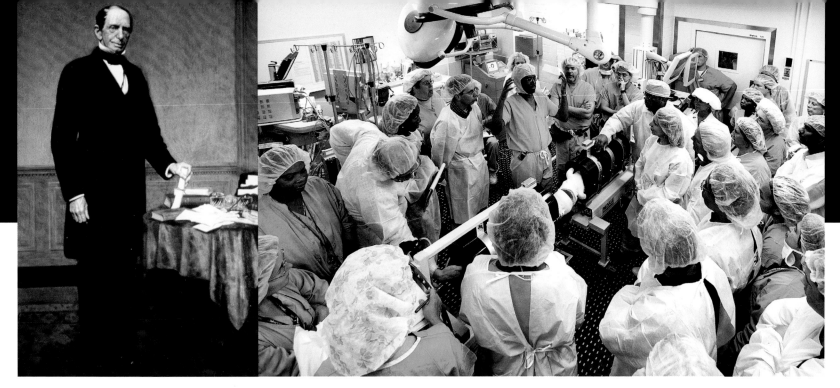

Although many people still think of the medical school and the original, flagship hospital as synonymous with Johns Hopkins, over the past decade Johns Hopkins Medicine has undergone unprecedented expansion. Johns Hopkins Bayview Medical Center, Howard County General Hospital, primary and home care, specialty outpatient centers, and a robust international presence constitute Johns Hopkins Medicine's modern-day, medical enterprise. Johns Hopkins Medicine also has created more than 100 affiliation agreements with other providers and hospitals; among the most significant are Anne Arundel Health System and Greater Baltimore Medical Center.

The Johns Hopkins Hospital—This institution, which draws the vast majority of its patients from Maryland, houses such world-renowned specialty centers as the Wilmer Eye Institute, the Brady Urological Institute, the Sidney Kimmel Comprehensive Cancer Center, the Johns Hopkins Heart and Vascular Institute, and the Johns Hopkins Children's Center. It has always adhered to the vision articulated by its intellectual architect, John Shaw Billings, who said in a letter to the first trustees, "This hospital should advance our knowledge of the causes, symptoms, and pathology of disease, and methods of treatment, so that its good work shall not be confined to the city of Baltimore or the state of Maryland, but shall in part consist in furnishing more knowledge of disease and more power to control it, for the benefit of the sick and afflicted of all countries of all future time."

Johns Hopkins Bayview Medical Center—This academic medical center provides acute, long-term, and preventive health care, with specialties including a comprehensive neonatal intensive care unit (NICU), an area-wide trauma center, the state's only regional adult burn center, and nationally renowned geriatrics programs. Most of the center's physicians hold full-time faculty positions at the Johns Hopkins University School of Medicine. Also on the campus are research facilities for the National Institute on Drug Abuse and the National Institute on Aging.

Howard County General Hospital—This facility, which joined Johns Hopkins Medicine in 1998, is a comprehensive, acute care medical center providing a full range of inpatient services. Specialties include women's and children's services, surgery, cardiology, oncology, orthopedics, gerontology, psychiatry, emergency services, and community health education.

Further Expansion—For primary and high-end specialty outpatient care in Baltimore County, Johns Hopkins at Green Spring Station in Lutherville houses some 250 physicians and 16 specialty services. Johns Hopkins at White Marsh offers primary care and specialty care in nine disciplines. In Anne Arundel County, Johns Hopkins at Odenton offers primary and specialty services. Johns Hopkins Community Physicians offers primary care at 17 sites in central and southern Maryland, on the eastern shore and elsewhere across the state.

Left: Johns Hopkins, the Quaker merchant, banker, and businessman who in 1873 left $7 million to create The Johns Hopkins University and The Johns Hopkins Hospital, was named for his great-grandmother Margaret Johns. Her last name became his first name. This idiosyncrasy has been confusing people ever since. Right: The Johns Hopkins Hospital has been ranked number one among America's Best Hospitals every year since 1991 by *U.S. News & World Report*, which also has consistently ranked the Johns Hopkins University School of Medicine one of the country's top two medical schools. Johns Hopkins medical scientists annually receive more federal research support than their counterparts at other American medical schools. Shown here is neurosurgeon Benjamin Carson, M.D.

Reaching Out—Johns Hopkins HealthCare

To provide high quality care to patients beyond the walls of Johns Hopkins Medicine's hospitals, the Johns Hopkins Home Care Group and Johns Hopkins HealthCare offer services for adults and children. The Home Care Group provides visits by nurses; physical, occupational, and speech therapists; home health aides; and social workers, and furnishes medical and respiratory equipment, infusion therapy, and pharmaceuticals. Johns Hopkins HealthCare, the managed care arm of Johns Hopkins Medicine, administers such programs as Employer Health Programs, the Uniformed Services Family Health Plan, and Priority Partners, a Maryland Medicaid managed care organization.

Thousands of patients from around the world annually come to Baltimore to see Johns Hopkins physicians, and in addition, Johns Hopkins Medicine takes its models for patient care, teaching, and research to the world, forging links with governments, health care consortia, physician groups, and academic institutions in more than 40 countries.

Education for a Lifetime

When The Johns Hopkins University was opened in 1876, its first president, Daniel Coit Gilman, embraced an idea entirely new in the United States: a university dedicated to advancing not merely students' knowledge but also human knowledge generally, through research and scholarship. The realization of this philosophy at Johns Hopkins—as well as at other institutions that later attracted Hopkins-trained scholars—has helped to revolutionize American higher education.

So it was fitting that in 1893, a trailblazing class at the fledgling Johns Hopkins University School of Medicine embarked on a radically new kind of training. Instead of learning only through lectures, as earlier would-be physicians had done, these students

had to meet rigid entrance requirements and then within their studies, interact with real patients. Their vastly upgraded curriculum was the first to treat medicine as a graduate-level pursuit instead of as a trade and the first to set up a rigorous four-year study program that emphasized the scientific method and incorporated bedside teaching and laboratory research. In addition, Johns Hopkins launched advanced training in specialized medical fields with the creation of the first post-graduate specialty internships. In a matter of years, the Johns Hopkins model would come to mean the very definition of excellence in medical education. Ever since, Johns Hopkins has been training physicians not only for the state of Maryland but also for the nation and the world.

Now Johns Hopkins has pioneered an equally visionary curriculum for the 21st century. Called Genes to Society, this curriculum reframes the context of health and illness so that students will consider all the interacting variables—including social, cultural, psychological, environmental, and genetic—that underpin each person's health.

Johns Hopkins Medicine provides additional information about the organization and its activities on its Web site at www.hopkinsmedicine.org.

Committed to the Community

The Johns Hopkins campus in East Baltimore is many things: a vibrant economic hub with more than 25,000 employees, a world-renowned medical center, and the home of groundbreaking research and education. But Johns Hopkins is also working with its East Baltimore neighbors to reach a shared goal: building a stronger community with bright opportunities for all.

Some projects are highly visible, such as the New East Side project, with which Johns Hopkins has joined federal, state, and local governments; area foundations; and other institutions as a partner. Overseen by East Baltimore Development Inc., this enormous project will transform much of the area north of the Johns Hopkins campus, create new housing for people of all incomes, and provide new economic opportunities for people who live and work in the community.

Other initiatives include the Johns Hopkins Urban Health Institute, which brings community-based approaches to health care focused on issues confronting disadvantaged city residents. Johns Hopkins also spearheads dozens of community projects, such as providing better health services to the area's growing Hispanic population and mentoring neighborhood students.

Altogether Johns Hopkins Medicine offers more than 130 programs to serve East Baltimore and invests more than $100 million annually to support community-benefit programs.

Left: As *Baltimore* magazine noted in its July 2007 issue on the area's best employers, Johns Hopkins employees have the benefit of working with "really, really smart people" and enjoy "solid benefits, a sweet tuition offer, plus the prestige of a well-respected institution." Shown here is David Nichols, M.D., vice dean for education. Right: Under construction are two 12-story buildings —the Sheikh Zayed Cardiovascular and Critical Care Tower and the Charlotte R. Bloomberg Children's Center at Johns Hopkins—that will replace half of the existing hospital. In addition to providing 1.6 million square feet of flexible new space, the buildings will include a single front entrance for the hospital as well as its pediatric and adult emergency departments.

Bravo Health, Inc.

Bravo Health provides a critical service to seniors: access to high quality, cost-effective health care. The company provides Medicare Advantage health plans to more than 65,000 members. Bravo Health also offers stand-alone prescription drug plans to nearly 200,000 Medicare beneficiaries in 46 states. Founded in 1996, Bravo Health has more than 600 associates and 30,000 contracted providers.

Medicare beneficiaries deserve solid choices as well as extraordinary value in the health care they receive. Traditional Medicare benefits alone can be costly, and do not provide all of the coverage that today's seniors need. People with low- to middle-range incomes often cannot afford to pick up where Medicare benefits leave off. They need an affordable alternative, which is why 10.1 million Medicare beneficiaries are enrolled in a Medicare Advantage plan; that is more than one in five of the more than 45 million people with Medicare as of April 2008.

With a competitive network of participating health care providers, excellent benefits, and a focus on providing superior service, Bravo Health, Inc. is dedicated to delivering outstanding value for its members. Led by a management team with more than 150 years of combined health care industry experience, Bravo Health has seen substantial growth in recent years—doubling its membership from November 2007 to July 2008. This growth is strong affirmation that the company is fulfilling its mission to be a leading health services company.

The key factor that sets Bravo Health apart in today's increasingly competitive health care marketplace is the outstanding service it provides to its customers. Bravo Health is committed to cultivating a deep understanding of health care delivery for seniors. Using that knowledge, the company strives to implement the most effective and creative programs to optimize value and health outcomes for members.

"Bravo Health takes its role in providing enhanced health benefits to people on Medicare very seriously," says Jeff Folick, chairman and CEO of Bravo Health. "We know our customers have choices. Competitive networks, excellent benefits, and exceptional service are the keys to satisfying our customers and growing our business."

Strong Partners, Superior Care

Bravo Health is only as strong as those who partner with the company to provide health care to its customers. To deliver the best outcomes, Bravo Health partners with outstanding physicians and hospitals in each of its communities. Members have access to hospitals and physician practices without having to pay high out-of-pocket expenses.

Bravo Health builds strong relationships with health care providers who offer care that meets high standards and endeavors to enhance that care through its quality improvement programs and performance-based evaluations. The company also works to develop and strengthen its provider network, collaboratively defining protocols that use resources efficiently and result in ultimate patient satisfaction.

Bravo Health emphasizes preventive services to promote health and prevent illness. All of its Medicare Advantage plans provide full coverage for physical exams, influenza and pneumonia vaccinations, and a variety of preventive tests such as mammography and prostate screenings—many of which are not covered under traditional Medicare. Bravo Health also offers enhanced benefits

Above center: An advertising campaign for Bravo Health, Inc. focuses on seniors enjoying their favorite hobbies and challenging their health care providers to keep up with their active lifestyles.

such as coverage for routine dental, vision, and hearing services, and limits members' out-of-pocket liability on many plans.

For many low-income beneficiaries, transportation can be the greatest barrier to receiving critical health care. Bravo Health bridges this gap by providing routine transportation to and from medical appointments for all of its plans designed for those who are dually eligible for Medicare and Medicaid.

Bravo Health is also the first company in the nation to join the American Heart Association's Healing Heart Society as a Champion Partner, a partnership that helps advance heart-related education and research.

Reaching Out to the Community

As part of its effort to bring even greater value to members in each of the communities it serves, Bravo Health invests time and energy to develop local relationships.

Bravo Health offers group and individual presentations and encourages caregivers, family, and friends to participate with members in the health care decision-making process. The company networks with local organizations to help disseminate information beneficiaries need to effectively access high quality health care.

Looking to the Future

Health care is changing, and more educated consumers of health care are driving that change. People who rely on Medicare today are more active in managing their own health than prior generations were.

Today's seniors are familiar with their medical history and try to take good care of themselves. They want to be in control of their own health, and want to be confident they will be able to receive the health care they need, when they need it.

The opportunities to serve older Americans are greater than ever. People are living longer, with the number of people aged 65 and over expected to increase 60 percent to 72 million by the year 2030.

Bravo Health looks forward to continuing its service to Medicare beneficiaries and is seeking to expand into more communities.

"Achieving our growth objectives is a clear indication that we are doing the right things to succeed in the marketplace," says Folick. "Whether we are improving our business in our core markets or expanding into new areas, Bravo Health is consistently focused on providing access to dependable, affordable health care coverage."

Bravo Health, Inc. provides more information about the company and its products on its Web site at www.bravohealth.com.

Above right: Headquarters for Bravo Health is located in the historic Baltimore neighborhood of Brewers Hill.
Above left: Jeff Folick is chairman and CEO of Bravo Health.

Bravo Health:

- Is a strong company dedicated to serving America's growing population of seniors.
- Plays a significant role in helping people who are most in need of access to critical health care services.
- Provides value by offering lower out-of-pocket costs and additional benefits over and above traditional Medicare that enhance quality of life and improve access to care.
- Manages health care effectively through efforts such as its Network Quality Improvement Program (NQIP) for primary care providers that aims to improve the quality and appropriateness of health care delivery.

Shah Associates M.D., LLC

For more than 30 years this private multispecialty medical practice has cared for and grown with the community. This innovative group, which includes more than 90 physicians representing 21 specialties, takes a creative approach to health care, operating clinics with extreme efficiency so its doctors have time to do what they are passionate about—care for patients.

'WHEN FACED WITH SERIOUS MEDICAL PROBLEMS, MOST PEOPLE— AMERICANS AND OTHERS AROUND THE WORLD—WOULD HAVE COMPLETE TRUST IN WHAT WE CAN DO AND RANK AMERICA AS THE BEST. HOWEVER, THE BEST IS NOT ENOUGH UNTIL IT REACHES THE REST.'

— *Vinod K. Shah, M.D.* —

- respect for the patient and family;
- comprehensive evaluation with timely, efficient assessment and treatment; and
- availability of the most advanced, innovative diagnostic and therapeutic technologies.

Shah Associates M.D., LLC is a multispecialty practice offering some of the most comprehensive outpatient medical services available throughout Southern Maryland. Established in 1974 as a three-physician practice, the group has grown to include 90 physicians and specialists in 14 locations, making its services highly accessible to patients. As a member of the American Medical Group Association, Shah Associates values physician leadership, teamwork across specialties, and continuous improvement of patient care.

The physicians are also guided by the Mayo Clinic Model of Care, which subscribes to:

- a team approach that relies on a diverse group of medical specialists working together to provide the highest quality care delivered with compassion and trust;
- an unhurried examination with enough time to listen to each patient;
- personal responsibility for directing care in partnership with the patient's primary care physician;

From India to St. Mary's County

In the 1970s, St. Mary's County was not a place that attracted young doctors looking for a place to settle. The county hospital used outdated equipment, struggled to pay workers, and did not have a single full-time specialist. In spite of delivering more than 600 babies per year, the hospital did not even have a pediatrician. Fortunately, this was also an era when the United States actively recruited international medical graduates to work in underserved rural and urban areas.

Above left: The founders of Shah Associates M.D., LLC are (from left) Dr. Ila V. Shah, Dr. Vinod K. Shah, and Dr. Umed K. Shah. Below right: Dr. Arpana Shah takes great pride in developing close working relationships with her patients.

Shah Associates M.D., LLC Medical Services and Departments

Primary Care
- Pediatrics
- Family Practice
- Internal Medicine

Medical Specialties
- General Radiology
  - CAT Scan and MRI
  - X-ray and Mammography
  - Ultrasound and Sonography
- Cardiology
  - Preventative Cardiology
  - Nuclear Cardiology/
    Stress Testing
  - Echocardiography

- Gastroenterology
  - Endoscopy
  - Colonoscopy
  - Colon Cancer Screening
- Neurology
  - Electromyography (EMG)
  - Nerve Conduction Studies
  - Dermatology
- Infectious Diseases
  - HIV/AIDS
  - Hepatitis
  - Lyme Diseases and Other
    Tick-borne Diseases
- General Dermatology
  - Age/Sun Spot Removal

- Laser Hair Removal
- Spider Vein Removal
- Endocrinology
  - Diabetes
  - Thyroid Disorders
  - Osteoporosis
- Pulmonary Medicine
  - Lung Function Test
  - Asthma and Allergy
- Outpatient Surgery
  - Laboratory Services
- Cancer Recovery Center
- Sleep Studies
- Geriatric Care
- Urgent Care Center

Understanding the dire need of this community, Vinod K. Shah, a cardiologist, and Ila Shah, a pediatrician, chose to commit their services to rural St. Mary's County. The Shahs, who received their medical training in Bombay, India, and in Washington, D.C., were excited about the difference they could make at St. Mary's Hospital, where Richard Martin, head of the hospital at the time, described them as "the answer to his prayers."

Feeling at home in Southern Maryland, the Shahs decided to open a medical practice in 1974. Vinod's brother, gastroenterologist Umed K. Shah, joined them in their endeavor. A few years later, they encouraged friends Dr. Anwar Munshi, Dr. Mohamed F. O. Lafeer, and Dr. Adinath Patil and family members Dr. Nayan Shah, Dr. Atul Shah, and Dr. Mahesh Shah to join their group. Shortly afterwards, Vinod's brother, cardiologist Anil K. Shah, came to Southern Maryland with his wife, Beena, a neurologist. As time went on, the Shahs recruited more friends and family members, including the remainder of Vinod's eight siblings, each of whom is a doctor or is married to one. Together they staffed Shah Associates, the largest private multispecialty practice in Maryland—which has treated the majority of the county's 110,000 residents.

Embracing the Community
Today, two generations of Shah doctors treat patients from all around Southern Maryland. Shah Associates has come a long way since the early days. As a result of the doctors' excellent professional skills and gracious demeanors, the group quickly

earned the community's trust. As local residents began to appreciate this hard-working family, the practice grew. Soon many local doctors joined the medical practice, which was and still is a model of efficiency and state-of-the-art technology.

In 1997, Vinod Shah opened the Philip J. Bean Medical Center in Hollywood, dedicating the building to the memory of a revered local physician who had delivered approximately 5,000 of the area's residents. Rather than naming the center after themselves, the doctors at Shah Associates decided to name it after Philip J. Bean, a man who was a role model within the physician community. It was their way of paying respect to a local hero. "The people of the community were overwhelmed by this noble gesture," commented Roy Dyson, Maryland State Senator.

Shah Associates physicians work out of the Bean Medical Center as well as 13 satellite offices. Donald W. Fisher, Ph.D., President and CEO of The American

Above: Shown are (clockwise from top left) the Philip J. Bean Medical Center in Hollywood, Maryland; Shah Associates nurses at the Bean Medical Center; and Dr. Ila Shah hugging a patient.

Shah Associates M.D., LLC

℘

'THE BEST INTEREST OF THE PATIENT IS THE ONLY INTEREST TO BE CONSIDERED.'
— *William James Mayo, M.D.* —

Above left: The Shah Associates business team includes, from left to right: Deven Desai, Judy Emerson, Alan Buster, Julie Slade-Williams, and Hari Kanagevelu. Above right: Dr. Vinod K. Shah describes the growth of Shah Associates to Maryland Governor Martin O'Malley.

Medical Group Association, "envisions a world in which multispecialty organized systems of care are the preferred model of health care delivery for coordinated, patient-centered, efficient quality medical care in America." The practice follows this methodology in that it operates as a "center of excellence," where patients have almost immediate access to physicians practicing 21 different specialties.

An important partnership was formed when Maryland HealthCare Associates (MHCA) became affiliated with Shah Associates in 2008. MHCA, a large primary care physician group in Southern Maryland, operates one of its two multispecialty medical centers in Waldorf, halfway between Washington, D.C., and the Bean Medical Center. Shah Associates helped to improve the efficiency of MHCA's billing system and upgrade the health records operations at MHCA's primary care facilities. "This was one of the most significant decisions that we made as a group, considering the current status of health care delivery in our society," say Dr. Howard Haft and Dr. Bill Tanner of MHCA.

Improved Care through Paperless Records

Mohamed Lafeer, the clinic's medical director of quality assurance and performance improvement, explains how tasks that can be performed electronically are outsourced to Health Prime International, a premier health care consulting company specializing in electronic medical record (EMR) implementation and revenue-cycle management. Says Lafeer, "Doctors are relieved of the burdens of paperwork, billing, and record keeping, giving them more time with patients, who may be scheduled for everything they need—including laboratory tests, diagnostics, and treatment—in one day at one place, saving valuable time and improving the quality of medical care."

Through Health Prime International, Shah Associates has simplified and standardized record keeping by transcribing physicians' patient records into an extensive computer database, enabling physicians to call them up with the touch of a button. Doctors can instantly access a patient's medical history without being slowed down by paper files or faxes. And patients need not waste time filling out repetitive forms as they go from doctor to doctor.

With its database of approximately 150,000 patients' health records, Shah Associates and Health Prime International can also identify patients who might be at risk of developing certain ailments, such as heart disease or diabetes. The names of these individuals can be distributed to their doctors, who may notify them of the need to make an appointment and begin the process of preventive health care.

PEDIATRICS

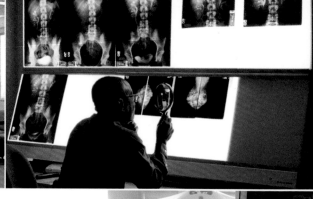

Investing in a Healthy Future for All

Providing such a large percentage of the population with medical care has given Shah Associates a unique perspective on health care. As part of a new partnership, specialists from Georgetown University Hospital and Washington Hospital Center will practice with Shah Associates in a new 66,000-square-foot addition to the Bean Medical Center. The partnership will enable the universities to study health patterns across generations, compiling information that might one day help researchers better understand hereditary conditions.

As the baby boomer generation continues to age, the American Medical Association reports that the country could be short as many as 200,000 doctors by 2020—a trend that will hurt underserved areas the most. Vinod Shah, who is President of the American Association of Physicians of Indian Origin, believes a shortage may be prevented by increasing the number of medical schools in the United States, relying more on physician assistants and nurse practitioners, and by allowing greater numbers of qualified international medical graduates to practice in the United States.

Every year Shah Associates hosts young, dynamic graduates from foreign medical schools, encouraging them to seek opportunities outside of big cities. In the summer of 2008, four graduates of Indian medical schools traveled to Southern Maryland for an education in American medicine. The graduates witnessed the Shah tradition of developing a rapport with their patients and listened as doctors made clinical recommendations or explained procedures regarding upcoming surgeries. Taking time to establish one-on-one interaction with patients enables

doctors to know their patients better and ultimately brings about better health care. For doctors in training, practicing physicians, and Southern Maryland residents, Shah Associates offers a win-win relationship.

Additional information about Shah Associates and its services is available on the organization's Web site at www.shah-associates.com.

Shah Associates Locations

Breton Medical Center—California, MD
By The Mill Road Medical Center—California, MD
Calvert Medical Arts Center—Prince Frederick, MD
Charlotte Hall Medical Center—Charlotte Hall, MD
Clinton Medical Center—Clinton, MD
Fort Washington Medical Center—Fort Washington, MD
Lexington Park Medical Center—Lexington Park, MD
Mechanicsville Medical Center—Mechanicsville, MD
Medical Arts Center—Leonardtown, MD
Philip J. Bean Medical Center—Hollywood, MD
Shanti Medical Center—Leonardtown, MD
Solomons Medical Center—Solomons, MD
Waldorf Medical Center—Waldorf, MD
Wildewood Medical Center—California, MD

Shah Associates

Top: Shown are images from the Philip J. Bean Medical Center, including (clockwise from top left) the in-house laboratory, the center's pediatrics department, a radiologist examining X-rays, and the facility's open MRI center. Bottom, both illustrations: These renderings depict new Shah Associates Maryland office buildings in Calvert (left) and Waldorf (right).

Upper Chesapeake Health

Committed to delivering 'Unparalleled Care Close to Home,' Upper Chesapeake Health combines advanced medical and surgical technology with outstanding and compassionate care from world-class physicians, creating a high quality setting that promotes healing and well-being.

UCH owns and operates Harford Memorial Hospital (HMH), Upper Chesapeake Medical Center (UCMC), Upper Chesapeake/St. Joseph Home Care, Harford Hospice, and Upper Chesapeake Health Foundation. The largest private employer in the area, UCH serves Harford County, western Cecil County, and northern Baltimore County with a team of more than 2,700 staff members and 550 physicians.

Upper Chesapeake Medical Center

A state-of-the-art hospital, UCMC is located in Bel Air, where the latest advances in medical technology are delivered in a healing and compassionate environment. Every room reflects a patient-oriented and family-centered model of care, resulting in an atmosphere where the patient and the family support person can be together at all times in a comfortable, relaxed, and private setting. With their home-like ambience, patient rooms are designed to enhance the healing process while also allowing the patient's needs to be the top priority.

Since it opened in 2000, UCMC has continued to grow in size and services. An expansive $39 million renovation project has brought a new Emergency Department, a new Critical Care Unit, five additional obstetric beds, 26 additional medical and surgical beds, as well as a new parking garage and physician office pavilion. Located next to the medical center are the Ambulatory Care Center of Harford County and Physicians Pavilions I and II, which house physician offices, outpatient imaging and laboratory procedures, outpatient preassessment testing, the Upper Chesapeake Cardiovascular Institute, the Upper Chesapeake Surgical Pavilion, Diabetes and Endocrine Center, Outpatient Rehabilitation, Anticoagulation and Lipid Management, Spine Center, Infusion Center, Center for Cancer Services, and administrative offices.

The medical center's awards and industry recognition are as impressive as its facilities. In 2007 and 2008 UCMC was named a Distinguished Hospital for Clinical Excellence by HealthGrades; was ranked number one in Maryland for Joint Replacement Surgery, also by HealthGrades; has been recognized by the Delmarva

Upper Chesapeake Health (UCH) has provided northeastern Maryland with outstanding quality care for almost a century. UCH cares for thousands of patients each year at its hospitals, emergency departments, Family Birthplace, home care and hospice, Upper Chesapeake Sports Medicine and Rehabilitation Center, Primary Care Clinic, Ambulatory Care Center, and Physicians Pavilion II.

Above: The Upper Chesapeake Medical Center campus of Upper Chesapeake Health is located in the heart of Bel Air in Harford County, Maryland.

With the vision of creating the healthiest community in Maryland, UCH is dedicated to maintaining and improving the health of its community members through an integrated health delivery system that provides high quality care to everyone. The organization is committed to delivering service excellence and compassionate care; maintaining a broad range of health care services, technologies, and facilities; and serving as a resource for health promotion and education.

Foundation as being in the top 10 percent of hospitals in Maryland for achievements in improving quality care to patients; and received accreditation for its oncology program from the Commission on Cancer of the American College of Surgeons.

Harford Memorial Hospital

HMH, located in historic Havre de Grace, successfully blends old-fashioned charm with progressive medicine. With a legacy of caring for the community since 1910, HMH opened in a 21-room Victorian home to serve a population of about 29,000. Today the hospital operates in a newly renovated facility surrounded by a brick facade that complements the town's architecture. An acute care nonprofit hospital, HMH offers a full complement of medical, diagnostic, and emergency care services to a community of some 250,000 people.

The hospital features state-of-the-art facilities for intensive care and a busy emergency department that cares for more than 50,000 patients a year. HMH offers specialized hospital-based services, including anticoagulation management, a Center for Wound Care, inpatient and outpatient behavioral health services, the Joint Center for hip and knee replacement, a Sleep Disorder Center, and a Bariatric Surgery Program that has been named a Center of Excellence by the American College of Surgeons.

For its excellent services and programs, HMH has received HealthGrades' five-star rating for joint-replacement surgery and treatment of patients with heart failure, pneumonia, and fibrillation; has been recognized by the Delmarva Foundation as one of the top 10 percent of hospitals in Maryland for achievements in improving quality care to patients; and the hospital's oncology program has received accreditation from the Commission on Cancer of the American College of Surgeons.

Upper Chesapeake Health provides additional information about its services and activities on its Web site at www.uchs.org.

The Healthiest Community

UCH is dedicated to the well-being of all the residents of the community from young children to seniors. It is committed to responding to the needs of individuals, whether they come to the system because of an emergency condition or for hospitalization, or when they are expecting a baby or need home care or hospice services. Upper Chesapeake Health supports the vision of creating the healthiest community in Maryland by demonstrating a culture of caring and excellence: "We create a healing and compassionate environment by providing the finest in care, courtesy, and service to all people with whom we interact."

Above left: Harford Memorial Hospital is situated in historic Havre de Grace, Maryland. Above right: Upper Chesapeake Health offers leading-edge cardiovascular technology and services, including a state-of-the-art, all-digital cardiac catheterization laboratory, a 64-slice computed tomography (CT) scanner, emergency cardiac angioplasty, inpatient and emergency cardiac care, primary acute stroke centers, Cardiac Rehabilitation programs, accredited echocardiography and vascular laboratories, and a Pulmonary Rehabilitation Program.

Pharmaceutics International, Inc. (PII)

This privately held company develops quality drug-delivery solutions to provide pharmaceutical companies with development services that range from preformulation to materials for clinical trials and commercial manufacturing. Based in Hunt Valley, Maryland, it has a global reach through its acquisitions and partnerships in the United States and Europe.

A leader in the pharmaceutical industry, Pharmaceutics International, Inc. (PII) provides contract drug development services, including formulation development, clinical trial materials (CTM) manufacturing, and commercial manufacturing. It delivers a quality dosage form development service to major multinational and virtual pharmaceutical companies primarily focused in the United States and Europe. Committed to meeting all of the needs of its clients, the company complements its services with analytical and regulatory support and provides exceptional customer service.

Founded in 1994, PII is headquartered in Hunt Valley, Maryland. Its facilities in the United States and Europe—which are regularly inspected by both the United

States' Food and Drug Administration (FDA) and the European Medicines Agency (EMEA)—total more than 300,000 square feet of space. PII's Hunt Valley location includes five analytical laboratories, a formulation development center, and 50 production rooms, which include 22 containment suites. In 2008 PII opened a new, 30,000-square-foot, state-of-the-art facility in Beaver Court in Hunt Valley, which is dedicated to development work, aseptic vial filling, and additional manufacturing.

Among PII's 400 employees is a diversified scientific team of scientists, pharmacists, chemists, and experienced technicians with diverse and extensive pharmaceutical industry experience.

A Broad Spectrum of Services

The drug development process begins with preformulation and formulation development. During these critical stages, PII takes into account the physical and chemical characteristics of the active pharmaceutical ingredient (API) as well as the intended use of the compound. The company's areas of expertise cover a wide range of dosage forms, including solids, semi-solids, and liquids.

Through its CTM manufacturing and packaging services, PII manufactures supplies for phase I, II, III, and IV studies. By using sound scientific practices and working closely with its clients, PII moves compounds from formulation development to the clinical stage in a timely manner. PII can manufacture and package batch sizes that range from one kilogram to 1,200 kilograms. To meet the needs of clinical studies, PII offers over-encapsulation and tamper-evident banding and can develop matching placebos.

PII uses cGMPs to commercially manufacture a variety of dosage forms. It follows client-approved protocols during the commercial manufacturing stage. Its state-of-the-art containment suites allow PII to handle high-potency and cytotoxic compounds. Additionally, PII is registered with the U.S. Drug Enforcement Agency (DEA) to manufacture schedule I, II, III, and IV compounds.

Emphasizing quality as the means to successful drug development, PII maintains a quality assurance department that comprises more than 10 percent of the company's workforce. This department is involved in all aspects of a project, from beginning to end. Among its important tasks are the inspection of all materials received, the qualifying of vendors, cleaning equipment and manufacturing rooms, and the final release of all products.

Growth and Development

Since 1994 PII has continually grown through organic expansion, acquisitions, and important industry partnerships. Adding to its service offerings, in 2008 PII acquired Pharmaterials Ltd, an experienced and well-regarded drug development company based in Reading, England, the United Kingdom.

Pharmaterials specializes in creating optimal physical forms and formulations of drug substances to facilitate the development of low solubility and poorly permeable drug substances and drug delivery to the lung. With a scientific approach and a strong technical understanding of the industry, Pharmaterials uses advanced technology to supply its clients with comprehensive early phase drug development services.

Pharmaterials was founded as a spin-off company from the School of Pharmacy at the University of London. Since its beginning in 2000, the company has experienced exponential growth. It operates out of state-of-the-art laboratories in Reading and also maintains offices in Tokyo, Japan.

Additionally, in early 2008 PII formed a partnership with Glasgow-based Bio-Images Research Ltd., which specializes in gamma scintigraphy—noninvasive imaging of internal body tissue designed to reveal the journey of a drug formulation from delivery site to final location. Working with Bio-Images, PII offers its clients expanded services and expertise in early phase drug development and clinical trials.

PII also works with Penwest Pharmaceuticals Co., a specialty company that provides drug-delivery technologies designed to optimize the performance of medicines—especially those related to diseases of the nervous system —and thereby improve patients' health. Through this partnership, PII conducts formulation work for drugs that use Penwest's proprietary oral drug-delivery technologies.

PII provides additional information about its services and capabilities on its Web site at www.pharm-int.com.

PII is dedicated to delivering quality drug development services to its multinational client base of major pharmaceutical companies. Through its growth, acquisitions, and partnerships, PII will continue to increase its global reach and provide extensive, comprehensive contract formulation services.

Above left: PII can manufacture a wide range of dosage forms covering solid, semi-solid, and aseptic filling.
Above right: The company's manufacturing personnel are specifically trained to work with drugs that require special handling procedures. PII offers 14 state-of-the-art containment suites for product manufacturing.

MedAssurant, Inc.

Dedicated to improving the quality, effectiveness, and efficiency of health care in the nation by assisting the organizations that provide care, this innovative Bowie-based company is committed to the development of advanced medical informatics tools that empower solutions across the health care landscape.

MedAssurant, Inc., a leading provider of superior health care quality, care management, and financial performance improvement solutions, combines the details of data with the goals of best-practice medicine to deliver a positive impact on the health care industry. The company goes beyond traditional data sources and interventional approaches to consider the uniqueness of every patient, practitioner, and health care organization.

MedAssurant distinguishes itself from other health care solution providers by enabling a deeper and more meaningful analytical insight in combination with the end-to-end intervention needed to turn the insight into meaningful and measurable impact. From data integration and analysis to the delivery of objective, valuable results, the company eliminates the need for fragmented achievement. An integrated platform approach provides superior scalability, efficiency of operation, and flexibility to health care improvements on a nationwide scale.

Across the country, MedAssurant's experienced and qualified personnel use the company's advanced technology infrastructure to provide local and national health insurance plans, care delivery networks, employers, pharmaceutical companies, regulatory bodies, and government organizations with services that address disease management, clinical outcomes, quality of care, cost improvement, risk adjustment, financial performance, and health care data verification.

Underlying these services is the company's vision: deep, data-driven insight can empower advanced solutions and meaningful results in health care delivery. Although the task is complex, MedAssurant has turned theory into practice for millions of people and the health care systems that serve them throughout the United States. For clients of MedAssurant, advances in health care data aggregation and analytics are truly translating into improved care and improved financial performance at a time when both are critically necessary.

Making a Positive Impact on Health Care

MedAssurant works with nearly 200 health care organizations across approximately 99.5 percent of all counties in the United States to affect the health care industry in meaningful ways. At the center of the company's efforts is a focus on improving the accuracy, insight, and impact of medical informatics. Informed by a deeper health care dataset, MedAssurant's advanced analytics achieve a more powerful insight to identify gaps in care, advance intelligence, enable change, and drive meaningful impact for patients, providers, and the health care community that serves them.

MedAssurant sets itself apart with its innovative, multidisciplinary approach to insightful solution design, comprehensive end-to-end implementation, and a steadfast dedication to realizing increased value. These focal differentiators are reflected in the company's suite of products—Clinical Outcomes and Quality of Care, Advanced Disease Management and Chronic Care Solutions, Claims Data Accuracy Analytics & Risk Adjustment, and Healthcare Data Intelligence. The combination of these core capability tools enables MedAssurant to give its clients an unmatched, end-to-end solution.

Right: MedAssurant, Inc.'s senior management team includes: (standing, from left to right) Scott Groom, vice president; Grey McLean, MBA, chief operating officer; David Norris, vice president; Phillip Traylor, vice president; Stephen E. Coy, vice president; Cary Sennett, M.D., Ph.D., chief medical officer; and Jason Z. Rose, MHSA, vice president; and (sitting, from left to right) Richard W. Lasch, executive vice president; Daniel L. Rizzo, CFA, chief product technology officer; Keith R. Dunleavy, M.D., president and CEO; Raymond K. Walheim, JD, vice president, general counsel; and Heather Ramsey, vice president.

Corporate Responsibility

At MedAssurant, improving the effectiveness and efficiency of patient care through high quality data accuracy and interpretation is just one of the ways the company makes the world a better place. The company is equally committed to supporting the communities where it works through philanthropic giving and participation.

Of particular interest are local and national charitable organizations that enrich the lives of community members as well as organizations committed to preserving the environment. MedAssurant's headquarters in the Bowie Corporate Center in Bowie, Maryland, is one of Prince George's County's first buildings to be certified by the U.S. Green Building Council's Leadership in Energy and Environmental Design (LEED).

In Maryland MedAssurant supports the Annapolis Area Ministries, Annapolis Wellness House, the Anne Arundel Medical Center Outreach Program, Box of Rain, the Maryland Hall for the Creative Arts, and the Chesapeake Bay Foundation. Nationally, the company supports the Boy Scouts of America, the Girl Scouts of the USA, the Cystic Fibrosis Foundation, and the National Medical Fellowships.

Along with the environment and charitable giving, MedAssurant devotes much of its efforts to customer satisfaction. The company strives to create a partnership with every client that results in their success. Upholding high standards for customers and employees is fundamental to the company's operations and at the core of its mission. Additional information is available on the company's Web site at www.medassurant.com.

MedAssurant Solutions

Healthcare Data Intelligence Systems (Insights™)

- Comparative Effectiveness Analysis
- Research, Development, and Clinical Trial Support
- Advanced Business Intelligence
- Registries and Custom Datasets
- Quality and Safety Surveillance and Monitoring Systems

Predictive Clinical Insight Systems

- Disease Presence Probability and Impact Analysis
- Disease Progression Predictive Analysis
- Care Consideration Gap Identification Systems

Disease Management and Care Support Solutions

- Advanced Disease Management (CCS Advantage™)
- Practitioner Decision Support Platform (ePASS™)
- Disease Identification, Stratification, Assessment, and Prioritization Systems (ISAP™)
- Multi-Initiative Care Management Coordination (CareSync Advantage™)

Clinical and Quality Outcomes Insight Systems

- Advanced Healthcare Data Aggregation (Discover™)
- NCQA HEDIS® Administrative Data Processing and Hybrid Medical Record Review (HEDIS Advantage™)
- Custom QI and Clinical Outcomes Analysis
- Audit and Data Validation

Risk Adjustment and Revenue Cycle Management Solutions

- Medicare Capitation Risk Adjustment (CARA™)
- Medicaid Capitation Risk Adjustment (CARA™)
- CARA-Rx™
- Risk Adjustment Claims Data Processing (CAAS™)

Left: MedAssurant's Bowie, Maryland, corporate headquarters houses its diverse team, made up of both medical and technology professionals, all of whom play a vital role in executing progressive, end-to-end solutions. Above right: MedAssurant's Bowie, Maryland, data center supports the company's operations. MedAssurant's methods and services are extremely beneficial to health plans, employers, physicians, and patients. Through its exclusive, multidisciplinary approach, advanced infrastructure of leading technologies, and exceptional personnel, MedAssurant provides comprehensive medical data targeting, capture, and abstraction. The company uses evidence-based discoveries from this expansive dataset to reveal and implement unequivocal health care innovations.

BD Diagnostics—Diagnostic Systems is a unit of BD (Becton, Dickinson and Company), a global medical technology company founded in 1897. This unit is the center of the worldwide BD health care diagnostics technology family.

Represented on all five continents, BD has the core purpose of "Helping all people live healthy lives." Products include instruments, test kits, and culture media to diagnose infectious disease, as well as microbiology products for testing food, monitoring the environment, and making biopharmaceuticals.

Headquartered in northern Baltimore County with six facilities in Sparks and Cockeysville, Maryland, BD Diagnostics—Diagnostic Systems employs more than 1,800 associates at these locations, in functional areas such as administration; finance; research and development, including life sciences, engineering, and software; medical and regulatory affairs; manufacturing; quality; logistics; and sales and marketing. The Maryland-based organization generated revenue of over $1 million in fiscal 2008.

for the American Red Cross. Following the success of this project, in 1955 BD acquired BBL.

Hynson, Westcott & Dunning (HW&D), a company founded in 1889 by two faculty members of the University of Maryland–Baltimore, was acquired by BD in 1972. HW&D was an early pioneer in dyes, specialty diagnostics, and immunodiagnostic processes, and most notably invented one of the first tests for syphilis.

Johnston Laboratories, Inc., founded by Baltimore investor Manuel Dupkin and acquired by BD in 1979, developed and patented the first automated device for detecting bacterial growth in culture media. This device, called the BD BACTEC™ Blood Culture System, is now in its 10th generation and is the leading method by which physicians detect bacteria and fungi in the blood of infected patients.

In 1997 BD purchased Difco Laboratories to help expand the BD line of industrial microbiology products. The BD Difco™ brand has a trusted reputation in providing microbiological testing products used to ensure safety, including food testing, environmental monitoring, and biopharmaceuticals production. Then in 2005 BD acquired GeneOhm Sciences, a company that offered rapid diagnosis of antibiotic-resistant bacteria, such as the superbug MRSA, using molecular detection techniques. And in 2006 BD acquired TriPath Imaging, a move that signaled the further expansion of BD in cancer diagnostics.

Above: BD Diagnostics has collaborated with the Foundation for Innovative New Diagnostics (FIND) to improve diagnosis of tuberculosis (TB) in HIV/AIDS patients and increase access to faster and more accurate diagnostic technology in developing countries.*

Strategic Building for Specialization

BD Diagnostics—Diagnostic Systems traces its roots to three companies developed and nurtured by scientists from the Johns Hopkins University and the University of Maryland and dating back to the 19th century. Baltimore Biological Laboratory (BBL) was founded in 1935 by two young scientists from the Johns Hopkins University—Theodore John Carski and Dr. Einar Leifson. Recognizing a need for the commercialization of dehydrated culture media, they set up a laboratory in the basement of Carski's row house and began manufacturing the media. The business did well and, in collaboration with BD, it eventually led to the development of the first sterile, disposable blood-donor kit, which became standard equipment

High Quality and Performance

Today BD Diagnostics—Diagnostic Systems develops and manufactures a range of products extending from simple, manual plated media products for growing and detecting microorganisms to more complex, fully automated microbiology culturing and detection systems. Since 1935 BD BBL prepared culture media products have brought microbiology laboratories the highest levels of quality and performance. BBL has manufactured and shipped more than 225 million plates annually from the facilities located in Cockeysville.

*The World Health Organization (WHO) estimates that nine million new cases of active tuberculosis (TB) and approximately two million TB deaths occur annually. The BD BACTEC™ MGIT™ 960 System is the test of choice in many developing countries because it provides faster results for mycobacterial growth and detection, as well as drug susceptibility testing, which may help improve patient care. In fact, WHO recently endorsed the use of liquid culture systems for TB diagnosis in high-burden countries.

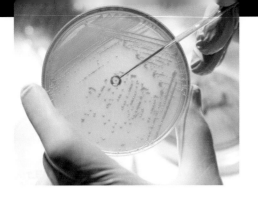

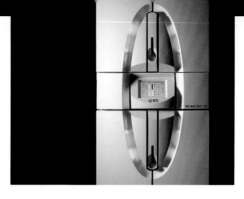

The patented BD ProbeTec™ and BD Viper™ platforms are used worldwide in diagnosing sexually transmitted diseases and are used by more health care institutions than any other molecular method. The BD Phoenix™ system is used in testing for bacterial susceptibility, providing results that allow physicians to offer appropriate antibiotic therapies. The launch in 2008 of the BD BACTEC™ FX Blood Culture System continues the innovations that make the BD BACTEC brand the leader in detection of blood infections in patients.

BD Diagnostics—Diagnostic Systems provides additional information about the company and its products on its Web site at www.bd.com/ds.

A Community Leader

BD Diagnostics—Diagnostic Systems takes seriously its role as a leader in the region and in Maryland's life sciences community. With its global business focus, the unit helps to drive the biosciences sector locally, and it actively pursues a comprehensive agenda of community service that supports its focus on the life sciences.

Recognizing that a science-literate workforce is necessary to Maryland's continued leadership in life sciences, BD supports initiatives in science education for children from kindergarten through college and beyond. In addition to funding, the company involves its researchers and executives in science-oriented initiatives and often opens its facilities to outside groups in order to help promote science education. As a health care leader, BD also supports groups that advance the region's ability to offer the effective delivery of health care—both acute and preventive. In doing this, BD is pursuing its corporate purpose. BD also links with the Johns Hopkins Bloomberg School of Public Health to globally address urgent health care issues in areas of greatest need.

Finally, BD recognizes the importance of its associates and their own commitments to community service. Through the BD Social Investing department, as well as its Diagnostic Systems Community Relations Advisory Board in Maryland, BD dedicates its giving to the areas in which the company focuses its business and to those causes in which its employees are most active.

From its humble row house beginnings, BD Diagnostics—Diagnostic Systems has evolved into a worldwide leader in infectious disease diagnostics, women's health, and cancer diagnostics, committed to the BD purpose of "Helping all people live healthy lives."

BD

Helping all people live healthy lives

This page: BD Diagnostics has created revolutionary health care diagnostic tools and tests such as (from left to right) BD BBL™ CHROMagar™ Plated Media, BD Viper™ System, BD BACTEC™ FX, and BD Phoenix™ System.

As the market leader in dynamic splinting, this company has built its success upon serving each individual patient, helping them to regain range of motion and quality of life. The company uses the finest materials and continually refines its products to ensure that its Dynasplint® Systems technology remains cutting edge.

Right: George Hepburn, P.T., founder and president of Dynasplint Systems, Inc., fits a patient with an Elbow Extension Dynasplint® System. A sales consultant fits each patient to ensure comfort and a proper understanding of the protocol they will follow to regain their range of motion.

At Dynasplint Systems, Inc. (DSI), the driving force behind the company's success is a commitment to restoring range of motion (ROM) in therapy patients, resulting in an improvement in their quality of life. In 1974 Baltimore native George R. Hepburn, P.T., CEO, and founder of DSI, launched his practice as a physical therapist. As he spent several sessions per week with each patient, Hepburn began to see a need for change and a better way to treat a common condition in the field of rehabilitative therapy called "contracture." A contracture can be the result of an injury, illness, or surgery and occurs when a joint becomes stiff and loses its ROM. When he

began, Hepburn might spend as much as five months assisting a patient in regaining their ROM, watching as the patient's gains slowly progressed. He recognized that this was not an ideal way to conduct rehabilitative therapy and that there had to be a more efficient method.

In 1981 the Dynasplint® System—a dynamic splint—was born. Today patients can be prescribed Dynasplint® Systems as soon as they are cleared for passive ROM therapy. The key to the system's effectiveness is a low-load, prolonged-duration stretch (LLPS) technology that delivers a biomechanically correct stimulus to create a permanent length change in shortened connective tissue. The device mimics a therapist's hands and gives an additional six to eight hours per day of gentle stretching, constantly seeking the end range in the affected joint.

Dynasplint® System's in-home use protocol restores the patient's ROM daily. This complements the therapy process for a speedier recovery. Studies have proven that the use of a Dynasplint® System in conjunction with physical therapy can restore lost ROM up to 53 percent faster than traditional methods.

Today DSI has more than 700 colleagues and a presence throughout the United States, Europe, and Canada. The company's corporate headquarters is located in Severna Park, Maryland, while its products are designed, manufactured, refurbished, and distributed from its facility in Queen Anne's County, Maryland. DSI operates as five divisions: Orthopedic, Neurological, Carpal Tunnel, Trismus, and Veterinary, and maintains an international unit. DSI offers a line of 95 systems in a wide variety, each designed to treat a specific peripheral body joint, from shoulder to finger and knee to toe, and the Trismus System for restoring function and for pain management of the jaw.

DSI has a unique sales model. Each patient is individually fit by a DSI sales consultant to ensure that the patient is comfortable and correctly positioned within the Dynasplint® System. The consultant works with patients throughout the entire

rehabilitation process, thereby providing an additional layer of care. Each year the top sales consultants gather together with Hepburn for a conference that he calls "organized chaos." Everyone has the opportunity to make comments and suggestions on how they would change and improve the company's products and to brainstorm new ideas. This continual refinement is designed to guarantee that DSI will continue to offer patients the best option for ROM rehabilitation and will maintain its position as the leader in its industry.

DSI is concerned not only about restoring patients' lives to the way they ought to be but also about restoring business and life in its community. The company sponsors and participates in many local events and continually looks for ways in which colleagues can come together, building relationships while serving people in need. Their efforts are chronicled on the Dynasplint® Cares Web site at www.dynasplint.org.

DSI continually seeks advancements in ways to be good stewards of the environment and its restoration. Being green is somewhat natural to the company as it seeks and leverages improved ways to increase efficiencies while also decreasing its environmental footprint. Most Dynasplint® Systems are rentals, and upon return each unit is completely refurbished. Cardboard shipping boxes are recycled, the metal infrastructure of the system is thoroughly cleaned and inspected, and then the unit is re-dressed with all-new cuffs, pads, and straps. In its corporate offices, new technologies are being put in place as the company works toward a virtually paperless internal system, saving cases of paper and acres of trees.

The company that began in 1981 as a one-person business has steadily expanded and undergone many changes throughout the years. The one core value that has held fast is the commitment maintained by DSI to provide each patient with the best possible treatment and service while focusing on doing what is right to restore people, business, and life the way it ought to be.

Dynasplint Systems, Inc. provides full information about its products and services on its Web site at www.dynasplint.com.

Left: Production welder Gregory Poulos welds just one component part of the Knee Extension Dynasplint® System, which is made up of more than 70 different parts. Once the various components are ready, the system is assembled, inspected, packaged, and shipped to the sales consultant who will individually custom fit it on a patient. Above right: Often paired in teams, sales support representatives work hand-in-hand with sales consultants, receiving orders and verifying the patient's insurance to obtain authorization for the use of the Dynasplint® Systems.

Dimensions Healthcare System

This nonprofit health care system and its member institutions offer a full range of health care services, community wellness programs, and medical education opportunity throughout Prince George's County and the surrounding area. Dimensions Healthcare System provides high quality, cost-effective, accessible health services to local residents.

Above: Prince George's Hospital Center, a Dimensions Healthcare System member, is Maryland's second-busiest trauma center. Right: Laurel Regional Hospital uses state-of-the-art equipment, such as this 64-slice CT scanner.

From prenatal care to behavioral health care to rehabilitation services, Dimensions Healthcare System provides comprehensive medical services to residents of Prince George's County and beyond. Formed in 1982 and headquartered in Cheverly, Maryland, the organization includes Prince George's Hospital Center in Cheverly; Laurel Regional Hospital in Laurel; Bowie Health Campus in Bowie; Gladys Spellman Specialty Hospital & Nursing Center in Cheverly; Larkin Chase Nursing and Rehabilitation Center in Bowie; Glenridge Medical Center in Lanham; and the Senior Health Center at the Cora B. Wood Senior Center in Brentwood.

Prince George's Hospital Center

An acute care teaching hospital and regional referral center, Prince George's Hospital Center was founded in 1944 and is the largest provider of health care services in the county. With 270 beds and 1,400 employees, the hospital offers a comprehensive range of inpatient and outpatient medical and surgical services including trauma and critical care services; cardiac care; open-heart surgery and therapeutic catheterization; surgical services; outpatient services; maternal and child health, including a Level III neonatal intensive care unit and a Perinatal Diagnostic Center; psychiatric care, including the designated sexual assault center for the county; and a graduate medical education residency program.

The hospital's intensive services pavilion has 10 operating suites, a 24-bed intensive care unit, catheterization laboratories, and endoscopy suites. The emergency department has private acute care treatment rooms, a six-bed resuscitation area, an observation unit, two trauma rooms, and a separate ambulatory and walk-in care area.

Laurel Regional Hospital

Laurel Regional Hospital (LRH) is a full-service community hospital serving northern Prince George's County and Montgomery, Howard, and Anne Arundel counties. With 132 beds and 630 employees, the hospital offers a comprehensive range of inpatient and outpatient medical and surgical services including behavioral health services, a cardiac catheterization laboratory, emergency services, an infusion center, maternal and child health services, outpatient addiction treatment, a sleep laboratory, and a wound care center.

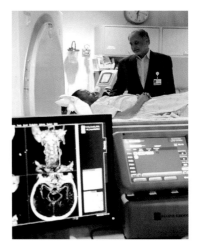

"No matter where you are in Prince George's County, you are never far from the health care you and your family need. We offer a full range of inpatient and outpatient services including medical, surgical, emergency, and long-term care. Whether you need neurosurgery, angioplasty, or have a high-risk pregnancy or diabetes, we provide sophisticated care and the latest technology to treat your needs. From major trauma and critical care services to cardiac care and obstetrics, we are here when you need us most."

— *G. T. Dunlop Ecker, President and CEO, Dimensions Healthcare System*

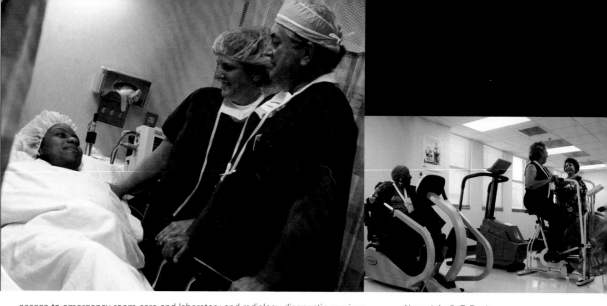

LRH has the only hospital-based, accredited inpatient rehabilitation unit in the county. Its facilities include expanded emergency services, a critical care area, and a pre-admission testing area. The hospital offers qualified interpreters, text telephones (TTYs), and other assistance for deaf and hard-of-hearing patients, free of charge.

Bowie Health Campus

This unique 50-acre property provides health care services for patients of all ages, from newborns to the elderly. Comprehensive facilities include Level II emergency services, after-hours pediatric care, laboratory services, and radiology services. The Dimensions Surgery Center offers ambulatory surgery and pain management and Bowie Physical Medicine offers rehabilitation services, physical therapy, occupational therapy, and speech therapy. The Mullikin Medical Center houses physician practices and specialties and is the site of the Bowie Pharmacy.

The Larkin Chase Nursing and Rehabilitation Center, a long-term care facility, is also located on the Bowie Health Campus. The facility has 119 beds and 140 employees and specializes in respiratory care, progressive wound care, dialysis, and rehabilitation therapies.

Gladys Spellman Specialty Hospital & Nursing Center

A 110-bed comprehensive care center and specialty hospital, this center offers long-term care services for patients with medically complex conditions. Located on the campus of Prince George's Hospital Center, the hospital provides immediate access to emergency room care and laboratory and radiology diagnostic services. A full range of diagnostic and treatment services includes rehabilitation, respiratory care, pain management, progressive wound care, intravenous therapy, dialysis, infectious disease management, and support services including speech-language pathology, physical therapy, occupational therapy, recreational therapy, psychological therapy, and social services.

Community Outreach

Dimensions Healthcare System works to improve and maintain the health of the community by delivering information and services people need to get healthy and stay healthy. The organization offers a wide range of services and programs— such as support groups, health screenings, and informative seminars—to help individuals make healthier choices and lifestyle changes.

Community outreach programs include Community Education, Dimensions Smoking Cessation Program, Faith Community, Senior Health Center, Speakers Bureau, Support Groups, and Volunteer Services. Volunteers who wish to give back to their communities will find many opportunities to make a difference in the lives of others and are considered a vital part of the Dimensions health care team.

Additional information about Dimensions Healthcare System is available on the organization's Web site at www.dimensionshealth.org.

Above left: G. T. Dunlop Ecker serves as Dimensions Healthcare System's President and CEO. Above center: The Dimensions Surgery Center on the Bowie Health Campus offers four well-equipped surgical suites and one special procedural room. The center strives to make surgical procedures efficient, eliminating the need for costly hospital stays. Above right: Prince George's Hospital Center, which serves Prince George's County and southern Maryland, offers a comprehensive range of inpatient and outpatient medical and surgical services, including cardiac rehabilitation.

Washington County Health System

This health system—the largest health care provider in Western Maryland—is located at the crossroads of Western Maryland, southern Pennsylvania, and the Eastern Panhandle of West Virginia. It brings highly skilled health care providers and advanced medical technologies to the vibrant tristate region.

Above: Washington County Health System's new regional medical center will feature single-patient rooms, expanded emergency care facilities, and state-of-the-art medical technologies in a patient-centered environment that focuses on quality health care and safety.

Washington County Health System, in Hagerstown, Maryland, is an integrated health care delivery system. As the largest employer in Washington County, it has a deep understanding of the needs of the business community. Its programs span the continuum of health care, ranging from inpatient care to occupational health services to physician practices and outpatient care. The system delivers patient care through two primary components, Washington County Hospital and Antietam Health Services.

Washington County Hospital

Located in Hagerstown, Maryland, this acute care hospital, which was opened in 1905, is a significant force in the provision of quality medical care for the region. It is building a new regional medical center, projected for completion in 2010, that will have 267 single-patient rooms, along with the most advanced medical technologies available.

Services that will move to the new site include a special care nursery, a Level III trauma program, a primary stroke center, a wound center, as well as a cardiac diagnostic laboratory. Other hospital services that address outpatient needs will continue to be available, such as the John R. Marsh Cancer Center, Total Rehab Care, the Center for Clinical Research, and the Center for Bariatric Surgery.

State-of-the-art medical technologies at the new facility will include new technologies such as advanced 3T magnetic resonance imaging (MRI), single-photon-emission computed tomography (SPECT) scanners, and cardiac interventions. Patients also will benefit from the convenient location of the new facility, which is adjacent to Robinwood Medical Center, operated by Antietam Health Services. With this proximity, patients can take advantage of an array of both inpatient and outpatient services. The medical mall houses a pharmacy, medical laboratory, an urgent care clinic, surgery centers, and diagnostic imaging services. In addition, there are numerous physician practices, offering a wide variety of medical specialties.

Antietam Health Services

Antietam Health Services (AHS), an affiliate of Washington County Health System, is a leading provider of ambulatory health care services in the tristate region. Its mission is to engage in ambulatory health care activities that complement the goals and objectives of Washington County Health System. AHS vigorously recruits physicians and other health care providers to the region to assure an adequate supply of physicians in many medical specialties. AHS has a very successful record of joint-venture relationships with physicians that has greatly benefited the well being of the residents of the tri-state area.

AHS includes a number of businesses and medical practices. It maintains two urgent care clinics, which are open seven days a week and work closely with primary care physicians, caring for patients with minor illnesses or injuries. Because numerous patients can be seen at these clinics, local physicians have more time to spend with regularly scheduled patients in their offices. AHS

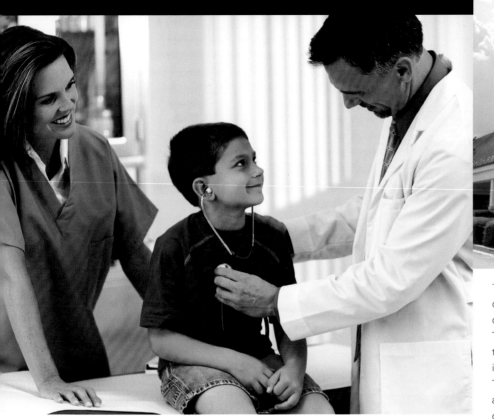

also manages the Robinwood Medical Center and provides durable medical equipment, ambulance transport, retail pharmacy, and child care services. It continually evaluates the health care needs of the community and plans ways to best meet these needs.

Additionally, AHS operates Health@Work, a comprehensive occupational-health service for employers and employees. The program coordinates a wide range of employment-related services. It helps to assess employees as they enter the workplace and to keep them healthy and on-the-job once they are hired. Health@Work offers employee-assistance programs, occupational medicine, and industrial rehabilitation.

THP—A Partnership to Improve Community Health

THP TriState Health Partners (THP) is a physician hospital organization owned by more than 200 physicians and Washington County Hospital. This partnership enhances the ability of its physician owners and the hospital to focus on technology and initiatives to improve quality and patient care outcomes in this community.

THP's mission is to be the region's most comprehensive health care solutions company, fostering collaboration with community practitioners and providers to create a fully integrated medical care delivery system. Clinical integration engages THP physicians in a cooperative effort to improve the quality of health care and the cost-effectiveness of health care services. Such clinical integration provides important benefits to physicians, patients, employers, and payers alike. It provides THP with a competitive edge by keeping the delivery of community health care and the decisions that impact this care in the hands of local physicians. The clinical integration program provides access to electronic health records for its members, develops evidence-based indicators to ensure achievement of measurable quality improvement, and augments case management and pharmacy benefits management to control costs. THP also provides employers with comprehensive medical management, including utilization management, case management, disease management, and wellness services.

Washington County Health System provides additional information on its Web site at www.washingtoncountyhospital.com.

The Future of Health Care in the Tristate Region

Future health care in the tristate region depends on medical care providers such as Washington County Hospital and Antietam Health Services as well as partners such as THP. Together, these entities bring their energies and considerable strengths to bear on meeting the medical needs of a rapidly changing region. They recognize that physicians want to provide the best care they can to patients in their local community. These providers work diligently with others in the region and focus on delivering first-class health care to local residents.

Left: Washington County Hospital is served by more than 300 physicians, who represent more than 30 medical specialties. Above right: The Robinwood Medical Center brings a variety of health services together in one medical mall, including more than 125 health care providers. Washington County Health System's new regional medical center will be built adjacent to the Robinwood Medical Center to make the best use of space for patients and their families.

Mercy Medical Center

This cutting-edge medical center is nationally recognized for its quality patient care, state-of-the-art facilities, and outstanding medical staff. Mercy Medical Center has been named one of the nation's top 100 hospitals, based on quality and performance standards, and houses one of the nation's top women's centers. Mercy is also a teaching hospital affiliated with the University of Maryland School of Medicine.

Mercy's History: A Legacy of Service to Baltimore

Today's Mercy Medical Center stands on the same location where six Sisters of Mercy arrived in 1874 to administer what was then known as the Baltimore City Infirmary. Through the Great Baltimore Fire of 1904, the Depression of the 1930s, and the postwar emergence of the suburbs, Mercy has remained a stabilizing part of downtown Baltimore. The question of moving the hospital to the suburbs has come up many times in Mercy's history, but each time, the Sisters of Mercy have held firm to their commitment to serving the community that has depended on them for generations. Today Mercy is a thriving institution that is successful and growing, and is recognized every year for excellence in quality of care, operational efficiency, financial performance, and respect and opportunity for its workforce.

Above right: The Mary Catherine Bunting Center at Mercy—a replacement hospital adjacent to Mercy's current campus—is one of the Baltimore region's most advanced hospital facilities.

Mercy's Mission: A Commitment to Quality and Excellence

Mercy's commitment to provide programs and services with uncompromising quality is grounded firmly in the tradition of Catholic health care and the values of the Sisters of Mercy. The organization remains committed to serving the poor and those who cannot afford the cost of their care. People count on Mercy to open its doors and hearts to their needs. Innovation, excellence, and hospitality are Mercy hallmarks.

Mercy Medical Center Highlights

- Founded in 1874 by the Sisters of Mercy
- Independent; governed by a 26-member Board of Trustees
- Teaching hospital affiliated with the University of Maryland School of Medicine
- One of the Baltimore region's largest employers
- Generates $500 million of economic activity each year

Mercy's Vision: A Commitment to Baltimore for Decades

Mercy's new Mary Catherine Bunting Center—an 18-story, 686,000-square-foot, replacement hospital located adjacent to Mercy Medical Center's current campus on St. Paul Place—will meet the health care needs of the Baltimore community for decades to come. The new hospital will provide 259 private inpatient rooms, including 32 critical care beds, 15 operating rooms, and advanced diagnostic and medical imaging.

For over 100 years, Mercy has enjoyed a special relationship with the Baltimore City Fire Department. Today Mercy is the exclusive provider of health care services to Baltimore's 1,700 firefighters and 3,200 police officers.

Excellent health care is offered to the community by more than 500 members of the Mercy Medical Staff through Centers of Excellence, primary care physicians with offices in downtown Baltimore and throughout the community, and private practices located at Mercy Medical Center.

Mercy is well-known for clinical excellence, compassionate care, and innovative treatment, evidenced through its many honors and distinctions. Mercy Medical Center has been named one of the nation's Top 100 hospitals by Solucient, based on quality and performance standards. Mercy is also known for the specialized programs of The Institute for Cancer Care; The Weinberg Center for Women's Health & Medicine, which was named one of America's 10 Best Women's Centers by *Self* magazine; The Vascular Center, the region's busiest center of its kind; the internationally recognized Institute for Foot and Ankle Reconstruction; and the regionally recognized Maryland Spine Center.

Additional information is available on the Mercy Health Services Web site at www.mdmercy.com.

Centers of Excellence at Mercy Medical Center

The Weinberg Center for Women's Health & Medicine
- The Gynecology Center
- The Hoffberger Breast Center
- The Center for Plastic and Reconstructive Surgery
- Tyanna O'Brien Center for Women's Imaging
- Center for Bone Health & Division of Endocrinology
- The Prevention and Research Center

The Institute for Cancer Care

The Melissa L. Posner Institute for Digestive Health and Liver Disease

The Orthopedic Specialty Hospital
- The Institute for Foot and Ankle Reconstruction
- The Maryland Spine Center
- Orthopedics and Joint Replacement

The Vascular Center

Urology Specialists of Maryland

Eye and Cosmetic Surgery

Center for Minimally Invasive Surgery

The Lung Center

Center for Interventional Pain Medicine

The Diabetes Center

Holy Cross Hospital

Committed to being the most trusted provider of health care services in the area, this mission-driven hospital has grown into one of the largest hospitals in Maryland. Offering a full range of inpatient and outpatient primary and specialty health care services and valuable expertise in specialized areas, it remains firmly dedicated to meeting the health care needs of its community.

Holy Cross Hospital is a faith-based hospital devoted to healing the mind, body, and spirit. An excellent place to work and an advanced place to learn about medicine, it was founded in 1963 by the Congregation of the Sisters of the Holy Cross. With 454 beds, the nonprofit hospital is now one of the largest hospitals in Maryland, treating and caring for more than 160,000 patients each year.

Located in Silver Spring, Holy Cross Hospital has a long-standing commitment to providing a full range of inpatient and outpatient primary and specialty health care services. It offers specialized expertise in surgery, neuroscience, cancer, women and infants' services, and care for seniors. Specialists at Holy Cross Hospital perform more inpatient gynecologic surgeries, deliver more babies, and care for more newborns who are critically ill than any other hospital in Maryland.

Above: Holy Cross Hospital is located in Silver Spring, Maryland.

The hospital serves the communities of Montgomery and Prince George's counties, providing health care services to all, including vulnerable and underserved people, whom the hospital cares for at no cost or through financial assistance. In the past five years alone, Holy Cross Hospital has provided more than $100 million in community benefit, according to reporting guidelines of the Maryland Health Services Cost Review Commission. The hospital's community benefit activities are tailored to the community's needs and provide services that might otherwise be unavailable.

As a teaching hospital, Holy Cross Hospital contributes to the future of health care by training physicians, nurses, and other health care professionals. The hospital's GATE Institute, a specialized training center for physicians who perform minimally invasive procedures, has trained thousands of clinicians since its inception nearly 20 years ago. The hospital hosts physician-residency programs affiliated with George Washington University, Children's National Medical Center, and Howard University. It also educates students from seven nursing programs and houses a state-of-the-art Nursing Simulation Laboratory.

Holy Cross Hospital provides additional information about all of its services on its Web site at www.holycrosshealth.org.

Holy Cross Hospital is the only hospital in Maryland to have been honored with the Workplace Excellence Award from the Maryland Work-Life Alliance every year from 1999 through 2009. This award recognizes the hospital's efforts to maintain outstanding employee benefits, programs, and policies that respond to the needs of employees and contribute to the organization's success. Holy Cross Hospital is noted for offering highly competitive compensation and reward programs for its employees.

As a member of Trinity Health, based in Novi, Michigan, Holy Cross Hospital is part of one of the largest health systems in the nation. The hospital employs 3,200 people, including 1,000 nurses. More than 1,200 physicians are affiliated with the hospital.

PROFILES OF COMPANIES AND ORGANIZATIONS
Insurance Services

Riggs, Counselman, Michaels & Downes, Inc. (RCM&D)

For 125 years this privately held insurance brokerage has sustained a strong reputation as a trusted provider of insurance, risk management, and employee benefit solutions to companies and organizations as well as personal insurance to individuals and families. Today it is ranked among the top insurance brokers in the country.

The history of Riggs, Counselman, Michaels & Downes, Inc. (RCM&D) can be traced back to 1885, when R. E. Warfield, a local insurance executive, was appointed resident manager for the Royal Insurance Company in Baltimore.

Warfield's insurance business continued to thrive in the early 20th century and was formally incorporated as the Henry M. Warfield–Roloson Company in 1923. One of the firm's first officers was F. Albert Roloson, the grandfather of RCM&D's current chairman of the board and CEO, Albert R. "Skip" Counselman.

By 1946 the continued growth of the firm led to its merging with Riggs, Rossman, and Hunter, Inc., and the firm's name was changed to Riggs, Warfield, Roloson, Inc. (RWR). In 1969 RWR merged with Michaels, Fenwick & Downes, and the firm's current name of Riggs, Counselman, Michaels & Downes, Inc. was adopted.

Today RCM&D remains an independent and employee-owned firm, managing more than $450 million in insurance premiums with offices in Baltimore and Bethesda, Maryland; Richmond and Virginia Beach, Virginia; and Harrisburg, Pennsylvania.

RCM&D is consistently recognized as one of the top 20 independent insurance brokers and risk and benefit consultants in the country and has a client retention rate of 98 percent.

Above: Riggs, Warfield, Roloson, Inc. was merged with Michaels, Fenwick & Downes in 1969, and the firm became Riggs, Counselman, Michaels & Downes, Inc. (RCM&D). Shown here, from left, are Albert H. Michaels Sr., Lawrason Riggs of J, Charles C. Counselman Jr., and William W. Downes. Right: The corporate headquarters for RCM&D is located in Baltimore, Maryland.

A Personalized Approach

RCM&D's current and future success is driven by the firm's staff of more than 275 dedicated insurance professionals who are committed to a personal approach to client service and RCM&D's core principles of honesty, trust, and integrity.

RCM&D is grounded by the premise that each client is unique. By devoting time and resources to understanding a client's specific risk and benefit needs, the team at RCM&D can translate that knowledge into comprehensive, tailor-made solutions.

An Unwavering Passion for Independence

Amid rapid consolidation in the insurance industry, RCM&D has gone against the trend of merging with or being acquired by larger national entities, remaining independent and employee owned.

RCM&D's independent structure allows the firm to focus on the long-term development of strategic solutions and client relationships. The businesses and organizations RCM&D serves demand foresight rather than hindsight; solutions, not products; and industry experts, not generalists.

The firm's passion for independence helps it attract and cultivate top risk and benefit professionals by promoting an atmosphere of collegiality, as opposed to a culture of competitiveness. This sense of teamwork contributes to RCM&D's outstanding level of client service.

Industry Specialization Fuels Growth

While RCM&D's history dates back more than a century, the firm has evolved significantly in recent years and is poised for continued success in the coming decades.

Recognizing extraordinary growth opportunities throughout the mid Atlantic area, RCM&D enacted an aggressive regional expansion plan. Through strategic acquisitions and recruitment, RCM&D added more than 100 employees, including talented executives with specialized talents and experience in industries such as health care, construction, education, and life science, and in nonprofit organizations.

The development of these dedicated industry resources has enhanced RCM&D's ability to deliver innovative solutions and measurable value to clients and continues to fuel the firm's strategic growth throughout the mid Atlantic region and beyond.

Responding to Evolving Needs

As RCM&D's client base has become more diverse, the demand for the firm to provide more complex services has increased significantly. RCM&D has worked hard to meet this demand.

In addition, RCM&D has dramatically increased its international business activity in response to its clients' need for services throughout the world.

While RCM&D remains mindful of its rich heritage, the extent to which it relies on past achievements is limited. The firm is constantly evolving, tirelessly searching for new solutions, and remains inspired by the vision of what it can achieve together with its clients.

RCM&D's history of high ethical standards, a commitment to the communities it serves, and a personalized approach to client service continue to define the firm today.

RCM&D provides additional information about all of its services on its Web site at www.rcmd.com.

A True Community Partner

Giving back to the communities it serves is the cornerstone of RCM&D's corporate philosophy. For the past 15 years, RCM&D has hosted an annual fall sailing regatta that has raised more than $300,000 for 20 different nonprofit organizations.

In addition, RCM&D sponsors a series of annual philanthropic events that cultivate a strong sense of camaraderie among employees, who help raise funds and guide where the dollars are donated.

Above left: In 1985, on the 100th anniversary of the firm, the cornerstone was laid for the RCM&D building. Chairman emeritus Charles C. Counselman Jr. and Catherine Counselman christened the new building. Above right: The Annual RCM&D Regatta has raised more than $300,000 for worthy nonprofit organizations.

IWIF Workers' Compensation Insurance

From the town of Accident in Garrett County to the town of Gratitude on the Eastern Shore, employers across the state of Maryland count on this insurer to provide accessible and fairly priced workers' compensation insurance coverage and just compensation for injuries incurred on the job.

Above right: Members of the IWIF Executive Team include, from left, seated, Rona S. Finkelstein, Esq., senior vice president, Legal Services and Human Resources; Thomas J. Phelan, CPA, president and CEO; Dennis W. Carroll, Esq., executive vice president and general counsel; and standing, Robert Marshall, vice president, Information Systems; Timothy K. Michels, Esq., executive vice president, Claims; George H. Matthews, AAI, executive vice president, Insurance Operations; Donna C. Wilson, senior vice president, Strategic Planning and Communications; Robert E. Merritt, CFA, executive vice president and CIO; and Paige Beck, CPA, executive vice president and CFO.

The Maryland state legislature created IWIF Workers' Compensation Insurance (IWIF) in 1914 to provide a stable source of workers' compensation insurance coverage. Throughout its nearly a century of service to Maryland, IWIF has ensured the availability of fairly priced workers' compensation insurance to all Maryland employers.

A Special Role in Maryland

IWIF is a fully self-supporting insurance organization operating with a social purpose and funded entirely by premiums and investment income. IWIF offers financial strength and stability, exceptional customer service, innovative product offerings, and in-depth knowledge about local business.

Building on Strength

With $1.6 billion in assets, conservatively built through decades of sound management, IWIF has the capacity to underwrite Maryland's entire workers' compensation market. The organization's unique status as a nonprofit insurer allows it to return profits to policyholders through the rate-making process, incentive plans, and dividend programs. By returning profits through its rate-making process, IWIF is in a position to establish the competitive pricing benchmark for Maryland's workers' compensation industry. IWIF assures that the cost of workers' compensation insurance in Maryland remains among the most competitive in the nation.

IWIF has emerged as a carrier of choice among Maryland employers, especially small-to-midsize companies. Small businesses paying as little as $3,000 over three years, for example, are able to enjoy premium discounts when they achieve good loss experience and maintain a safe workplace—a benefit that private insurance companies usually reserve for only their largest policyholders.

A Service Commitment

IWIF is a specialist in the field of workers' compensation, with all efforts concentrated on elevating the services and operations of this one line of insurance. By focusing

solely on workers' compensation insurance, IWIF is continually expanding and improving upon the services it provides.

IWIF also excels in managing claims and the medical components of workers' compensation health care. Through IWIF's best-practices approach to claims management and with the IWIF network of health care providers, IWIF claimants are able to access Case Managers who are local and who therefore have firsthand knowledge of Maryland medical providers. IWIF's leadership and strong market share in Maryland reflect the quality and value that IWIF provides for its policyholders.

A Champion for Workplace Safety

Maryland employers choose and depend on IWIF to help protect their greatest resource—their employees. IWIF helps to keep Maryland companies financially sound by guiding them in ways of preventing workplace accidents.

From assisting a small start-up business to implement its first workplace safety program to helping a larger, established business recognize the financial benefits of an exemplary safety record, IWIF's expert Loss Control Consultants assist policyholders every day with lowering the frequency and severity of workplace accidents and injuries and thereby lower their rates.

As a workplace safety champion, IWIF conducts and participates in an array of safety workshops, policyholder seminars, and conferences. IWIF creates and produces extensive safety literature, including Safety Tip Sheets, available in both English and Spanish, and all materials are available on its Web site (www.IWIF.com). Without a doubt, IWIF is passionate about its basic benefit message to all Maryland businesses that "Safety Saves with IWIF."

Quality Care for Injured Workers

For those Marylanders who do become injured on the job, IWIF embraces the social and humanitarian principles of fair and equitable benefits for the

compensable injuries of Maryland's workers. IWIF created the "Guide for the Injured Worker," which is distributed to all claimants. This pamphlet educates injured employees about their benefits and responsibilities.

A major focus of IWIF's claims service is to ensure that an injured worker receives the highest quality medical care in a timely manner. IWIF's commitment is to provide the services, information, and benefits that make workers' compensation function the way it is intended to work.

As committed as IWIF is to the fair treatment of injured workers, it is equally committed to investigating and prosecuting workers' compensation fraud. IWIF pioneered the creation of an in-house fraud unit and is leading the cause in Maryland to reduce unnecessary costs resulting from fraud.

A Promise Kept

When IWIF was established, the goal was to ensure that all Maryland employers, regardless of the size or risk profile of their businesses, could offer insurance to their workers for on-the-job injuries. Today, IWIF is still the only guarantor of that promise. "Accessible, affordable, and accountable" have been the hallmarks of IWIF's service to Maryland—a dependable resource that is destined to continue to serve generations of Maryland workers to come.

> **IWIF**
> - Founded in 1914
> - Located in Towson, Maryland
> - $1.6 billion in assets
> - 380 employees
> - 26,000 policyholders
> - 28 percent market share
> - 25,000 injured workers receiving benefits and services

Above left: IWIF is located in Towson, Maryland. Above right: Members of the IWIF board of directors include, from left, R. Bruce Alderman, board vice chairman; Leonard "Bud" Schuler, board member; Patricia McHugh Lambert, board secretary; Rocky V. Gonzalez, board chairman; Frank D. Boston Jr., board member; Joseph M. Coale, board member; Kenneth Nwafor, CPA, board member; Charles Dankmeyer, board member; and (not shown) Queen Logan Gladden, board member.

AEGON Direct Marketing Services, Inc.

With more than 35 years of experience, this company offers a different approach to purchasing insurance by executing a variety of marketing techniques that enable customers to choose the insurance products they need at a convenient time and place. With its large product portfolio, the company possesses the expertise and experience to develop custom-designed products that meet its customers' changing needs.

Above: AEGON Direct Marketing Services, Inc. (ADMS), a leader in the direct marketing of life and supplemental health insurance, employs more than 2,300 staff members. Right: A group of ADMS employees takes part in one of many ADMS-sponsored community projects.

AEGON Direct Marketing Services, Inc. (ADMS) is a leading direct marketer of life, supplemental health, and specialty insurance products as well as fee-based programs.

Using diverse marketing methods, ADMS provides convenient alternatives to buying insurance for customers, who can choose the products they need from ADMS's large product portfolio at a time and place of their choice. For more than 35 years, ADMS has helped individuals, families, and businesses protect what is important.

With major operations in Baltimore, Maryland, North America, Asia Pacific, Europe, and Latin America, ADMS services nearly 19 million insurance policies around the world and employs more than 2,300 people. ADMS is an AEGON company. AEGON is one of the world's largest insurance organizations, headquartered in The Hague, the Netherlands.

Direct Marketing Expertise

ADMS uses a variety of direct response techniques to deliver convenience and access to its customers. These techniques include inbound and outbound telemarketing, point-of-sale marketing, direct mail, television advertising, statement inserts, Internet marketing, and more.

ADMS's expertise and longevity in direct marketing have made it a valued partner to many leading financial institutions, associations, retailers, credit unions, catalog publishers, and employer groups in the United States and around the world. ADMS uses the endorsement of these sponsoring organizations to develop and execute co-branded marketing programs. It works directly with its business partners as well as through brokers, agents, and third-party administrators to create programs custom-designed to respond to the unique needs of each of its clients. These programs range from a full package of product development, administrative, technology, and marketing services to the delivery of a single product or a single service, such as product underwriting.

ADMS provides additional information about its products and services on its Web site at www.aegondms.com.

Serving the Community

ADMS has a strong commitment to the communities in which it operates, and it actively supports the health and welfare initiatives supported by its employees. The ADMS team based in Baltimore is actively involved with United Way of Central Maryland, Habitat for Humanity, My Sister's Place, and other community organizations. Support is offered through financial and in-kind donations, and volunteerism.

Building the Future

Looking to the future, AEGON Direct Marketing Services, Inc. is building on its history of providing innovative solutions and support to customers, business partners, and the community.

GEICO

This Chevy Chase, Maryland–based automobile insurance company provides affordable coverage for more than 15 million automobiles, trucks, and motorcycles owned by nine million policyholders. The company is known for its exceptional customer service and for its consistent reliability.

In 1936, some of the most memorable U.S. automobiles were the Lincoln Zephyr, the Ford V-8, the Chrysler Airflow, and the spectacularly well-engineered Hudson, and despite lingering frugalities of the Great Depression era, drivers were buying cars in record numbers. People could not wait to get out on the open road and see where it took them.

That is when Leo Goodwin confirmed his thinking that the automobile insurance industry was precisely the right business to be in. He founded GEICO — Government Employees Insurance Company — in Washington, D.C., in 1936, and made every effort to provide the right coverage and prices for government employees and members of the military, most of whom were more than ready to plunk down hard-earned dollars to get in the driver's seat.

With the right direct marketing messages and upfront savings for customers, Goodwin got GEICO off to a healthy start.

America's love affair with the automobile never dimmed.

By the 1950s, GEICO was insuring hundreds of thousands of motorists, making plans to open offices in several locations around the country, and sensing that there were limitless opportunities ahead.

In 1959, to help house GEICO's growing staff of 1,100 insurance professionals, the company opened its 27-acre campus in Chevy Chase, Maryland, which remains GEICO's headquarters today.

Right: The GEICO gecko was introduced during the 1999–2000 television season and has since become the GEICO mascot. Far right, top: GEICO has been insuring motorists since 1936. Far right, bottom: GEICO opened its Chevy Chase campus in 1959.

Early photos show GEICO surrounded sparsely by housing and shops. Over the years a dynamic neighborhood grew up around the campus, and GEICO is now in the heart of one of the area's liveliest retail centers.

Today GEICO is the third-largest private passenger automobile insurer in the United States, and works to meet the needs of nearly every driver. In addition to automobile insurance, GEICO offers customers insurance products for their motorcycles, all-terrain vehicles, boats, homes, apartments, and mobile homes. Identity theft protection, life insurance, and personal umbrella coverage are also available. GEICO provides complete details about GEICO products on its Web site at www.geico.com.

Leo Goodwin would be quite proud that GEICO has become a household name through its popular advertising and humorous branding. And he would probably be delighted that GEICO's small green gecko has become such a powerful spokescreature for the company.

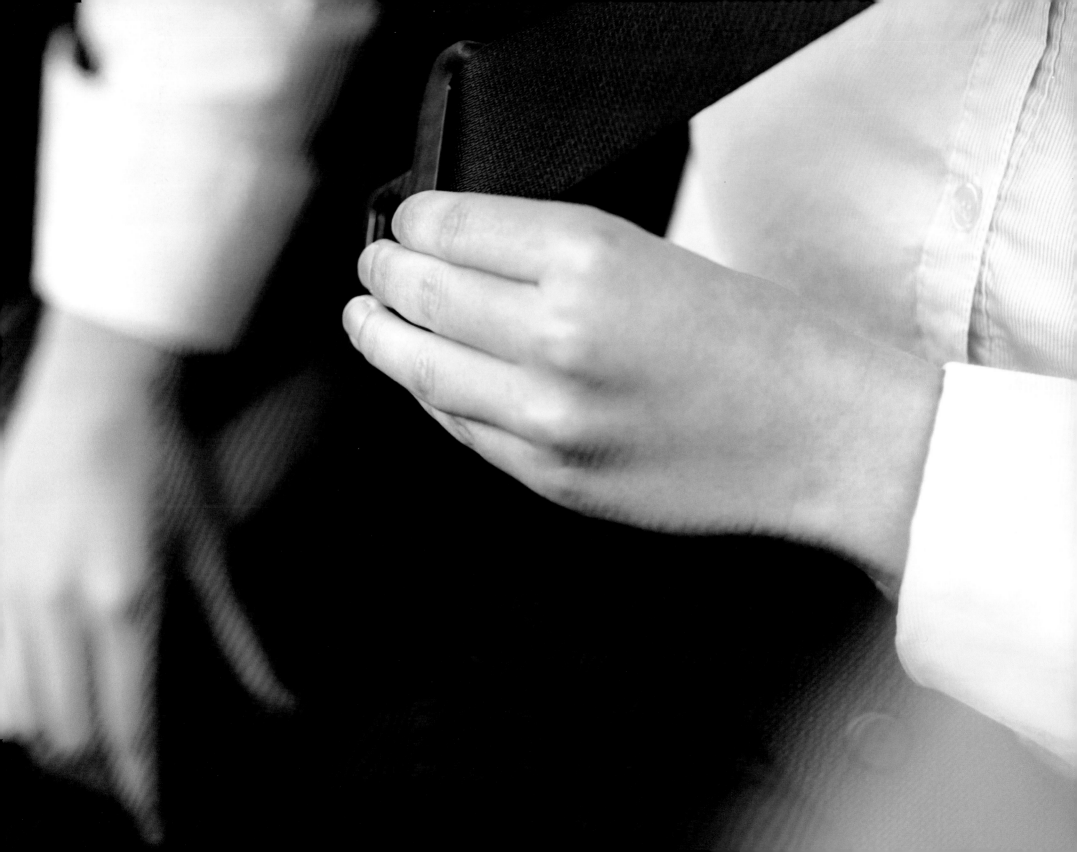

Kelly & Associates Insurance Group, Inc.

This company offers employers integrated services for managing their employee-benefits and payroll processes. It maintains alliances with the top life, disability, dental, and vision insurance carriers, suppliers, and brokers in the region and applies advanced technology to provide employers of every size with customized, employee-benefits plans, administration, and services.

With businesses today facing complex, fast-changing employee-benefits challenges, Kelly & Associates Insurance Group, Inc. (KELLY) of Hunt Valley, Maryland, offers cutting-edge solutions designed to not only save employers time and money but also help them retain their best people. KELLY is renowned for providing its clients with its *Total Benefits Solution*®, which combines advanced employee-benefits technology with the highest quality of customer service. KELLY is the largest employee-benefits administrator in Maryland and one of the largest and fastest-growing group-insurance administrators, brokers, and consultants in the mid-Atlantic region. In addition, KELLY's payroll and workers' compensation solutions—KTBS*Payroll* and KTBS*WorkComp*— which are divisions of Kelly & Associates Financial Services, Inc., a KELLY affiliate, have quickly become leaders in their areas.

The firm began in 1976 when Frank and Janet Kelly started a small health and life insurance agency in the basement of their home in Timonium, Maryland. By 1994 the Kellys, with their sons, Frank III, John, David, and Bryan, had built a business of 20 employees and $25 million in annual premiums. Today KELLY, headquartered in Hunt Valley, Maryland, has expanded to more than 300 associates working in metropolitan Baltimore; suburban Washington, D.C.; northern Virginia; Wilmington, Delaware; and Atlanta, Georgia. The company administers or manages more than $1.5 billion in total

annualized premiums for more than 10,000 corporate clients and hundreds of thousands of workers. KELLY attributes this phenomenal growth to a number of factors, including

- A passion for their mission
- A core belief in innovation
- A combination of superior technology and personal service
- A powerful, proprietary online tool, KTBS*Online*
- The ability to offer a unique and powerful *Total Benefits Solution*
- Living up to its commitment that "The customer always comes first"
- Valuing its employees' contributions because it knows that they make the difference
- Maintaining a laserlike focus on integrity, professionalism, and excellence

KELLY's benefits solutions are packaged in a secure and easy-to-use online tool that provides seamless, real-time information and clear-cut results. The company serves businesses of all sizes, gives agents and brokers the most-advanced value-added technology, and offers expert consultations on a client company's benefits needs. The company's products KTBS*Payroll* and KTBS*WorkComp* integrate payroll and workers' compensation insurance solutions with a benefits package—all accessed through a single point of entry. This streamlines billing and enhances cash flow, eliminating surprises, and makes managing these tasks fast, efficient, and stress-free. KELLY provides more information about its products and services on its Web site at www.kaig.com.

As the marketplace continues to evolve, companies face increasing employee-benefits challenges. KELLY considers this to be an opportunity to make life less complicated and more profitable for its clients. That is the KELLY way.

Above right: The Kelly family includes, from left, John Kelly, Francis X. "Frank" Kelly III, Senator Francis X. Kelly, Janet Kelly, David Kelly, and Bryan Kelly. Below right: Kelly & Associates Insurance Group, Inc. is headquartered in Hunt Valley, Maryland.

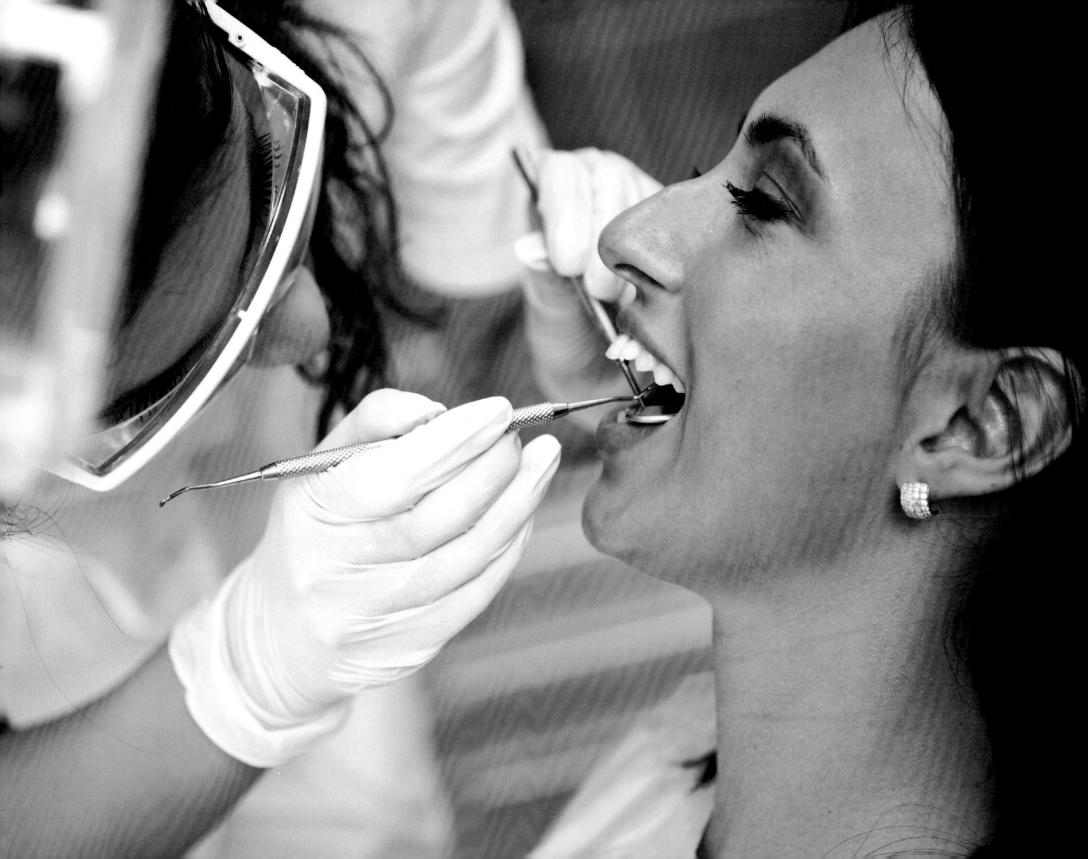

while Corporate Fleet Driver Training may be conducted by AAA Mid-Atlantic at the participating company's place of business.

Free programs conducted by representatives of the Mid-Atlantic Foundation for Traffic Safety and Education, the nonprofit arm of AAA Mid-Atlantic, are held daily on a variety of safety issues at schools, senior centers, and other public facilities throughout the state. They include road safety, motorist and pedestrian safety, and school safety. One of the foundation's oldest and most recognizable programs is the AAA School Safety Patrol Program, which was established in 1920. AAA School Safety Patrollers help safeguard the lives of millions of young boys and girl as they go to and from school each day. Nearly 30,000 Maryland students serve as AAA Safety Patrollers on behalf of the Mid-Atlantic Foundation in Maryland. The AAA School Safety Patrol Program uses nationally accepted methods to alert motorists to drive carefully and to use caution because school children are present in the area.

Most commonly recognized for roadside assistance in an emergency, the club offers roadside service that is a lifesaver for drivers who are out of gas, in need of towing, or experiencing other difficulties. The roadside assistance fleet is composed of approximately 100 drivers and 80 vehicles in Baltimore and Landover. These operations are supplemented with an extensive contract network composed of more than 100 contract facilities, with an estimated total of 800 drivers and 1,000 trucks, ensuring full coverage of the entire state.

One of the largest AAA clubs in the nation, AAA Mid-Atlantic operates 11 retail branches in the state: Arnold Station, Bel Air, Frederick, Germantown, Hagerstown, Largo, Maple Lawn, Salisbury, Timonium, Westminster, and Wheaton. Members can visit their local AAA office to take advantage of almost 300 different benefits or they may access the club online at www.aaa.com, where they will find a member guide offering helpful links, information about vehicle ownership and maintenance, and many travel-related products and services.

Above: For more than a century, AAA Mid-Atlantic has been the motorist's guardian angel, helping to improve roads and routes and reassuring drivers that emergency assistance is always at hand.

As more and more drivers take to the road throughout the 21st century, AAA Mid-Atlantic, which serves Maryland, Delaware, Washington, D.C., and parts of Virginia, Pennsylvania, and New Jersey, remains a strong and vibrant member services organization that has been serving automobile drivers for more than 100 years. From roadside assistance and car insurance to travel reservations, discounts, and maps, the club and its associates are dedicated to prompt, personal, and effective member support.

AAA Mid-Atlantic has a significant presence in Maryland, with nearly 900,000 members in the state and employing nearly 300 associates. From its administrative offices in Towson, AAA Mid-Atlantic is home base for Public and Government Affairs, Insurance Claims, Traffic Safety, and Approved Auto Repair personnel. A second administrative office in Bowie manages the auto club's driving programs and serves as the location for the Advanced Driving Program.

Other driving programs, such as Mature Defensive Driving and an Approved Driving School Network, are located at the Wheaton and Maple Lawn branches,

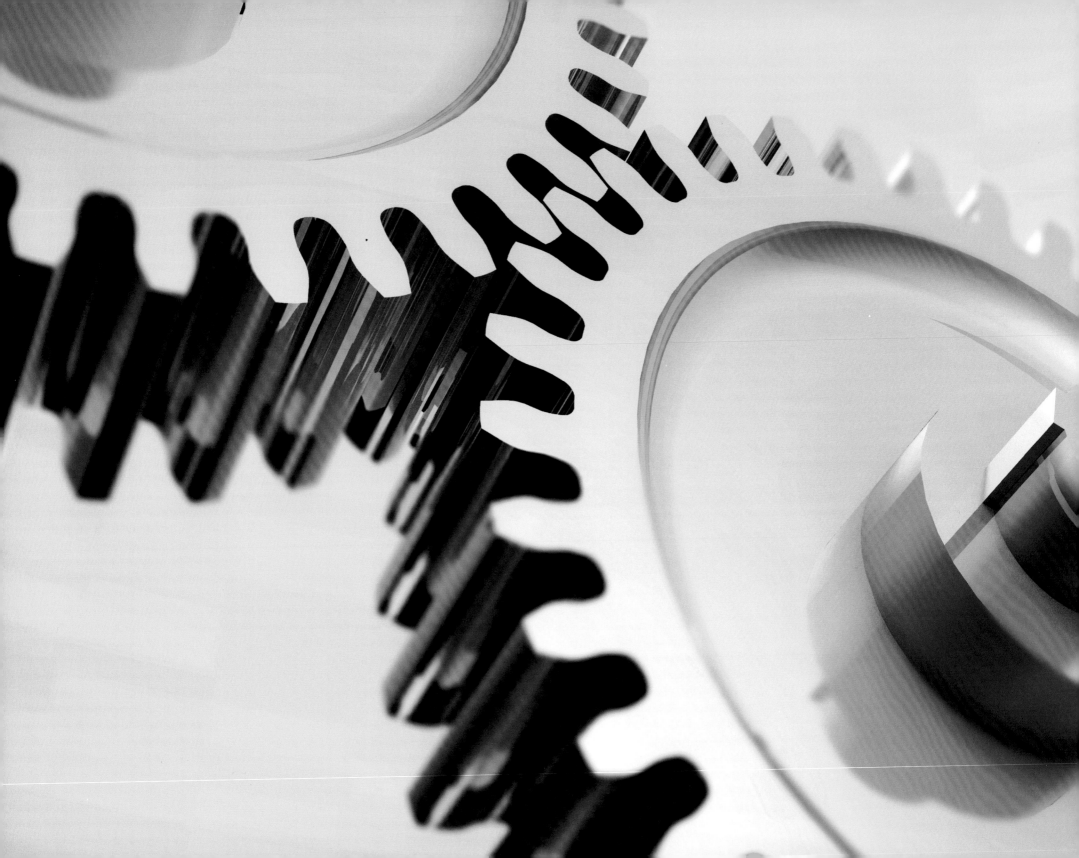

PROFILES OF COMPANIES AND ORGANIZATIONS
Manufacturing

Under Armour, Inc.

This entrepreneurial company has created technically advanced apparel engineered with superior fabric construction, exclusive moisture management, and proven innovation—all designed to be cool, dry, and light and improve athletic performance. Its New Prototype launch in 2008 heralded the company's Performance Training line of footwear. An innovative line of custom running footwear was introduced in 2009.

Above: From its inception in 1996, the Under Armour, Inc. "UA" logo has evolved much like the company's brand. Today the logo is a global symbol of the company's commitment to developing revolutionary performance apparel, footwear, and accessories. Right: Former University of Maryland special teams captain and founder and CEO of Under Armour, Kevin Plank started with an idea for a moisture-wicking T-shirt in 1995 and has developed an entire company devoted to making all athletes better, with a full line of performance apparel and footwear.

Under Armour, Inc.—a $725 million company as of the end of 2008—began small, with a simple plan to make a superior T-shirt. The T-shirt would keep athletes cool and dry when worn with their uniforms or other sportswear. Unlike traditional cotton T-shirts, which absorb moisture and remain wet, this successfully engineered product would provide compression while removing perspiration from the skin, help to regulate the athlete's body temperature, and enhance performance.

In the process of pioneering its moisture-wicking synthetic fabrics, Under Armour engineered an ideal sports T-shirt and revolutionized the industry. Today the company's performance gear—HeatGear®, ColdGear®, and AllSeasonGear®—work as hard as the athletes who wear them do. From its original T-shirt concept, Under Armour has branched into a full line of athletic performance apparel for men, women, and youths, including not only T-shirts, but also tank tops, mock turtleneck shirts, sweatshirts, outerwear, pants, leggings, underwear, bras, socks, hoods, caps, cleated footwear, and more. In 2008 it launched Performance Training footwear, branching out into the noncleated sports shoe category. In winter 2009 the company introduced its line of running footwear, which showcases the company's belief that all runners are athletes and all athletes run. Each shoe is specifically engineered to maximize the performance of today's generation of professional, collegiate, high school, and amateur athletes who are running as a sport or incorporating running as an essential component in their training regimen.

Creating the technology underlying Under Armour's diverse product assortment is complex, but gaining the benefits is simple: athletes are advised to wear HeatGear when the weather is hot, ColdGear when it is cold, and AllSeasonGear when

temperatures fall between the extremes. Comfort for the athlete was also the motivation behind the company's LockerTag heatseals, which display the player's jersey number clearly and stylishly on the garment. LockerTags have eliminated the need for an inside garment label and have become one of Under Armour's most recognized trademarks.

Lighter. Faster. Stronger. Better.

Under Armour was established *for* athletes *by* athletes, which means that the company's associates understand the demands of competition. Kevin Plank, founder and CEO of Under Armour, developed the concept in 1995 during his senior year as a student at the University of Maryland, where he majored in business management and was special teams captain of the football team.

Plank was dissatisfied with the players' cotton T-shirts—which became so wet and heavy with perspiration that they had to be changed in the middle of a game—so he began to search for fabrics that would offer an alternative. He tested designs for his performance shirt with former teammates, some of whom had begun playing in the National Football League (NFL). The result was a lightweight, synthetic undershirt that does not retain moisture or the weight of perspiration, dries in minutes, and fits comfortably and as closely as a second skin.

Under Armour's product line that began in 1996 with a superior undershirt for athletes has evolved into a wide array of sports gear that covers nearly every season, climate, and condition. Under Armour incorporates only the finest microfiber fabrics in its Moisture Transport System—which manages moisture to enable garments to slide over the body while keeping players cool, dry, and light throughout the course of a game or workout. Today the company continues to be devoted to discovering new product technologies designed to enhance athletic performance.

Across the Country and Around the Globe

Under Armour products enjoy a large following with athletes across the United States and in other countries as well. With headquarters in Baltimore, Maryland, the company's U.S. distribution includes its own specialty retail stores and numerous retail sporting goods chains. Under Armour also has official outfitter relationships with a number of college sports programs, and it is an authorized supplier of footwear to the NFL. Its international distribution is focused on the United Kingdom, France, and Germany, and there are third-party distributors in Australia, New Zealand, Italy, and the Benelux union of Belgium, the Netherlands, and Luxembourg, plus a licensee in Japan. Under Armour is the official kit supplier for the Welsh Rugby Union and the German soccer team Hannover 96, and it is the official Performance Product sponsor for the Toronto Maple Leafs National Hockey League team. The company maintains offices in Toronto, Canada, and in Hong Kong and Guangzhou, China; its European headquarters are at Amsterdam's Olympic Stadium.

Under Armour also makes its products available through the company's Web site located at www.underarmour.com.

Supporting Community Causes

Under Armour gives its time, energy, and support to a variety of organizations that focus on improving the well-being of children, fostering environmental initiatives, and finding a cure for cancer. The company also gives back to the community through in-kind donations, products, and financial assistance.

Above: Under Armour opened the first full-price retail specialty store in 2007 in Annapolis, Maryland. Greeting customers with the sounds of a stadium and a giant "Screaming E" statue, the Under Armour Specialty Store combines a passion for sports with state-of-the-art technology that defines the foundation of the brand.

Under Armour, Inc.

Under Armour team members prepare dinner several times each month for families staying at the Ronald McDonald House of Baltimore and support the charity's local chapter. Under Armour supports the V Foundation for Cancer Research, and the Under Armour Power in Pink campaign honors, supports, and strives to inspire women who are fighting breast cancer. The company believes that an active, athletic lifestyle and attitude can play a key role in battling the disease.

Under Armour supports the initiatives of the nonprofit Conservation Fund, which is dedicated to protecting the most important landscapes and waterways in the United States for future generations. Under Armour also provides monetary contributions, as well as donations of its many products, to the Rock Foundation, whose mission is to educate, empower, and enrich the lives of children worldwide. The Rock Foundation's physical-fitness and obesity-prevention program and its educational worldwide giving program are designed to improve the health and build the self-esteem of children and educate them about healthy eating, nutrition, and the life benefits of physical exercise.

UNDER ARMOUR: HIGHLIGHTS ON THE FAST TRACK TO SUCCESS

Above: Since 2004, Under Armour's Power in Pink campaign has worked to raise awareness, research, and treatment for breast cancer. A portion of sales from all Power in Pink Under Armour products are donated to multiple breast cancer organizations.

1995

Kevin Plank begins to explore the possibilities of creating his own line of performance undergarments for athletes.

1996

Plank puts his T-shirt design into production and markets the products with the Under Armour trademark. He and his partners build the business, working from a relative's basement and relying on word of mouth, high quality, and outstanding customer service to sell the product. The athletes also use their personal contacts in the sports industry to market their revolutionary T-shirt.

1998

The National Football League Europe signs Under Armour to be the official supplier of performance apparel for its teams. The company adds HeatGear®, ColdGear®, AllSeasonGear®, and LooseGear®—a version of HeatGear with a roomier fit—to its lineup.

1999

Warner Brothers contracts the company to outfit actors to play football in two forthcoming movies. Under Armour signs on with Eastbay, The Athletic SportsSource, and becomes the fastest-selling soft good product line in the Eastbay catalog's history.

2000

Under Armour becomes an official supplier to Major League Baseball. Under Armour products are distributed by more than 1,500 retail outlets.

2001

Under Armour becomes an official supplier to the National Hockey League and USA Baseball. The company's devoted clients include Olympic athletes, NASCAR drivers, amateur and professional athletes, and members of law enforcement and the military. Four of the top five sports apparel chains in the nation begin selling Under Armour apparel.

2002

Under Armour becomes the official outfitter to Major League Soccer and the U.S. Ski Team, and the company is named the best apparel supplier of the year by Sporting Goods Business magazine and The Sports Authority, one of America's largest full-line sporting goods retailers.

Going the Distance

In 2008 Under Armour found yet another way to fulfill its mission—by developing the TNP (The New Prototype) Performance Training program, which gives amateur and world-class athletes access to the latest methodology, drills, and knowledge to reach their athletic potential. The program combines proven training methods and techniques with the company's superior apparel and footwear to help athletes prepare for competition.

In 2009 Under Armour introduced its first-ever running footwear collection, with Cartilage® footwear technology. This independent suspension system serves as the "connective tissue" between a runner and the environment to enhance performance and provide an exceptionally stable and smooth workout. Under Armour created a multifaceted marketing campaign to showcase its running footwear and apparel. The advertisements depict world-class athletes training to run and running to train in a unique and poignant light.

For Under Armour, the principles that have proven successful on the playing field have led the company to prosperity. By striving to reach the highest standards in its business practices and the quality of its products, Under Armour, Inc. has created an environment of business growth and teamwork within the company. As a graduate of the University of Maryland, Kevin Plank is an inspiration and a mentor to students of all ages—for his business ethics and supplier code of conduct, for his accomplishments as an entrepreneur, and for his commitment to philanthropy.

Left: In 2009 Under Armour unveiled an innovative campaign to showcase running footwear and apparel. The advertisements highlight Under Armour's position that all runners are athletes and all athletes run. Above right: Under Armour announced its entrance into noncleated footwear in May 2008 with The New Prototype campaign, launching the company's first line of training footwear. Each shoe is specifically engineered to maximize an athlete's performance.

2004
Under Armour is named one of the 25 Leaders to Watch in the Sports Industry by the Sporting Goods Manufacturers Association.

2005
Plank is named Industrialist of the Year, which celebrates Maryland's visionary business leaders, by the Baltimore Museum of Industry. The company's Protect this House® marketing campaign is named Campaign of the Year by the Baltimore chapter of the American Marketing Association.

2006
Plank is named the Ernst & Young Entrepreneur of the Year National Winner in the Retail and Consumer Products Category. Under Armour enters the footwear business with the launch of cleated footwear. The company becomes an authorized supplier of footwear to the National Football League (NFL).

2007
Under Armour opens its first specialty retail store in Annapolis, Maryland. By year-end the company also operates 17 retail outlet stores and has 1,400 employees working at its Baltimore headquarters, distribution centers, and retail stores.

2008
Under Armour launches Performance Training footwear and opens a second specialty retail store in Aurora, Illinois. The company signs a five-year, $17.5 million contract with the University of Maryland (UM), College Park, to be the exclusive outfitter for all of UM's 27 varsity sports.

2009
Under Armour launches its first line of running footwear in January. In addition, the company becomes the presenting sponsor of the 2009 NFL Scouting Combine and announces a long-term partnership with Ripken Baseball. By April, Under Armour has 27 Factory House outlet stores and four specialty retail stores across the United States.

McCormick & Company, Inc.

Headquartered in Maryland, McCormick & Company, Inc. produces a wide range of food products that bring flavor and excitement to any eating occasion. The company is so prevalent in the food industry that the odds are good that almost everyone enjoys a McCormick product every day.

Above, all photos: McCormick & Company, Inc. is a leader in its industry because it provides consumers with products designed to help create restaurant-quality meals at home. The many well-known brands within the McCormick portfolio, such as those seen above, are evidence of McCormick's abilities in flavor development.

McCormick & Company, Inc. is a global leader in the manufacture, marketing, and distribution of spices, herbs, seasonings, specialty foods, and flavors to the entire food industry. The company focuses on adding flavor to all types of eating occasions, whether cooking at home, dining out, purchasing a quick service meal, or enjoying a snack. McCormick offers consumers a range of products from premium to value-priced.

From locations around the world, its consumer brands reach nearly 100 countries. The leading brands in the Americas are *McCormick, Lawry's,* and *Club House*. The company markets authentic ethnic brands, such as *Zatarain's, El Guapo, Thai Kitchen,* and *Simply Asia*; specialty items such as *Billy Bee* honey products; and seafood complements under the *Golden Dipt* and *Old Bay* labels. In Europe, the Middle East, and Africa, spices and herbs are sold under the *Ducros, Schwartz, McCormick,* and *Silvo* brands; the *Vahine* dessert line of products is sold in Europe. McCormick uses cutting-edge innovation to support the growth of its industrial

customers around the world. The company provides flavors for convenience foods, cereals, snacks, and beverages to leading food manufacturers. Global restaurant customers use McCormick coating blends, seasonings, and sauces to enhance their dishes.

Quality and Consistency

McCormick has a long history of selling products made with the best available ingredients. The company was founded in Baltimore in 1889 with the motto "Make the Best—Someone Will Buy It." Customers today benefit from McCormick's expertise in sensory testing, culinary research, food safety, and flavor applications, along with its commitment to quality.

McCormick relies on product development and innovation to help drive sales, which exceeded $3.1 billion in 2008. Customer demands—such as the desire for convenience, product quality, flavor trends, and natural ingredients—propel product

development. In January 2007, the company formed the McCormick Science Institute—an independent research organization—to investigate and deliver information about the health benefits of herbs and spices.

McCormick & Company, Inc. provides additional information about its U.S. brands on its Web site at www.mccormick.com and about the company at www.mccormickcorporation.com.

A Worldly Corporate Citizen

McCormick is part of an industry that for centuries has built a legacy of developing and participating in the global market. The company, mindful of its leadership position, maintains ethical business practices that include respect for its industry, its employees, and its communities.

As an agriculture-based business, McCormick is aware of the need to protect the Earth's resources. Its unparalleled global sourcing program continues to have a deep respect for the environment. It strives to conserve the natural resources used in its operations through reductions in energy, water, electricity, and fossil fuel usage; there are also solid waste disposal and solid waste recycling programs in place.

All italicized brands are registered trademarks of McCormick & Company, Inc.

McCormick's 7,500 employees form a diverse, worldwide team. Its Multiple Management philosophy encourages employees at all levels to take part in the decision-making process and to work together to expand the business.

The company considers that its charitable giving has no geographic boundaries. McCormick and its employees donate time and money to civic, educational, cultural, and health and wellness organizations in local communities.

In the United States and some of its foreign operations, the company holds an annual Charity Day, on which employees work an extra day and donate their wages to community charities. The company matches their donations. Initiated in 1941, this program today contributes over a million dollars annually to McCormick communities. The McCormick Unsung Heroes Awards program grants scholarships to high school athletes in the Baltimore area who demonstrate sportsmanship and teamwork. In 2004, the company introduced the McCormick Community Service Award to recognize employees who are exceptionally dedicated to improving their communities through volunteerism.

For more than 120 years, McCormick has been and continues to be driven by its "passion for flavor."

Above left: Convenience is as important as taste for today's busy consumer. McCormick creates meal solutions that save time while still delivering great flavor. Above center: The company is focused on innovation and responds to current trends that are in line with modern lifestyles. Above right: McCormick's expertise is also used to create flavors and ingredients for some of the world's most well-known food manufacturers. It is the flavor of McCormick that people enjoy in many popular food brands.

Redland Brick Inc.

Building on more than a century of producing brick in Maryland, this company operates one of the few plants in the country where genuine moulded bricks are still made by hand. It also offers machine-moulded and extruded styles of brick, along with special shapes and genuine clay pavers, providing bricks at every price range in an array of colors, shapes, and textures for residential, institutional, and commercial building projects.

Above: Redland Brick Inc.—one of the nation's leading manufacturers of hand-made brick, moulded and extruded-face brick, clay pavers, and shapes—provided specially made Redland Camden–blend modular bricks for Oriole Park at Camden Yards.

Redland Brick Inc.'s Cushwa plant in Williamsport, Maryland, has been making quality bricks the old-fashioned way—by hand—since 1872, and authentic Cushwa-hand-moulded bricks have played a role in the architecture of Maryland. Through the same, time-honored process that has been used for centuries—a process that cannot be replicated by any of today's brick-making machines—skilled, experienced brickcrafters press clay into one sand-coated wooden mould at a time. Cushwa products are distinct with an antique texture, soft contours, rich color, and individualism that allow a project to become an instant classic. These bricks can be found on diverse projects ranging from prestigious buildings and complexes to dream homes. In Maryland, they are used in Oriole Park at Camden Yards, the Baltimore Ravens home M&T Bank Stadium, and in some of the state's finest residences. At its Rocky Ridge plant located outside of Thurmont, Maryland, Redland Brick also makes machine-moulded brick products. The Cushwa and Rocky Ridge plants are established as premier moulded-brick producers in the United States.

Redland Brick operates four conveniently located plants. Along with its Cushwa plant in Williamsport, where the company is headquartered, and its Rocky Ridge plant, it operates the Harmar plant in suburban Pittsburgh, Pennsylvania, and the KF plant in South Windsor, Connecticut. Redland Brick is a wholly owned subsidiary of Belden Holding & Acquisition, Inc. Both companies are ISO-9002 certified and their brick products are distributed across the United States and Canada.

Using natural resources such as fireclay and red shale, Redland Brick's numerous product lines, including its hand- and machine-moulded bricks as well as its extruded bricks, are available in a spectrum of colors, textures, shapes, and sizes. In 2008 Redland Brick launched its Tuscan Collection of genuine clay pavers. The Tuscan Collection is the industry's first line of mass-produced, six-inch by nine-inch and six-inch by six-inch moulded brick pavers. It will complement the company's existing clay paver products. Redland Brick's diverse portfolio appeals to home-owners, designers, architects, and developers for use in residential, institutional, or commercial applications.

Technologically Advanced Manufacturing

At its Rocky Ridge plant, Redland Brick combines modern technology with its brick moulding to make its machine-moulded bricks. In 2006 the company revamped this facility with advanced processes that streamline manufacturing, thereby increasing its production capacity to meet increased product demand. The Rocky Ridge plant's machine-moulded bricks are fired in energy-efficient, computer-controlled kilns, maximizing production of the plant's uniquely textured moulded bricks.

The company's Harmar and KF plants also make extruded bricks, which are produced by forcing mud through an opening to form long ribbons that are sliced into specific sizes. At its Harmar plant, which was constructed in Pittsburgh in 2001, Redland Brick uses modern, state-of-the-art, fully automated equipment. It manufactures fireclay, red shale, and sand-coated extruded bricks with ingredients mined from the clay and shale deposits it has on-site at the Harmar plant. Redland Brick's Harmar products are known for their high quality, strength, consistent size, and durability.

At its KF plant in South Windsor, Redland Brick uses leading-edge manufacturing technologies to create new products in response to customer desires. This plant makes extruded brick for territories in New England and the mid-Atlantic region. In order to match the bricks that were used in early-20th-century buildings in these regions, the KF plant puts to use unique firing methods. Its product line has a broad spectrum of colors and textures custom-designed to fit the brick styles and architecture of early New England and Colonial America.

Redland Brick provides additional information about its products on its Web site at www.redlandbrick.com.

Respecting the Environment

By nature, bricks are construction materials of intrinsic durability, making them ideal for recycling and thereby reducing waste. Additionally, the company contributes to a greener environment through its energy-efficient, clean-burning, natural gas kilns. There is no greener building product than brick. Made from an abundant supply of clay and shale, brick also features a 100-year or longer lifespan. Brick is 100 percent recyclable, able to be used either on another building or as landscaping or fill material. Even more impressive—Redland Brick's policy is that after it mines the shale from a quarry, it adds back topsoil, plants grasses, and reverts the former mine back into a wildlife habitat or sets it aside as conservation property. And given the close proximity of its two Maryland plants to the state's largest metropolitan areas, the company is also reducing greenhouse gases with short transport distances.

The versatile products of Redland Brick—from its authentic handmade or machine-moulded brick to its modern architectural extruded brick—are created by a company that continually builds on its long experience in making high quality bricks. Redland Brick is proud of its history of supplying brick for Maryland's buildings since 1872.

Above left: The facing on this private residence was constructed with Redland Shenandoah antique over-size with a Victorian accent brick. Above right: This Long & Foster Real Estate building is an outstanding example of different types of special handmade blends of Redland bricks.

Alcore Inc.

This leading manufacturer of high quality structural honeycomb core materials combines advanced processing technologies and longtime expertise with superior customer service. It has expanded its facility, located in Edgewood, to accommodate aerospace companies' and other manufacturers' growing needs for its durable, lightweight products.

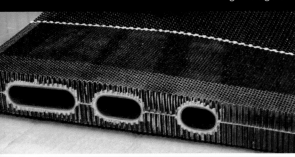  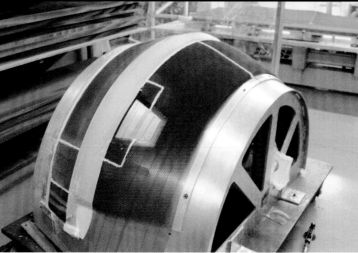

Above, all photos: Alcore excels in value-added processing for both nonmetallic Aramid fiber honeycomb and aluminum honeycomb. Aluminum honeycomb core materials made by Alcore are available in varying cell sizes and densities to accommodate the needs of aerospace, commerce, and industry. Opposite page: Alcore technology recently expanded to include a 50,000-square-foot facility that houses complex, five-axis machining of advanced commercial and military aircraft honeycomb structures.

A leader in providing high quality, lightweight structural honeycomb core materials to the aerospace, marine, construction, rail, and other industries, Alcore Inc. is a customer-focused company. By offering a variety of structural core materials, along with sophisticated machining and processing and broad engineering expertise, the company successfully delivers products that are fully responsive to its customer's precise needs.

Honeycomb core material forms a lightweight, rigid, and durable component when placed between sheets of metal or other composite materials. Alcore manufactures aluminum honeycomb core for the aerospace industry and other sectors that need materials offering crush resistance, impact resistance, and energy absorption. For aerospace use, honeycomb is machined and formed into components for engine nacelles, acoustics panels, thrust-reverser panels, landing-gear doors, and more.

Honeycomb core material is also used in nonaerospace applications, such as lightweight interior furnishings for mass-transit rail cars and high-speed, ocean-going ferries; sandwich panels in high-performance hulls for yachts; clean-room partitions and laser cutting tables; and the exteriors of high-rise buildings.

Alcore can perform special processing for both metallic and nonmetallic honeycomb, ranging from simple operations such as trimming and chamfering to more complex processes such as potting densification, five-axis computer numerical control (CNC) machining, and core splicing and stabilization. It offers in-house computer-aided design

and manufacturing and provides customer support throughout each process, from the concept stage until the finished product is fabricated to exact specifications.

Located in Lakeside Business Park in Edgewood, Maryland, Alcore employs a highly skilled workforce of 200 people. This includes a skillful engineering and production staff that is focused on lean manufacturing techniques designed for minimum waste and on-time deliveries, as well as an experienced team of service professionals who are dedicated to providing the finest service and sales support, prompt and accurate replies to customer inquiries, and overnight delivery. Alcore provides additional information about its products and services on its Web site at www.alcore.com.

Alcore's history dates back to 1958, when its predecessor company Bloomingdale Rubber began making adhesives and honeycomb core. Today Alcore is part of the M. C. Gill Corporation in El Monte, California, which provides access to a full line of Nomex and Kevlar honeycomb core and expands Alcore Inc.'s clientele worldwide.

PROFILES OF COMPANIES AND ORGANIZATIONS

Professional Services

Murthy Law Firm

'We know immigration matters!℠' is the slogan of this high-profile U.S. immigration law firm, which strives to help every person who has the dream of becoming a U.S. citizen. Its experienced attorneys and staff develop legal and ethical strategies and provide outstanding service, while educating clients and the entire immigrant community on continually changing immigration laws and regulations.

Upon reflection, Sheela Murthy often recalls her entire family—her parents and the three small girls—riding together on the family's only mode of transportation: a scooter her father had managed to purchase as a young engineer serving in the Indian army. Growing up in India, Murthy learned the value of an education. She was a diligent student in a country where educating daughters was uncommon. Allowed to pursue a profession in law, she ultimately earned an LLM from Harvard Law School and is now a regular guest speaker at her alma mater.

After working in prestigious firms in New York and Baltimore, Murthy became an entrepreneur in 1994, starting her own law firm focused on U.S. immigration law. Having personally endured the difficult process of becoming a U.S. citizen, Murthy was motivated by the lack of care and service provided by her own immigration attorney, who was unconcerned about the fear and anxiety experienced by his client while she pursued her American dream. Murthy began humbly, with a fax machine on her dining table, however she empathized with her clients and was passionate about their cases; and she did something unusual in the legal profession—she provided free information, explaining U.S. immigration laws and regulations to anyone who contacted her.

Left: Sheela Murthy is president, managing attorney, and founder of the Murthy Law Firm.

Today the Murthy Law Firm is considered to be a world leader in U.S. immigration law, helping businesses across the nation to bring the best and the brightest to American shores. Talent from abroad complements and augments a strong U.S. workforce, keeping the country competitive in a global market and enabling companies to maintain their operations in the United States. Murthy's original, unconventional practice continues to serve those with questions, as evidenced by the popularity of the firm's Web site, which was accessed an average of two million times per month in 2008. The site provides hundreds of articles that explain the law in layperson's terms. The firm's attorneys apply their wealth of knowledge and experience in representing clients that include professors, researchers, physicians, and highly skilled workers, as well as technology companies, universities, hospitals, and businesses of all sizes to find creative options within immigration law. Murthy's ethics and philosophy, her international recognition for her legal skills, her marketing savvy, and her philanthropy are all reflected in the firm's slogan "We know immigration matters!℠"

A member of the World Trade Center Institute, the Murthy Law Firm is a successful Maryland company and a valuable member of the community, employing a dozen attorneys and more than 50 paralegals and support staff members. Led by the example set by Murthy as the firm's president, managing attorney, and founder, staff members are dedicated to helping their clients who endure the complex and often grueling process toward living and working in the United States.

The caring and generous spirit with which the firm began flows into community projects supported by the family foundation—the MurthyFoundation—begun by Murthy and her husband, Vasant Nayak, following the events of September 11, 2001. Remaining connected to their native India and grateful to their adopted homeland of America, the couple has sought to give back. Murthy and Nayak believe that a business should not be "all brain and no heart." The MurthyFoundation is at the heart of the Murthy Law Firm, offering support to the most vulnerable members of society. In 2008 Murthy committed $1 million to United Way of Central Maryland for specific programs to help U.S. immigrants as well as women and children in Baltimore and in Bangalore (Bengaluru), India.

A few of the projects supported by the MurthyFoundation in and around Baltimore are the Multi-Ethnic Domestic Violence Project of the Women's Law Center of Maryland, Inc.; the Girl Scouts of Central Maryland's Beyond Bars program; and

at Harvard Law School, the endowment of a financial aid fund for LLMs and an immigration law travel fund to highlight immigration law while focusing attention on immigration as a symbol of the rich heritage of Americans as a people.

In India, among other programs, the MurthyFoundation provides support for 80 women in adult literacy and microlending programs in Delhi and Neemrana through Khushii; fights dowry burning, torture, and death through support to Vimochana Development Society; and helps provide breakfast, uniforms, transportation, and some scholarships for approximately 1,900 children of the Chennakeshava School in Bangalore. Also supporting the goal of United Way International by helping to expand that organization's operation in India, the MurthyFoundation believes, "From Baltimore to Bangalore, Each Life Matters!℠" More information on the Murthy Law Firm, as well as hundreds of articles on U.S. immigration laws and regulations, is available on its award-winning Web site at www.murthy.com.

Above left: Attorneys at Murthy Law Firm develop legal strategies with a commitment to excellence.
Top right: In Neemrana, India, Murthy stands with a group of women who are empowered by health and microlending programs supported by the MurthyFoundation.
Above right: Understanding that hungry children cannot learn, the MurthyFoundation provides breakfast at the Chennakeshava School.

The Mergis Group

This leading full-service recruiting and staffing company provides solutions designed to meet the specialized needs of businesses from small-to-midsize companies and Fortune 500 corporations in many industries. The Mergis Group places qualified, high-caliber professionals in positions from full-time to project-based assignments through a nationwide network of offices.

The Mergis Group is an expert at bridging the gap between opportunity and high-performance talent. With offices in Baltimore, Bethesda, and Columbia, Maryland, the company enables working professionals to advance their careers while helping small-to-midsize businesses and larger corporations hire the best talent available. Through the use of time-efficient and cost-effective methods and a nationwide network of offices, the company matches a broad range of specialized professionals for direct hire and project-based assignments with companies that need their skills.

Above: The Mergis Group builds loyal relationships—with both clients and candidates—that translate into high-value results.

The Mergis Group's successful search process begins with learning about an organization and its recruitment needs. It continues with interviewing both the client and candidates and is followed by making an official offer and counseling the candidate regarding the career opportunities.

The Mergis Group staff of specialists possesses strong recruiting skills and specific industry knowledge within their fields. The company applies a proven 11-step search process, offering many advantages that have a direct impact on its clients' success, including a full understanding of the client's industry, corporate environment, operations, and staffing needs; and the ability to respond quickly to identify cost-effective solutions to these needs.

Making Connections that Work

The Mergis Group's operations are divided into specialty areas.

- **Interim Executives**—Interim placement of executive-level accounting and finance professionals to help with business start-ups, initial public offerings,

Sarbanes-Oxley compliance, corporate relocations, business closures, financial restatements, and special projects;

- **Finance and Accounting**—Direct hire and interim placement of chief financial officers, controllers, tax specialists, financial analysts, senior and staff accountants, and bookkeepers;
- **Sales and Marketing**—Recruitment of sales and marketing specialists in all industries, including financial services, telecommunications, and technology;
- **Banking**—Recruitment of portfolio managers, banking and trust officers, treasury analysts, marketing and investor relations specialists, commercial loan officers, operations officers, telemarketers, managers of customer service centers, and executive division managers;
- **Mortgage Banking**—Recruitment of retail and wholesale mortgage loan officers, loan processors, loan closers, post-closers, and secondary marketing specialists;
- **Human Resources**—Recruitment of human resources administrators and vice presidents, compensation and benefits managers and directors, compensation analysts, and human resources generalists;
- **Engineering and Manufacturing**—Placement services for managers of design, quality, materials, energy, and special projects;
- **Technology**—Full life cycle recruitment of permanent and contract information technology (IT) specialists, including programmers, analysts, help-desk administrators, system administrators, and IT directors.

Serving the Mid-Atlantic Region

The Mergis Group was founded in1979 as Don Richard Associates of Baltimore. It continually expanded, and in 1996 it became The A. J. Burton Group. The company grew to become the largest accounting and finance recruiting company in the region, gaining a reputation for service excellence, for its commitment to the highest ethical standards, and for building strong relationships with clients and the business community.

In 1998 A. J. Burton merged with Interim Services, which is now staffing industry leader Spherion Corporation. In early 2007, Spherion launched The Mergis Group as a separate division of 36 offices nationwide focused on professional skills.

The Mergis Group is a division of the recruiting and staffing company Spherion, which is headquartered in Fort Lauderdale, Florida, and operates more than 630 offices throughout North America. Spherion has been a pioneer in its industry for more than 60 years and is one of North America's largest employers. It delivers innovative workforce solutions that help businesses improve their performance by screening and placing workers in positions ranging from flexible to temporary-to-hire to direct hire. The Mergis Group provides additional information about its services on its Web site at www.mergisgroup.com.

Above: The Mergis Group works closely with clients to fully understand the key drivers of their business so they receive the highest return on their talent investment.

First Data

A recognized leader in developing innovative technologies and solutions that support commerce around the world, this payment processing company uses its data-intelligence expertise to help merchants, financial institutions, and government agencies reduce costs, drive revenue, and manage risks while making consumer transactions easy and secure.

Headquartered in Denver, Colorado, First Data serves more than 5.3 million merchant locations, more than 2,000 card issuers and their customers, and millions of consumers worldwide. Over 26,000 employees provide transaction processing, mobile commerce, loyalty programs, data analytics, gift card solutions, and fraud and risk management services to clients worldwide.

Gathering Intelligence from Transactions

First Data's award-winning analytics technology helps its clients make smarter, time-sensitive decisions to detect and prevent fraudulent transactions, deliver relevant loyalty offers, and predict likelihood to pay overdue balances. With cutting-edge innovation, knowledge, and expertise, First Data provides clients with not only the highest level of data integration to optimize business decisions, but also a unique customer support model to deliver continuous business improvements in operation efficiency, revenue generation, and customer experience.

First Data's vision is "to accelerate the evolution of commerce around the world by being the global leader in processing transaction data of all kinds, harnessing the power of that data, and delivering innovations in secure infrastructure, intelligence, and insight." In other words, whenever people use a debit or credit card, visit an ATM, buy a gift card, or write a check, First Data will most likely be part of the process that makes it happen.

Local Operations

First Data's Hagerstown, Maryland, office is dedicated to merchant services, providing operational and sales support to customers, and enhancing client relationships through first-response service centers. Employing more than 2,100 people, the First Data Maryland facility houses multiple support areas, including the company's Global Customer Service Operations unit, which runs a 24-hours-a-day, seven-days-a-week call center and handles more than 58 million calls annually to service merchant clients all over the world. The Compliance and Dispute Operations division handles approximately

Above: A leading provider of electronic commerce and payment solutions, First Data helps businesses safely and efficiently process customer transactions and interpret information related to those transactions.

First Data believes that the way people pay for things tells a story. By listening to that story, and the information it reveals, companies can increase sales and revenue. A global technology leader in electronic commerce, First Data helps businesses process customer payments safely and efficiently while also helping them understand valuable information about their customers' buying habits. The company enables financial institutions, merchants, government agencies, and other businesses to build stronger, more profitable customer relationships and offers those same customers a secure, fast, and easy way to process purchases.

three million transaction disputes on behalf of merchant clients each year. The Hagerstown office is a recent recipient of a Workplace Excellence Award, an award presented by the Alliance for Workplace Excellence that recognizes businesses in the greater Washington, D.C., area that demonstrate outstanding commitment to balanced leadership and to the overall success of a company's workforce.

Partnering with Communities

First Data believes in staying connected to the communities in which its employees live and work by providing jobs and through active social involvement in each community. The company demonstrates its values through philanthropic sponsorships, employee volunteerism, employee gift-match programs, disaster relief efforts, and product donations. In 2008 First Data made a global charitable impact of more than $4.5 million; employee volunteers gave more than 4,500 hours to charitable organizations; and First Data was ranked sixth on *Fortune* magazine's 2008 list of America's Most Admired Companies for the Financial Data Services Industry.

In addition to donating time, talent, and other valuable resources, the company makes meaningful investments in business entrepreneurship and financial literacy programs that fuel the economy and build the business leaders of tomorrow.

Additional information about First Data can be found on the company's Web site at www.firstdata.com.

Above: First Data allows businesses and consumers to feel secure about electronic payment transactions. Left: First Data supports the communities it serves in many ways, such as financial education programs.

This Rockville-headquartered company provides a broad range of research and professional services primarily to the federal government. The company was founded in Colorado in 1963 and moved to Maryland in 1965. It also maintains research offices in Bethesda, Maryland, and in Raleigh, North Carolina; Atlanta, Georgia; and Houston, Texas, as well as in several international locations.

Westat is an employee-owned research organization. In 2008 it had a salaried staff of more than 1,900 people. Its total full-time equivalent employment is more than 3,500 with the inclusion of its nationwide data-collection staff. For more than 30 years, employee ownership has helped the company attract and retain outstanding employees and has played a vital part in its success. Employee ownership at Westat motivates employees and also gives the company the freedom and incentive to build new capabilities with long-term investments. Its staff capabilities are in statistical design and analysis, survey operations, scientific and clinical research, program evaluation, and computer systems. Many of its staff members have experience in important subject and program areas.

Since Westat's beginning, its growth has reflected the increasing importance of high quality research and timely information to its clients. Its projects serve a broad range of needs, such as assessing the educational achievement of students, understanding health and environmental risks, gaining new knowledge of the causes of disease, evaluating the performance of social programs, and supporting the development of policy and regulations in many areas of government. In meeting these needs, Westat combines a well-established reputation with a constant effort to innovate and build new capabilities.

In recent years Westat has expanded to serve new clients in the foundation sector and in state and local governments, to deliver Internet-based public-information services, and to conduct health research studies and clinical trials for government and biotechnology clients, both domestic and international.

The Westat campus on Research Boulevard in Rockville is the home office for the vast majority of the company's salaried staff. With 430,000 square feet of office space, a modern conference and training center, and data-collection and methodological research facilities, the campus enables project teams to work closely across multiple assignments and to stay in close proximity to many of their clients.

Westat provides additional information about its services on its Web site at www.westat.com.

Right: Members of the Westat Operations Committee, from left, seated, are James Smith, senior vice president; Joseph Hunt, president; Graham Kalton, chairman of the board; and Veronica Nieva, vice president; and, standing, Thomas McKenna, executive vice president; Alexander Ratnofsky, senior vice president; Renee Slobasky, senior vice president; Stephen Durako, vice president; and David Morganstein, vice president.

Westat®

PROFILES OF COMPANIES AND ORGANIZATIONS

Security and Protection Services

BFPE International
(Baltimore Fire Protection & Equipment)

This privately held woman-owned full-service fire protection and security company has earned the reputation for quality service and integrity by maintaining a highly trained workforce and a customer-focused culture. Founded in 1970, the company specializes in providing its customers with Total Fire Protection and security systems installation and service solutions.

BFPE's customers range from small-to-midsize companies to Fortune 500 corporations. BFPE also provides installation and inspection services for local, state, and federal government projects (and holds high-level security clearances, if required). The company's products and services are equally diverse. BFPE installs and provides service for fire detection and alarm, sprinkler, clean agent fire suppression, early-warning smoke detection, restaurant-cooking-equipment fire suppression, and security systems, along with portable fire extinguishers. BFPE also provides Underwriter Laboratories (UL)–listed central station monitoring.

Life safety is the paramount goal of BFPE International. A tightly knit group of experienced employees are trained and dedicated to fulfilling this goal. The company's sales, engineering, and outside technical personnel are required to obtain National Institute for Certification in Engineering Technologies (NICET) training and certification, as well as continual manufacturer's training.

From Pennsylvania to South Carolina and from Ohio to Delaware and Maryland, BFPE International (Baltimore Fire Protection & Equipment) provides customers with full-service fire protection and security systems from installation to preventative maintenance and testing. Headquartered in Hanover, Maryland, BFPE has branch offices in Chesapeake and Sterling, Virginia; Lancaster and York, Pennsylvania; Dover, Delaware; and Wilmington, Clayton, and Laurinburg, North Carolina. Every office provides sales, installation, inspection, testing, maintenance, and engineering services.

The Original Spark

When James "Jim" Boyer founded BFPE in 1970, he was a history teacher with an entrepreneurial streak and the courage to take a risk. Boyer saw an opportunity to start a business when he learned that Baltimore's municipal regulations regarding fire prevention were becoming more stringent—especially for restaurants with commercial cooking equipment. Boyer began his fire protection business in his grandmother's basement with a thousand dollars of borrowed money. Boyer sold fire extinguishing systems during the day, and he and his brother installed the equipment in the evening. Gradually the company gained clients, and by 1971 the business had moved from its basement operation into an industrial space in Cockeysville, Maryland.

Boyer chose his wife, Pam Boyer, to manage the service department, setting the stage for the company's future. Determined to overcome objections she encountered in a male-dominated arena, she began learning the business herself by watching and working with service technicians in the field. For the next 20 years the Boyers built BFPE into one of Baltimore's leading fire protection companies.

Building for the Future

In 1994 Jim Boyer passed away and his wife found herself at the helm of BFPE. Determined to carry on the business, she continued serving customers with the guidance of her husband's philosophy: "Take care of the customer and the rest will take care of itself."

By this time, the company had opened multiple offices on the East Coast and changed the name from Baltimore Fire Protection & Equipment to BFPE International to better reflect the out-of-state growth. Under Pam Boyer's leadership, and with the help of the BFPE team, the company continued to flourish through acquisitions and expanded services.

BFPE evolved from a company that specialized in specialty gases, portable fire extinguishers, and restaurant-fire-suppression systems to a company that supplied Total Fire Protection for all clients. Many businesses wanted a single-source vendor that could provide all of their fire-protection needs as opposed to subcontracting multiple companies that could provide service for only a part of

their property's fire protection. BFPE became an industry pioneer in interconnecting these services, resulting in significant business growth.

From 1994 to 2007, the business grew and annual revenues increased from $9 million to more than $60 million. Today BFPE is the leading fire protection company in the Baltimore region, one of the top such companies in the nation, and rated the largest woman-owned company in greater Baltimore by *Baltimore Business Journal*. Its reputation for quality, service, and integrity has spread around the world, leading to customers in Bermuda, Germany, Italy, Egypt, and Saudi Arabia. Pam Boyer and a dedicated team of more than 500 employees work diligently to uphold the founder's legacy; using talent, energy, imagination, and time to help others have better, more enjoyable, and safer lives.

BFPE provides additional information about its services and products on its Web site at www.bfpe.com.

Above left: Pam Boyer, owner and president of BFPE International, was featured on the cover of *Baltimore SmartCEO* magazine. Above right: Pam Boyer is shown with her late husband, Jim, who founded the company in 1970.

PROFILES OF COMPANIES AND ORGANIZATIONS
Technology, Information Technology, and Telecommunications

The Knowland Group™

Serving over 1,000 clients across the United States, Canada, Mexico, and beyond, this multimillion-dollar company helps hotels and convention centers ensure that their meeting spaces do not go unused. The Knowland Group knows that its success is based on its clients' success, so it works to increase each client's bottom line and competitive advantage.

research services as they expanded across multiple time zones. The firm now services more than 1,000 hotels in over 100 metropolitan areas from Alaska and Hawaii to Western Europe and the Middle East. Since its founding, the company has expanded its product offerings, creating a family of solutions designed to increase bookings for its hotel and convention center clients.

Year	Clients	Markets	Workers	Revenue Growth
2005	63	23	38	–
2006	226	61	125	558.9%
2007	507	70	158	161.4%
2008	902	103	188	104.4%

Above: The Knowland Group™ services hotel and convention center clients in more than 10 time zones worldwide. Right: Knowland CEO Michael K. McKean believes in innovation and in rethinking accepted and entrenched business practices.

Company Overview

The Knowland Group™ is one of the fastest growing providers of sales and marketing products and services to the meetings and conventions segment of the hospitality industry. Offering one of the most comprehensive databases of organizations with meeting needs in the world, The Knowland Group has become a premier provider of software solutions, marketing intelligence, hospitality sales–lead generation, and hotel and conference center booking services.

Fast Growth from the Start

Started in 2004 with only two employees, Knowland had expanded to over 250 clients by the spring of 2007 when the company opened a 7,000-square-foot call and operations center on the Eastern Shore of Maryland. With space for more than 100 specialized workers, the location has served the firm well, supporting field

The focus of Knowland Group CEO Michael K. McKean has always been to create cutting-edge products that add value for customers' businesses. "I like finding creative, talented people who can internalize our company's vision: to not only develop and support innovative software solutions, but also to rethink accepted business processes in a new light," says McKean. "We look for opportunities where we can prove ourselves quickly and then scale up in a defined target market. The group sales segment of the hotel industry has been a great success, and we are excited about future opportunities within the global travel industry."

The Knowland Event Booking Center

In April 2007 Knowland opened its Event Booking Center (EBC). Designed to provide outsourced hotel sales and sales support services to the firm's clients worldwide, the EBC has proven a huge success. Throughout its short history, demand has grown steadily as highly trained workers carry out hundreds of client requests per day. From researching corporate meeting plans and upcoming event schedules to quality control follow-up calls, sales appointment and site visit scheduling, and complete outsourced group booking services, thousands of hoteliers depend on Knowland personnel to help keep their meeting venues filled to capacity every day.

Knowland Group Products: Revolutionary Software Solutions

In addition to the Event Booking Center, Knowland offers a family of cutting-edge software solutions—ranging from market intelligence applications designed to give real-time visibility into a client's competitors to robust sales force automation and customer relationship–management tools—that are used by thousands of hoteliers every day. Just one example of Knowland's products is the software tool INSIGHT. Launched in 2007 and now used by over 400 hotels, this product is based on a database of virtually every organization that holds events in North America. Designed as a lead-generation tool for sales managers, INSIGHT quickly and easily generates thousands of qualified leads for its users.

In 2009 Knowland launched its Group Rating technology. With multiple patents pending, Group Rating is designed to identify high-probability sales leads for clients based on an organization's past meeting activity. This solution combines proprietary data-mining and microtargeting techniques developed by the firm's engineers with an easy and intuitive user interface. Group Rating was rolled out across multiple products and is poised to revolutionize the industry.

Exciting Future

The Knowland Group's continuous stream of innovative products and its ongoing development of value-added services for its customers ensure its position as a premier provider of marketing intelligence, lead-generation, and sales solutions for the hospitality and event planning industries. Additional information is available on the company's Web site at www.knowlandgroup.com.

Above left: Employees at the Knowland Event Booking Center carry out hundreds of client requests each day. Above right: Thousands of hoteliers depend on Knowland personnel to keep their meeting venues filled every day.

Verizon

Strengthening the Maryland economy, this innovative and leading-edge telecommunications company is dedicated to delivering high quality communication, entertainment, and information services through its advanced, all-fiber network that takes fiber-optic technology to its clients' homes and businesses.

Verizon Wireless's extensive and reliable network provides wireless voice and data services to 80 million customers across the United States. And with the recent acquisition of Alltel, Verizon Wireless is now the nation's largest wireless provider.

Verizon Business provides integrated communications solutions and Internet backbone services to businesses and governments around the world.

Technology Innovator

Verizon is investing in Maryland's economic future by deploying an advanced network infrastructure. William Roberts, regional president of Verizon Maryland and the District of Columbia, believes that a robust communications network is "key to the state's economic success." Through an investment that exceeds $1.4 billion, Verizon is bringing innovative technologies and a superior network to Maryland that will contribute to and advance the state's economy. Verizon's 12,000 employees in Maryland maintain more than three million telephone lines and serve more than two million customers.

Verizon's capabilities allow Maryland businesses to compete with their counterparts anywhere in the world. The company can support any application or bandwidth needs that businesses require, including Ethernet data and voice services.

Pioneering Fiber-Optic Technology

Verizon is the first telecommunications company to use fiber-optic technology as it updates its copper wire to homes and businesses. Verizon's Fiber to the Premises (FTTP) connects the company's clients to its network by means of fiber, which delivers nearly unlimited bandwidth and faster connections; is more reliable and easily monitored and maintained; and enables a variety of uses, including interactive content.

Above: Maryland shoppers can experience the innovative features of Verizon's all-fiber-optic FiOS TV and FiOS Internet services at one of several local stores.

Formed through a merger in 2000, Verizon has become a leader in the telecommunications industry, delivering a variety of wireline and wireless services through its multiple business units.

Verizon Telecom offers communication, information, and entertainment services to customers in 28 states—including Maryland and the District of Columbia.

In 2004 Verizon began installing its all-fiber network in Maryland. With more than 57 million feet of fiber in the state, FTTP is currently available in six counties in

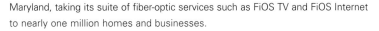

Maryland, taking its suite of fiber-optic services such as FiOS TV and FiOS Internet to nearly one million homes and businesses.

- Verizon's FiOS TV services deliver high quality images and sounds and include more than 1,000 all-digital channels, an expanding number of high-definition channels, video on demand, interactive media, and multicultural programming.
- The company's FiOS Internet services include the fastest connection available in the United States with download speeds up to 50 megabits per second (Mbps) and upload speeds up to 20 Mbps.
- Its 20/20 symmetrical service is ideal for online activities such as videoconferencing, social networking, digital media uploading, and multiple player online games.

High-Speed Internet

Verizon continues to expand delivery of its high-speed Internet service over its existing copper network. Over 80 percent of households in Maryland served by Verizon have access to this high-speed Internet service. Verizon has equipped 100 percent of Verizon switching stations across the state with this technology. This widespread broadband product offers speeds of up to 7.1 Mbps. Verizon is clearly bringing the benefits of broadband to Maryland. Additional information is available on Verizon's Web site at www.verizon.com.

A Good Employer

Verizon is one of the top employers in Maryland, providing meaningful employment to over 12,000 employees across the state. A good employer, Verizon provides its

Maryland workers with among the best compensation and benefits in the telecommunications industry, paying over $200 million annually in employee health care benefits alone. Verizon sets the standard in the industry for minority business contract rates, and is the first in the telecom industry to require that network-hardware manufacturers help to reduce energy consumption by meeting challenging new standards for upgrades to their networks.

A Good Neighbor

Verizon is a good corporate citizen, giving back to the community with a focus on literacy and education; health and safety; and the awareness, recovery, and prevention of domestic violence.

Verizon's employees in Maryland maintain this spirit of giving and volunteerism by donating their time and resources to the community. In 2008 Verizon Maryland employees and retirees volunteered nearly 48,000 hours for nonprofit organizations. The Verizon Foundation, the company's charitable wing, matched employee charitable donations with nearly $792,000 through its matching gifts program. The Verizon Foundation also donated over $1.5 million to 864 nonprofit groups in Maryland in 2008.

Verizon's free *Thinkfinity* Web site is the company's keynote vehicle for delivering powerful educational and literacy tools to teachers, librarians, students, parents, and nonprofits.

Verizon's *HopeLine* program is a phone recycling and reuse program begun by Verizon Wireless in 2001. It has distributed 80,000 phones with 160 million minutes of free wireless service to domestic violence agencies for their clients' use.

Verizon is delivering advanced communication, information, and entertainment services to homes and businesses and creating a stronger economy in Maryland. The company plans to invest even more in its sophisticated network infrastructure and in community programs across the state.

Above left: Verizon's Maryland headquarters office is located in the heart of downtown Baltimore. Above right: Verizon employees show their spirit of giving and teamwork as they race for charity in support of Catholic Charities Dragon Boat Races.

TeleCommunication Systems, Inc.

By engineering and delivering highly reliable wireless communications technology, this innovative company is a leader in text messaging, location-based technology that includes E9-1-1 services and commercial applications, and secure satellite-based communications systems. The company's cutting-edge solutions are valuable to global wireless and VoIP carriers, cable MSOs, and the U.S. Departments of Defense, State, and Homeland Security.

Above: TeleCommunication Systems, Inc. (TCS) engineers and supplies highly reliable wireless and messaging technology to wireless carriers, the government, and first responders.

Whether providing a highly secure communications link in remote places, connecting people to life-saving emergency services, or pioneering new messaging and location-based services and applications, helping people make "Connections that Matter" is what TeleCommunication Systems, Inc. (TCS) (NasdaqGM: TSYS) does best. As a leading provider of mission-critical wireless data solutions to government customers, public safety providers, and leading wireless communications carriers, TCS develops wireless data technology designed to handle the need for security and reliability.

The company has earned its standing as an industry leader. Through aggressive research and development, TCS has been awarded more than 70 patents for software, systems, and services used by its customers and have approximately 222 more patents pending. Headquartered in Annapolis, TCS was founded in 1987 by U.S. Naval Academy graduate Maurice B. Tosé. Since that time, TCS has expanded globally, with regional offices in Tampa, Florida; Seattle, Washington; Overland Park, Kansas; and Manassas, Virginia, and international offices in London, England; Calgary, Alberta, Canada; and Manama, Bahrain.

TCS wireless products include secure deployable communication systems and engineered satellite-based services; location-based wireless and voice over Internet protocol (VoIP) enhanced 9-1-1 services; messaging and location service infrastructure for wireless operators; and commercial location applications, such as traffic and navigation, using the precise location of a wireless device. Customers include leading wireless, cable multiple-system operators (MSOs), and VoIP carriers around the world, as well as a number of U.S. government departments.

Serving Wireless Carriers

TCS is a trusted partner to many leading wireless communications carriers, supplying comprehensive messaging, location, and enhanced 9-1-1 solutions.

The company's messaging products bring carriers new sources of income, enable inter-carrier messaging, and serve as the engines for today's text messaging mania. In providing text-messaging software to wireless carriers, TCS technology delivered an estimated 214 billion text messages in 2008 alone—nearly triple the number of text messages delivered in the previous year. Location technology proves to be the next wireless data success story, and TCS's location-based products and applications can be found on five continents around the globe.

Wireless carriers use TCS's Xypoint® location platforms to provide a broad range of applications to their subscribers, including navigation, social networking, and emergency services; and TCS provides the underlying location platforms and applications that support these new revenue-generating solutions.

Serving Public Safety Providers

TCS works in partnership with leading wireless carriers, cable MSOs, and public safety providers, pioneering enhanced 9-1-1 (E9-1-1) solutions that allow wireless and VoIP providers to supply the location of a caller in need of emergency services. Today TCS provides wireless, VoIP, and Next Generation E9-1-1 service to more than 100 million subscribers in the United States for more than 38 wireless carriers and handles more than 120,000 potentially life-saving calls daily.

Broadly, services by TCS include wireless E9-1-1, a hosted solution using the Xypoint Location Platform, the highly precise SnapTrack Position Determination solution, and the traditional landline network to enable wireless carriers to handle E9-1-1 calls; VoIP E9-1-1 Service, which provides a public safety solution for new IP-based communications; an award-winning real-time address validation engine for 9-1-1 (RAVE911), which unifies nationwide master street address guide data; and an automatic location identification (ALI) database, which uses reference data managed by the TCS Service Bureau to determine the appropriate routing for emergency calls.

Serving the Government

TCS provides seamless secure connectivity between the government's home operations at fixed facilities and its field activities. The company successfully meets the information technology and communications needs of government and military customers with innovative services, highly reliable deployable communications solutions, and managed satellite services.

SwiftLink® is an exclusive TCS suite of products that provides voice, video, and data links designed to enable field personnel to communicate with each other as well as with distant decision makers. SwiftLink solutions make possible rapid deployment of highly secure fixed and transportable communications systems using wireless, satellite, and terrestrial networks. The company's proven portfolio of solutions includes baseband IP kits, continuity of operations, disaster recovery, global satellite services, information assurance services, information technology professional services, telecommunications expense management, and solutions using very small aperture terminals (VSATs).

TCS supplies the government with SwiftLink products and in addition, secure communications solutions for teleport landing facilities; systems maintenance and support; communications engineering; program management; continuity of operations planning; telecommunications expense management; and help-desk outsourcing. Its customers include the U.S. Department of State, Department of Homeland Security, Department of Defense, military special operations, Defense Telecom Services–Washington, D.C., and Directorates of Information Management. TeleCommunication Systems, Inc. provides additional information on its Web site at www.telecomsys.com.

Above left: The TCS National Operations Center (NOC) provides enhanced 9-1-1 solutions, enabling wireless, cable MSOs, and VoIP operators to provide life-saving emergency services. Above right: TCS meets the communication needs of government and military customers with innovative services, highly reliable fixed and deployable communication solutions, and managed satellite services to provide seamless and secure connectivity between home operations and field activities.

The MIL Corporation

Serving federal government departments and agencies with professional assistance in the areas of finance, information management, and quality assurance, this firm recognizes that delivering sustained, high quality solutions is the most important contributor to its success. It is committed to providing a level of service that far exceeds the requirements of its contracts.

The MIL Corporation (MIL), based in Bowie, Maryland, was established in 1980 to provide the federal government with financial, quality assurance, and information technology–management services. After signing its first contracts with the Energy Information Administration of the U.S. Department of Energy, MIL went on to secure multiyear, multimillion-dollar contracts with 17 federal agencies by 2009. Its client roster includes such diverse entities as the U.S. Department of the Navy, the U.S. Department of State, and the Library of Congress.

Strategically sited midway between the Maryland state capital at Annapolis and the nation's capital in Washington, D.C., MIL has achieved some 30 years of steady growth due to a company culture that emphasizes superior quality of effort, individual creativity, and an entrepreneurial approach to performing work for the government. Since its inception, MIL has concentrated on providing its clients with high quality, on-site services.

MIL considers its ongoing ability to attract and keep the best employees to be key to its growth in both size and reputation. Its 450 professionals bring an average of eight years of on-the-job experience to the table, while the firm's managers average more than 15 years of experience. Staff members include certified public accountants (CPAs), certified government financial managers (CGFMs), and Microsoft Certified System Engineers and other Microsoft Certified Professionals.

MIL is accomplished at retaining expert staff members in many complex and expanding technical areas. Tasks are distributed among the firm's Financial Management Services, Financial Systems Support, Information Technology (IT), Quality Assurance, and C4I Integration and Lifecycle Support teams.

The Financial Management Services team sees to processes such as accounting operations, U.S. standard general ledger (USSGL) support, advisory services for federal chief financial officers, and audit assistance and business risk analysis. The Financial Systems Support team covers systems implementation, legacy system integration, and e-government (E-Gov) support services for better reconciling the needs of citizens, businesses, and government, among other services. The IT team embraces a library of help that includes infrastructure and network support, help-desk services, business intelligence collection, data warehousing and data mining, and systems administration. The Quality Assurance team sees to independent verification and validation (IV&V) (functional and technical), accreditation and certification, testing and information assurance, and performance testing. Finally, the C4I Integration and Lifecycle Support team handles command, control, communications, computers, and intelligence (C4I) training and support issues.

MIL is large enough to ensure that the job is done right, yet also small enough to be responsive to its clients' needs. These needs can be exacting indeed. MIL serves clients at the federal department level, including the U.S. Departments of Energy, the Navy, the State, the U.S. Departments of Commerce, the U.S. Air Force, Health and Human Services, Housing and Urban Development, and the Library of Congress. The firm also serves the U.S. Food and Drug Administration, the Federal Aviation Administration, the U.S. Government Accountability Office, the U.S. Commodities Future Trading Commission, and the U.S. Environmental Protection Agency, as well as federal courts. Each client presents its own set of unique challenges—challenges that MIL meets quickly, accurately, and thoroughly.

MIL holds four Federal Supply Service schedule (FSS) contracts authorized by the General Services Administration (GSA). FSS contracts give procurement managers the peace of mind of knowing that all legal obligations have been negotiated for them. That simplifies acquisitions and allows government customers to engage MIL professionals with confidence that their projects will move forward.

MIL's four FSS contracts are Schedule 70 IT Services (GS-35F-4670G), Financial and Business Solutions (FABS) (GS-23F-0034J), Mission Oriented Business Integrated Services (MOBIS) (GS-10F-0274P), and Travel Service Solutions (TSS) (GS-33F-0030P). Schedule 70 provides for such IT services as desktop support and applications development; FABS provides accounting, budgeting, reporting, and other financial services; MOBIS provides organizational and business-improvement services; and TSS provides answers to travel management and e-travel initiatives.

MIL also holds government-wide acquisition contracts (GWACs) such as a Commerce Information Technology Solutions (COMMITS NexGen) contract, which is the U.S. Department of Commerce's GWAC of choice for small and minority-owned busi-nesses, and SeaPort-e, which is the U.S. Department of the Navy's platform for acquiring electronic support services. MIL's COMMITS NexGen (Tier 2) GWAC allows MIL to compete for jobs valued between $5 million and $40 million.

To assist it in optimizing its services to clients, MIL maintains membership in the American Society of Military Comptrollers, the Association of Government Accountants, the Armed Forces Communications and Electronics Association, and the American Council for Technology/Industry Advisory Council.

The MIL Corporation provides additional information about its services on its Web site at www.milcorp.com.

Above, both photos: The creative, highly skilled professionals at The MIL Corporation are experts in federal financial management, systems design/build, management, and e-business.

Government and commercial satellite operators around the globe depend on this innovative company for reliable and cost-effective command, control, and communications systems for ground, air, and space. Customers have relied on the Integral Systems family of companies for over 27 years to deliver on time and on budget for more than 250 satellite missions.

Serving many of the world's satellite operators—including many of the leading commercial satellite operators, the U.S. military, the National Aeronautics and Space Administration (NASA), the National Oceanic and Atmospheric Administration (NOAA), and many more—Integral Systems, Inc. believes that a satellite is only as good as its network. Headquartered in Columbia, Maryland, Integral Systems builds revolutionary systems that incorporate the company's expertise in satellite ground systems and network operations, spectrum monitoring, signal processing, and signal interference detection and geolocation.

Ground systems are a critical component for successful satellite operations and satellite-interfaced networks. Ground systems track and control satellites and process and analyze the information they gather. The company's EPOCH Integrated Product Suite (IPS) is a command and control system designed to operate many satellites from various manufacturers with a minimum of personnel, making their operation highly cost-effective. The company's commitment to systems relying on open architecture, state-of-the-art user interface, and automated monitoring and control features allows operators to control their satellite fleets and networks.

Serving the Government and Commercial Sectors

For the government, Integral Systems provides the full services of a prime contractor, including requirements analyses, mission and systems engineering, custom design and development, operations support, and lifecycle maintenance, in addition to supplying its commercial off-the-shelf products. The company also deploys mission-specific systems built to government specifications for the entire range of space applications, including satellite simulations, planning, scheduling, and payload data processing.

Commercial satellite operators requiring a single ground system to operate all their satellites choose EPOCH IPS because it is compatible with satellite buses manufactured throughout the United States, Europe, Asia, and Latin America. EPOCH products contain integrated automation capabilities, enabling more cost-efficient satellite control operations. Operators can place their satellites in any orbit and can locate their remote receive stations anywhere in the world, knowing that Integral Systems will provide the ground system and global support for continuous operations.

A Family of Companies

Integral Systems' subsidiaries play an important role in the company's track record of delivering more than 250 satellite missions on time and on budget. They include SAT Corporation, Newpoint Technologies, RT Logic, Lumistar, and Integral Systems Europe (ISE).

SAT Corporation in Sunnyvale, California, is a worldwide supplier of automated radio frequency (RF) signal monitoring systems for satellite and terrestrial spectrum

management applications. These systems serve as communication management tools for commercial network owners/operators and telecommunications service providers to guarantee and maintain the quality of service they provide to their customers. They are also used by satellite owners and operators, teleport and gateway earth station operators, and government regulatory and security agencies.

Newpoint Technologies in Manchester, New Hampshire, is an industry leader in satellite and terrestrial network management systems for data control, Internet, broadcast, telecom, and hybrid networks. The company has been the industry's dominant supplier of software and systems for equipment monitoring and control and delivers a range of services, from standard software to complete turnkey solutions that manage large enterprise-level infrastructure systems. Principal customers include commercial satellite operators, telecommunications companies, and broadband service providers.

RT Logic in Colorado Springs, Colorado, designs, develops, and delivers innovative signal processing systems for the space and military communications industry. The Telemetrix product line is used for satellite test, launch vehicle telemetry, on-orbit satellite control, Satellite Communications (SATCOM) airborne communications, spectrum monitoring, and interference detection. Telemetrix products also support satellites launches out of Cape Canaveral and Vandenberg Air Force Base and support the Global Positioning System (GPS).

Lumistar in Carlsbad, California, designs and manufactures board-level telemetry products for PCI, VME, cPCI, and ISA computer buses. These boards are integrated into desktop, rack-mount, or rugged portable computers for quick-look telemetry applications, and stand-alone products such as bit synchronizers, telemetry receivers, and diversity combiners. The company also provides airborne telemetry components such as data and video transmitters, bit synchronizers, and receivers.

ISE in Toulouse, France, established in 2001, serves as the focal point for the support of Integral Systems' international business. ISE supports satellite ground systems, antenna, and earth-station integration for customers in Europe, the Middle East, Africa, and Asia. ISE has achieved ISO-9001 certification.

Additional information about Integral Systems is available on the company's Web site at www.integ.com.

Above left: Integral Systems Executive Dashboard software allows senior managers and executives to view and monitor critical data from across the entire ground system on a single display. Above right: Staff of Integral Systems, Inc. celebrates ringing the NASDAQ closing bell in December 2008.

TIG Global

Providing interactive solutions for the hospitality and travel industry, this award-winning firm offers an array of Internet-marketing services for its global client base, generating direct revenue, building brand awareness, and increasing market share and return on investment. TIG Global is dedicated to providing best-of-breed services to its clients, while also caring for its employees and supporting its community.

Established by hoteliers during the infancy of online travel distribution, TIG Global has grown to become the leading Internet-marketing company for the hospitality and travel industry. As an accomplished Internet-marketing firm consistently in the forefront of innovation, TIG Global blurs the line between art and science—combining leading-edge creative talent with high-touch account management and proactive marketing services. TIG Global's comprehensive online marketing plans are precisely engineered to each client's unique needs and are focused on driving direct revenue, increasing client market share, and improving brand awareness and customer loyalty.

Headquartered in Chevy Chase, Maryland, TIG Global serves an extensive portfolio of clients worldwide, including hotels, resorts, hospitality ownership and management groups, restaurants, spas, and destination marketing organizations. Several state, city, and island tourism boards and destination marketing organizations rely on TIG Global for marketing services, along with an array of hotel brands including Preferred Hotel Group, Hyatt Hotels & Resorts, and LXR Luxury Resorts & Hotels. In 2007, TIG Global broadened its international reach with the opening of an office in downtown London.

TIG Global's diverse spectrum of services includes designing and developing Web sites, search-engine optimization, paid search marketing, online advertising and strategic linking, and e-mail marketing. TIG Global also offers an array of social media solutions designed to facilitate customer interaction and generate consumer trust. Its most popular social media solution, HotelProtect, is a proprietary service that analyzes travel reviews and brand infringement online. All of TIG Global's services are accompanied by a true dedication to client service and consultation. In-depth analyses and proactive recommendations are made on a continuous basis based on each client's online marketing results.

Since its beginning, TIG Global has been recognized each year for its outstanding creative Web site design and successful online marketing efforts. It has received top honors in such competitions as the Adrian Awards, Summit Creative Awards, WebAwards, and the Internet Advertising Competition. TIG Global has also been consistently recognized for its workplace. Formerly located within the Washington, D.C., city limits, TIG Global was named one of the area's best places to work by *Washingtonian* magazine and the fastest-growing company in D.C. by *Inc.* magazine.

TIG Global believes that an energetic and motivated workforce contributes to a successful firm and satisfied clients. Implementing an open-door policy and a reward system, TIG Global has developed a positive work environment at its offices. To foster teamwork and promote fresh ideas, TIG Global's newly designed Chevy Chase, Maryland, office space is based on an open layout and includes themed meeting rooms, a putting green, and a game room with ping pong. TIG Global employees are encouraged to spend time together outside of the office giving back to the community, regularly contributing money, time, and services to various charitable organizations. As a company, TIG Global has made it a priority to support the community where it works and plays. Employee donations are continuously matched, and corporate volunteer efforts aid the Sabin Vaccine Institute and the Hoop Dreams Scholarship Foundation, among others.

A leading, fast-growth firm, TIG Global is dedicated to helping its clients, employees, and community succeed. Additional information about TIG Global and its services can be found on its Web site at www.TIGglobal.com and on its blog at blog.TIGglobal.com.

Above right: Trip Schneck, at left, is co-founder and president of TIG Global, and co-founder Frederic W. Malek is the company's CEO.

PROFILES OF COMPANIES AND ORGANIZATIONS
Tourism, Entertainment, and Hospitality

DavCo Restaurants, Inc.

Dedicated to creating a positive dining experience for every guest, this Wendy's franchisee has a passion for consistently providing quick-service food made for each customer with fresh, quality ingredients and presented with excellent service. Its passion extends to enriching its work environment and to embracing its community by supporting the local 'Wendy's Wonderful Kids' program, managed by the Dave Thomas Foundation for Adoption.

DavCo Restaurants, Inc.—which operates more than 155 Wendy's Old Fashioned Hamburgers restaurants—is one of the largest franchisees in the Wendy's family and an industry leader in progressive and professional management. DavCo, which was named after the Davenport family, the original franchise owner, purchased the franchise rights for Baltimore, Maryland; Washington, D.C.; and St. Louis, Missouri, in 1976. Today DavCo is the exclusive franchise owner/operator in the Baltimore, Salisbury, and Washington, D.C., markets, and has grown and prospered by maintaining the company's high standards of customer satisfaction and by working to measurably improve the business every day.

Wendy's is a leader in offering quality hamburgers and its varied menu includes chicken sandwiches, baked potatoes, chili, and warm chicken salads as well as their famous Frosty Dairy Dessert. The chain's recipe for success is commendable: serve a fresh, never frozen hamburger, accompanied by the guest's choice of condiments, in a clean and friendly atmosphere as quickly and as accurately as possible. This effective philosophy—outlined by Wendy's founder R. David Thomas—has enabled the chain to expand into one of the most successful restaurant companies in the world.

Great Food, Service, and Value

The Davenport family was not new to the restaurant business when it bought the Wendy's franchise. They were the founders of the Krystal Company, a major quick-service restaurant chain in the southeastern United States. The Krystal chain was built on a similar philosophy of great food, quality service, and fair value, which turned the company's 70 restaurants into cultural icons throughout its geographic territory.

Between 1976 and 1980 DavCo opened 44 Wendy's restaurants and made plans to open many more. Harvey Rothstein, who became the company's chairman and CEO in 2005, led the company through a period of appraisal, acquisition, and real estate financing for the development of new Wendy's restaurants throughout DavCo's exclusive territory. The company's aggressive growth strategy resulted in operating 100 restaurants by 1988.

In 1994 DavCo acquired Southern Hospitality Corporation, a 35-restaurant Wendy's franchise in Nashville, Tennessee. DavCo continued to expand, making an ambitious commitment to build between 50 and 60 Wendy's restaurants. In 1998 the company was taken private by Rothstein and then–president and CEO Ronald D. Kirstien, giving DavCo more control over company decisions and positioning it for future growth. In 1998 and 1999

Right: Guided by the philosophy of the founder of Wendy's, R. David Thomas, DavCo Restaurants, Inc. serves its "Old Fashioned Hamburgers" fresh, never frozen, with the guest's choice of condiments. Shown here is Wendy's quarter-pound single hamburger, "Made to order each and every time."

the St. Louis and Southern Hospitality business units were sold, enabling DavCo to focus on the mid-Atlantic market.

A Mission for Success

One of the top 10 largest employers in the mid-Atlantic region, DavCo is committed to a forward-thinking mission and core values. The company's mission is to be recognized by guests and employees as the premier restaurant company within its operating areas and corporate systems, dedicated to delivering excellence consistently through a strong network of caring employees who value personal and professional growth.

DavCo values people as its most important asset; values honesty, integrity, trust, and ethical behavior and pledges to uphold these beliefs with guests, employees, vendors, and neighbors; values internal growth and recognizes its obligation to continually teach, providing resources for its people to realize rewarding career opportunities; values and demands the highest operating standards and will not compromise them; values quality leadership and example setting and believes leaders take full responsibility and accountability for their team's performance; and values innovation and improvement in the work environment, operating systems, and general business practices.

Actively Caring for the Community

The Dave Thomas Foundation for Adoption established in 1992 is a special organization that is embraced by DavCo and many other Wendy's franchise owners. An adopted child himself, Wendy's founder was determined to help foster children find a home to call their own. The foundation is a nonprofit public charity devoted to increasing the adoptions of more than 150,000 children in North America's foster care systems. It is the only foundation of its kind and is guided by one of Thomas's basic values: "Do what is best for the child."

DavCo supports the Dave Thomas Foundation for Adoption as well as Wendy's Wonderful Kids, the organization that provides recruiters who find adoptive homes for foster care children. DavCo uses donations from Wendy's customers to fund the salaries of adoption recruiters in its region. DavCo also supports local charities and worthy causes that are active throughout the company's franchise territory.

Successfully Growing

Founded in 1969, Wendy's is headquartered in Dublin, Ohio. By 1976, when DavCo became a franchisee, Wendy's restaurants numbered 500 and in 1980 the number of stores quadrupled to an impressive 2,000 restaurants. During the 1980s Wendy's became one of the largest quick-service restaurant companies in the world. Today Wendy's includes more than 5,000 restaurants in 35 countries. As one of the world's largest Wendy's franchisees, DavCo Restaurants is prepared to grow successfully throughout the 21st century and continue operating restaurants where pleasing guests is the top priority. DavCo Restaurants, Inc. provides additional information on its Web site at www.davcorestaurants.com.

Center: Wendy's Frostys, made in several flavors, include the Original Frosty, Frosty Shakes, the Twisted Frosty, and this one, the vanilla Frosty Float, made like an old-fashioned soda shop float.

Skye Hospitality, LLC

Headquartered in Baltimore, this corporation was founded in 1995 to develop, construct, manage, and operate state-of-the-art hotels within the Hilton and Marriott systems. Focused on hospitality, this company operates nine award-winning hotels in White Marsh, Hanover, and Baltimore City, Maryland.

Above: Skye Hospitality, LLC's Hampton Inn at Camden Yards is steps from the Baltimore Orioles' Oriole Park and the Baltimore Ravens' M&T Bank Stadium and a short walk to other popular destinations in Baltimore.

Skye Hospitality, LLC understands that people come first, and that in order to be truly successful each hotel must exceed its customers' expectations. The company, which has won numerous awards for outstanding guest satisfaction, cleanliness, and building construction, believes that in today's highly competitive industry travelers and meeting planners expect a full range of services in well-maintained facilities. Founder and CEO James T. Dresher sums up the Skye philosophy, "We are not in the hotel business. We are in the hospitality business."

Guided by its continuous quest for quality, Skye Hospitality carefully selects its business partners, locations, and building materials to ensure the development of the best properties. Success begins with matching the right product with the surrounding community and its culture and is followed by careful site selection and thoughtful planning of the parcel, building placement, and presence of the property. By the time groundbreaking takes place on any new hotel, Skye Hospitality is halfway into the complete schedule.

The company applies the same high standards and hands-on involvement to the staffing, decorating, and grand opening of its hotels. Skye Hospitality hires experienced professionals to manage the property in a manner that exceeds the customer's expectations at every level. The company builds and staffs each property for long-term performance, first-class service, and outstanding property maintenance. In Maryland, Skye Hospitality operates nine hotels in three regions: White Marsh, Arundel Mills, and Camden Yards.

White Marsh—A Retail Hub

Skye Hospitality serves the White Marsh region with four distinctive hotels and free shuttle service to and from the shopping district. The hotels are minutes from Baltimore's Inner Harbor and are surrounded by 10 restaurants, 175 stores, and a 16-screen theater, making them ideal for active weekend sojourns. Conveniently located near Martin State Airport, Lockheed Martin, Franklin Square Hospital, and The Johns Hopkins Hospital, all four hotels are 14 miles north of Baltimore City. An excellent choice for business and leisure trips, the hotels are also near the White Marsh Mall, the Shops at the Avenue, and IKEA–White Marsh.

Hampton Inn—Renovated in 2004, this 127-bed hotel offers a 24-hour business center, a fitness center, a complimentary hot breakfast bar, and meeting and banquet facilities.

Hilton Garden Inn—This hotel features banquet and meeting facilities that accommodate up to 200 guests. Spacious guest rooms offer excellent value: refrigerator, microwave, and coffeemaker; free high-speed Internet access; and an ergonomic work station. The hotel offers extensive computing and business services.

Residence Inn by Marriott—This updated hotel features a library with business center and billiards room, guest suites with separate living and sleeping areas, grocery shopping service, laundry facilities, and an always-attentive Marriott staff.

Fairfield Inn & Suites by Marriott—Featuring spacious guest rooms with a well-lighted work desk, two phones, and data ports, this hotel also provides complimentary wired and wireless high-speed Internet access for its guests.

Arundel Mills and BWI Marshall Airport

Skye Hospitality serves the Arundel Mills region with four hotels and free shuttle service to and from the nearby Arundel Mills shopping, dining, and entertainment complex and Baltimore/Washington International Thurgood Marshall Airport (BWI Marshall). The hotels are also close to Fort Meade and several Annapolis and Baltimore attractions.

Hampton Inn & Suites—Offering a full range of amenities, this boutique hotel's French country decor, lobby with ceramic-tile fireplace, and complimentary hot breakfast bar are just some of the reasons that guests continually return.

Residence Inn by Marriott—This hotel features apartment-style guest suites, a multipurpose SportCourt, and a billiards room and library with complimentary Business Center services.

SpringHill Suites by Marriott—An excellent choice for business and leisure travelers, this hotel offers stylish guest suites that are 25 percent larger than at many comparably priced hotels, offering guests a generous space in which to relax.

TownePlace Suites by Marriott—This hotel specializes in making life comfortable for extended-stay travelers. Affordable and convenient, TownePlace offers three floor plans with separate living and sleeping areas, well-equipped kitchen, and complimentary high-speed Internet access.

Hampton Inn Baltimore—Camden Yards

In the Camden Yards region, Skye Hospitality offers the Hampton Inn, an upscale urban retreat in the heart of downtown Baltimore. Nearby attractions include the Baltimore Orioles' Oriole Park at Camden Yards; M&T Bank Stadium, home to the NFL's Baltimore Ravens; the Baltimore Convention Center; and Baltimore Inner Harbor; as well as several of the city's historical and cultural points of interest. The Hampton Inn's 126 guest rooms feature free, high-speed Internet access; flat-panel LCD television with premium cable and movie channels; and a complimentary hot breakfast daily.

Skye Hospitality provides additional information about all of its hotels on its Web site at www.skyehospitality.com.

Just as every hotel of Skye Hospitality, LLC strives to exceed the expectations of its guests, all of the company's employees pursue excellence in their performance. Employees are selected for their principles and values, which must reflect the company's high quality standards. The expertise and commitment of Skye associates has resulted in numerous industry awards. Among these are Marriott International's Circle of Excellence Awards, the J. D. Power and Associates Guest Satisfaction Award, Hilton's Lighthouse Award, Marriott Residence Inn's Diamond Awards and Cleanliness of Suite Awards, and a Marriott Hotels & Resorts' Top Operations Award.

Above left: Skye Hospitality hotels offer both comfort and grace for guests. Above right: The most discriminating travelers marvel at the elegance of Skye Hospitality hotels.

Chase Suite Hotel Hunt Valley

Featuring spacious, well-appointed one-bedroom and two-bedroom suites with full kitchens and luxurious bedding, this hotel is a fine choice for all types of travel, from overnight trips to extended-stay lodging to special-occasion gatherings. Conveniently located in the northern suburb of metropolitan Baltimore, the hotel is an excellent destination for the business or leisure traveler.

At the Chase Suite Hotel in Hunt Valley, Maryland, guests experience luxury, sophistication, and value at every turn. Visitors quickly discover why so many guests call Chase their home away from home. Its amenities include luxurious beds and bedding, complimentary hot breakfast buffet daily, weeknight social hour with hors d'oeuvres, complimentary wireless Internet access in the clubhouse, and personal service from a well-trained staff. Chase offers the charm of a bed-and-breakfast inn, the unique ambiance of a boutique hotel, and the assurance of a seasoned establishment.

Conveniently located in the city's northern suburb, Chase is just a few miles from the Maryland State Fairgrounds, Hunt Valley Towne Centre, and Oregon Ridge Park. The light rail is within walking distance, offering convenient transportation to the city's exciting and entertaining Inner Harbor. Visitors find many attractions nearby: the National Aquarium in Baltimore, the Maryland Science Center, Oriole Park at Camden Yards, M&T Bank Stadium, and the popular sports-themed restaurant ESPN Zone.

Comfort and Convenience

Whether traveling for work or leisure, guests enjoy a comfortable stay in the hotel's generously sized, well-appointed suites. Business travelers also appreciate the express office bar, complete with computer terminals and printers. In addition, the hotel features a Sport Court, fitness center, outdoor swimming pool, whirlpool spa, and guest laundry facilities. Visitors with an eye for sophistication combined with great value consider Chase a preferred choice of accommodations when visiting Baltimore.

Chase offers studio suites with the choice of a king-size bed, a queen-size bed, or two queen-size beds. The living space includes a sleeper sofa and flat-panel television, and the fully equipped kitchen provides a stove, microwave oven, refrigerator, and breakfast bar, as well as a data port.

For guests who are traveling with their families or planning an extended stay, the hotel's two-bedroom penthouses are roomy and homelike. A full living room and fully equipped kitchen area are set apart by French doors from the main bedroom and bath. Penthouses also feature a loft bedroom and an additional full bath. These penthouses provide ample room in which families can unwind after exploring the sights of the city. Two-bedroom penthouses are also an excellent place for family and friends to gather while attending a celebration.

The hotel's close proximity to many restaurants, shopping venues, and entertainment options provides guests of all ages with options for activities to be enjoyed when visiting the area. Complimentary shuttle service is offered within a five-mile radius of the hotel. For guests who wish to dine in, staff members are available to handle grocery shopping.

The Hardage Group Vision

Chase Suite Hotels is owned by the Hardage Group, a hotel management, franchise, and development company headquartered in San Diego, California. The company's philosophy of hospitality is to always be accountable for guest satisfaction and to treat guests in a way that is memorable long after their stay. The company's vision also includes both charitable and environmental initiatives that involve continually seeking new ways to be an exemplary corporate citizen.

The Hardage Group contributes both time and resources to the communities where it operates. After a property is renovated, its used furniture and decorative items are donated to local charities. Hardage also provides financial assistance to worthy community projects. In following this mission, employees are encouraged to volunteer their time and talent for the cause of their choice.

In addition to supporting outside organizations, the Hardage Group created its own Vision of Children Foundation, which is sponsored by the company's 13 Chase Suite

Hotels and three Woodfin Hotels. The foundation's goal is to improve the lives of visually impaired youth and their families by giving these children a chance at gaining their sight. The Vision of Children Foundation supports research leading to the prevention and treatment of blindness and is a primary information source for affected families, the public, and the medical community.

Giving back to the planet is also part of the Hardage vision. The company strives to reduce its impact on the environment: laundry policies are designed to save the planet's valuable resources by preventing detergent from entering the soil and conserving water. Even the company's memos are printed on 100 percent recycled paper. Every possible step is taken toward fostering a greener world.

Chase Suite Hotels are located in Hunt Valley and Rockville, Maryland; Overland Park, Kansas; Salt Lake City, Utah; Newark and Brea, California; Baton Rouge, Louisiana; Des Moines, Iowa; Dublin, Ohio; El Paso, Texas; Kansas City, Missouri; Lincoln, Nebraska; and Tampa, Florida.

Chase Suite Hotel Hunt Valley provides additional information on its Web site at www.chasehotelhuntvalley.com.

Above left: The spacious living area in each suite features a sleeper sofa, a fireplace, and flat-panel television. Above right: Each suite features a fully equipped kitchen, offering a stove, micro-wave, refrigerator, and breakfast bar, plus a data port.

Tremont Grand

This event facility provides a gracious, versatile setting for meetings, conventions, and social affairs of all types and sizes. One of Baltimore's architectural gems, the Tremont Grand is connected to the Tremont Plaza Hotel and offers numerous, well-appointed space options for groups ranging from executive symposiums to gala family gatherings and civic receptions.

BALTIMORE'S
TREMONTS
HISTORIC VENUE AND ALL-SUITE HOTEL

The Corinthian Room also offers an excellent setting for business events, which can reach new heights with meeting and planning packages when held at the Tremont Grand. Conference facilities include wide spaces, luxurious carpeting, a marble speakers' platform, and advanced technological capabilities, and provide ample room for up to 300 attendees. For smaller groups, such as executive conferences and board

Above left: The reception area at the Tremont Grand, located in downtown Baltimore, offers the accommodating atmosphere of gathering spaces providing comfort, elegance, and flair. Above right: The venue offers advanced technological capabilities for meetings and events of every kind.

Artfully restored and elegantly furnished, Baltimore's Tremonts offer state-of-the-art meeting space for a wide variety of events and luxurious accommodations for business and leisure travelers. A majestic and historic venue, the Tremont Grand affords the comfort, function, and service of Baltimore's most unique meeting place and the elegance of a grand ballroom. One of Maryland's largest event facilities, the Tremont Grand is close to downtown Baltimore's many attractions, the Inner Harbor, and Mount Vernon, and is connected to the 303-room all-suite Tremont Plaza Hotel.

The Tremont Grand's 19 flexible meeting rooms offer a combined 40,000 square feet of space throughout five floors. Among the venue's many distinctive rooms are the Marble Room, a grand ballroom with stained-glass windows that date back to 1866, and the Corinthian Room, an impressive ballroom of 4,500 square feet with glistening chandeliers and classical architecture.

meetings, the Tremont Grand offers the stately Library and the Boardroom. Visitors experience five floors of remarkable 19th-century architecture at Baltimore's newly restored Tremont Grand. Guests are awed by the impeccable service, exquisite cuisine, unique menus, devoted Wedding Coordinators, and all-suite guest rooms, all making for the most memorable day of a lifetime.

At the Tremont Grand, every event is customized by the venue's superior on-site culinary team with outstanding menu options, valet parking service, wireless high-speed Internet access, state-of-the-art audiovisual equipment, and individual lighting control. Unforgettable events take place daily at this unique facility, where sophistication, modern functionality, and a prime downtown location add up to a premium package. Baltimore's Tremonts provide additional information about the Tremont Grand on the company's Web site at www.tremonts.com.

In a city that is one of America's most popular meeting destinations, Baltimore's Tremonts stand out. Offering outstanding service in an unconventional setting, the Tremont Plaza Hotel and the Tremont Grand feature a historic ambience that is unique, with first-class service, gourmet dining, and the finest amenities. Throughout the property —from the Tremont Plaza's 303 luxurious suites to the adjoining Tremont Grand's 40,000 square feet of meeting space—this classic venue exceeds guest expectations.

To satisfy people's hotel needs, the Tremont Plaza offers three configurations of suites: studio-style plaza suites, one-bedroom premier suites, and two-bedroom chairman's suites. Whether guests desire extra work space, a game table, an additional bedroom—the Tremont Plaza can accommodate their wishes. Its comfortable, well-appointed suites are enhanced by attentive service.

All suites at the Tremont Plaza provide remote-controlled television and complimentary high-speed Internet access and feature a kitchenette with refrigerator, toaster, microwave, and coffeemaker.

- Studio-style plaza suites of 450 square feet offer a sitting area and the option of three bedding choices—a king-size bed, a queen-size bed, or two queen-size beds.
- One-bedroom premier suites provide 750 square feet, including a living room with a large seating area and a sleeper sofa, and a separate bedroom with a king-size or queen-size bed.
- Two-bedroom chairman's suites offer superior comfort at 1,400 square feet. The combined living and dining room features a sofa, coffee table, armoire, and

six-seat dining area. There are two bedrooms, one with a king-size bed, the other with a queen-size bed; three remote-controlled, flat-screen televisions; a walk-in closet; and two bathrooms. The chairman's suite includes three telephones, and the kitchenette is fitted with a full-size refrigerator.

Located in the heart of downtown Baltimore, the Tremont Plaza is a property of Baltimore's Tremonts and is connected to another of the company's properties, the Tremont Grand—a site for meetings and other events. Nearby are the Inner Harbor, Mount Vernon, the National Aquarium in Baltimore, the Maryland Science Center, and other attractions. Also, within walking distance are a variety of shopping, dining, and historical sites. And conveniently, Baltimore/Washington International Thurgood Marshall Airport (BWI Marshall) is just 10 miles away.

Guests who stay at the Tremont Plaza are delighted by the personal service, thoughtful amenities, and elegant accommodations of this fine hotel. Baltimore's Tremonts provide additional information about the Tremont Plaza Hotel on the company's Web site at www.tremonts.com.

BALTIMORE'S
TREMONTS
HISTORIC VENUE AND ALL-SUITE HOTEL

Above right: The Tremont Plaza Hotel in downtown Baltimore provides a luxurious respite amid the activities of business destinations and tourist attractions and services. Above left: The all-suite hotel features comfortable accommodations for every guest and offers a full complement of services and modern amenities.

HMSHost Corporation

A recognized leader in food, beverage, and retail shop concessions, this company serves people on the move at motorway travel plazas in North America and in airports worldwide. It is known for offering dining and shopping favorites and for showcasing the character and spirit of each region, thereby appealing to local residents and travelers alike.

HMSHost Corporation is a world leader in creating innovative dining and shopping services for travelers at airports and on motorways, offering an unparalleled blend of preferred local, regional, and international brands. For more than 110 years, HMSHost has used its experience and global reach to make the traveler's day better at travel venues in Maryland and around the world. Its operations at Maryland Turnpike travel plazas and Baltimore/Washington International Thurgood Marshall Airport (BWI) deliver exceptional food, beverage, and retail experiences to millions of people on the move.

In the early 1980s, HMSHost became the first to introduce brand-name concessions into airport and travel plaza environments. Today it has more than 350 familiar and unique restaurant and retail shop brands in its portfolio. Among these are exclusive relationships with hundreds of brands that consumers prefer.

Above: HMSHost Corporation's Maryland House Travel Plaza welcomes visitors with the traditional Phillips Seafood Express restaurant and other premium dining venues as well as Travel Mart—a convenience store created by HMSHost.

HMSHost offers a welcome respite at more than 100 travel plazas for motorists and families driving on U.S. toll roads from Maine to Florida; in Ohio, Pennsylvania, Indiana, and Illinois; and in Canada, from Windsor to Cornwall. The Maryland House Travel Plaza in Aberdeen, Maryland, and Chesapeake House Travel Plaza in North East, Maryland, are favorite stops for Maryland Turnpike travelers.

Motorists stopping at the Maryland House are pleased to find a Phillips Seafood Express restaurant, which represents a high quality Maryland tradition and creates a great experience for travelers. Popular Maryland House venues also include Sbarro, Roy Rogers, Starbucks Coffee, and Cinnabon, as well as Travel Mart, a convenience store created by HMSHost. At Chesapeake House, motorists can enjoy Burger King, Starbucks Coffee, Popeye's Chicken and Biscuits, Cinnabon, and Quiznos Sub, as well as another retail brand created by HMSHost—Z Market, a convenience store offering gourmet food for takeout.

As airports have become a new gathering place, travelers want to make the best use of their time. Today they expect enhanced dining and shopping opportunities. At more than 100 airports worldwide, HMSHost and its affiliates HMSHost Europe and HMSHost Asia Pacific are providing air travelers with fine shops and restaurants.

Maryland residents and travelers will recognize the restaurant brands operated by HMSHost at BWI, including Phillips Seafood, Starbucks Coffee, Manchu WOK, and HMSHost's own Varsity Grill, as well as the specialty jewelry and giftware shop Talie.

One of Montgomery County's top local businesses, HMSHost employs 500 associates at its worldwide headquarters in Bethesda, Maryland, and more than 1,200 associates statewide. A part of Italy's Autogrill S.p.A.—the world's largest provider of food, beverage, and retail services for travelers—HMSHost has 33,000 associates worldwide and annual revenues of more than $2.6 billion. HMSHost provides additional information on its Web site at www.hmshost.com.

Brewer's Alley Restaurant & Brewery
Fountain Rock Management Group

This state-of-the-art brewery and restaurant in the heart of Historic Frederick's downtown district has revived the town's legacy of producing outstanding fermented spirits and has provided local residents and tourists with an upscale establishment ideal for dining and relaxing. All beers are brewed on-site and the extensive menu promises something for everyone, from local specialty dishes and old favorites to exciting new recipes.

Located in the historic Maryland town of Frederick, Brewer's Alley Restaurant & Brewery is a favorite destination for local residents and worldwide travelers. This distinctive establishment offers a wide variety of handcrafted beers as well as fine wines, cognacs, and scotch complemented by a lengthy menu of outstanding culinary creations. Patrons can enjoy a casual lunch, unwind after a long day, or celebrate a special event in a unique atmosphere that blends 18th-century architecture with modern hospitality.

Restaurant owner Phil Bowers traded in his software engineering job in 1996 to open Brewer's Alley, Western Maryland's first brewpub. After a short period of serving as the brewmaster and hiring out the restaurant management tasks, Bowers realized he needed to learn the restaurant business quickly to keep his dream alive. Today Bowers—who in 2007 was named Maryland Restauranteur of the year by the Restaurant Association of Maryland—oversees Fountain Rock Management Group along with operations manager Nezih Pistar. Fountain Rock operates three unique restaurants within one block of each other in Downtown Frederick. Brewer's Alley has been the driving force of Downtown Frederick's revitalization. In 1999 Isabella's Taverna & Tapas Bar opened, offering a Spanish flair and an amazing tapas menu. In 2002 Acacia Fusion Bistro—a restaurant with a California-style atmosphere serving new-American cuisine—opened directly across the street from Brewer's Alley.

Tom Flores was hired as the Brewmaster for Brewer's Alley in 1997. He became interested in brewing beer when he was a teenager, inspiring him to pursue an education in this unique specialty. Flores graduated from the University of California–Davis in 1994 with a master's degree in Food Science and Technology, with an emphasis in brewing. He has developed five year-round favorites—Kolsch, India Pale Ale (I.P.A.), Nut Brown

Ale, Oatmeal Stout, and Hefeweizen—as well as many seasonal varieties. The brewery boasts these and many other award-winning varieties of beer. In 2006 the brewery responded to the increasing popularity of and demand for these brews by offering its beers in bottles, which are available through many local and regional retail outlets.

The town of Frederick is known for its appreciation and masterful production of fermented spirits, a tradition that Brewer's Alley is proud to continue. The original Brewer's Alley—a long line of breweries that occupied space along the banks of Carroll Creek—was a fixture in the social and economic landscape of Frederick for 153 years. The historic three-story brick building that houses today's restaurant is one of the city's earliest and most important structures. The building was raised in 1769 to accommodate the first Town Hall and Market House, served this function for more than a century, and witnessed the birth of the city of Frederick. As the town prospered, the building became the site of government offices and then served as an opera house and theater.

Today Brewer's Alley continues to carefully enhance and preserve the building's original design. The restaurant has three distinctive dining areas: an outdoor patio where guests may dine in Frederick's fabled streetscape atmosphere, an indoor dining room surrounded by Greek-style columns and ceilings with smooth faux-marble surfaces with a sports-bar atmosphere, and two casual indoor areas with stained-glass windows and expansive views of the historic city.

The brewery's banquet facilities and catering services accommodate groups of between 12 and 100 guests. The professional staff of Fountain Rock Restaurant Management Group fashions each affair to suit the needs and personal style of the customer. An extensive and varied catering menu includes the preparation of a wide selection of dishes that are carefully planned and executed and elegantly presented. A friendly and attentive wait staff and detail-oriented catering director contribute to the success of every event. Additional information about the restaurant and its catering services is available on the restaurant's Web site at www.brewers-alley.com.

Both pages, all photos: Housed in a historic brick building in the charming town of Frederick, Brewer's Alley Restaurant & Brewery offers specialty beers brewed on-site, a full array of menu items, and indoor and outdoor dining areas.

PROFILES OF COMPANIES AND ORGANIZATIONS
Transportation and Logistics

Knorr Brake Corporation

With extensive experience in mass transit passenger rail systems, this Carroll County–based company manufactures braking systems, passenger doors, and climate-control equipment for all types of rail lines such as metro, light rail, high-speed train, commuter rail, and monorail, among others. It also offers complete OEM braking systems, parts, and overhaul and maintenance services.

Mass transit is changing the face of cities across the world, and Knorr Brake Corporation (KBC), of Westminster, Maryland, has had its hand on the wheel for more than three decades. The company provides top-of-the-line pneumatic and hydraulic braking systems; door systems; and heating, ventilation, and air-conditioning (HVAC) systems for all types of passenger rail vehicles across North America, ranging from the Baltimore metropolitan area transit system and the Washington Metropolitan Area Transit Authority (serving Maryland, Virginia, and Washington, D.C.) to the high-speed Acela trains for Amtrak and the Sky Train vehicles in Vancouver. Each railway on which KBC systems are installed—including metros, light rail, and high-speed—not only offers a safe, reliable, comfortable ride but also fosters invaluable confidence among its passengers.

KBC began modestly as the three-person U.S. office of Knorr-Bremse Group. Knorr-Bremse, based in Munich, Germany, is one of the world's leading manufacturers of braking systems for rail and other commercial vehicles. The stateside location began operations in Rockville, Maryland, in 1973, where it established itself as Knorr Brake Corporation. Continued growth prompted a move in 1991 to larger facilities in Westminster, Maryland, where the company's headquarters and manufacturing plant continue to operate today.

Acquisitions enabled the company to expand significantly in the new millennium. Innovations for Entrance Systems (IFE), one of the world's leading producers of automatic door systems and drives for rolling stock, is also a part of the Knorr-Bremse group. In 1999 a U.S. operation for this group was also launched. Merak (formerly Stone Ibérica), a world leader in HVAC systems for railroad vehicles, joined KBC in 2005. Together these companies have more than 130 years of experience on five continents. Both now operate from the KBC complex in Westminster.

Dedication to quality has always been the primary concern of KBC. This guiding principle was rewarded in 2007, when KBC became the first company of its kind in North America to be recognized for excellence in manufacturing by International

KBC president Richard Bowie believes that furthering the education and work experience of students in the community is a valuable path to establishing a continually improving economy and quality of life in Carroll County. Following this philosophy, the company supports numerous educational programs. Many local high school and college students work for the company as interns, serving in departments ranging from finance and marketing to engineering. Many of these students are considered for employment when positions become available. The company also supports Business and Schools Involved in Creative Strategies, a Carroll County organization that assists teachers and administrators in observing businesses in action and offers course credits for selected master's degree programs.

A company culture is supported by its employees, and at KBC, employees are the heart of the company's philanthropic efforts, supporting numerous local charitable causes such as United Way. Employees not only donate their time and money but also organize annual fund-raising events such as Neighbors in Need, Daffodil Days (in support of breast cancer research), and chili cook-offs for various charities.

With its international ties and ever-increasing business, KBC is moving ahead as quickly as the mass transit railways that use its systems. Its heart is at home in Carroll County, where its efforts are helping to provide a better life. Knorr Brake Corporation provides additional information about its products, services, and activities on its Web site at www.knorrbrakecorp.com.

Railway Industry Standard (IRIS). IRIS is a globally recognized standard for the railway industries for the evaluation of management systems. IRIS certification embodies the requirements of the railway industry and fills gaps in ISO-9001:2000 certification. In an interview for the February/March 2009 issue of the county's *Carroll Magazine*, Gary St. Onge, KBC director of quality, said, "IRIS certification is a real feather in our cap. It shows our commitment to producing quality systems, and we gain more business because of it."

KBC is committed to striving for quality in all areas of its operations, including a focus on its workforce and its community. This world-renowned manufacturing leader attracts employees from around the globe and hires a good portion— approximately 40 percent—of its 220-strong workforce from Carroll County, where it dedicates its academic, economic, and philanthropic efforts. With a less than 2 percent employee turnover at its Westminster facilities, the company is clearly succeeding in these efforts.

Opposite page: Knorr Brake Corporation, headquartered in Westminster, Maryland, designs and manufactures customized braking systems for passenger rail transit vehicles, including subway cars and light rail vehicles. This page, left: Knorr's friction brake systems, Merak's HVAC systems, and IFE door systems can all be found on various series of Washington Metropolitan Area Transit Authority (WMATA) transit railcars. This page, top right: Knorr's electronic system for railway applications (ESRA) has unsurpassed reliability. This page, below right: Knorr's oil-free piston compressor is quickly becoming the standard for compressed air supply control on trains.

Maryland Port Administration

A job provider and major source of revenue for the State of Maryland, this organization is dedicated to promoting economic activity for the Port of Baltimore, while also sustaining its reputation as an environmental leader and a highly secure port. In 2007 it handled general cargo that reached record highs in tonnage and dollar value, and it received the acclaimed Presidential "E" award for contributing significantly to increase U.S. exports.

The Maryland Port Administration promotes, protects, and manages the bustling Port of Baltimore. Above: The Port of Baltimore's Dundalk (foreground) and Seagirt (background) marine terminals are two of the busiest in the United States. Opposite page: With an average of 37 container moves per hour, the Port of Baltimore's Seagirt Marine Terminal is considered to be one of the most efficient container terminals in the nation.

The Maryland Port Administration (MPA) was created in 1956 to modernize and promote the Port of Baltimore. However, Baltimore's port has been serving the state's economy for more than 300 years. Today the MPA continues to support the port's economic activity through the maintenance of Baltimore's six public marine terminals, including 73 buildings, water and electrical infrastructure, and technologically advanced storage facilities with fast, accurate automated systems. The MPA also maintains the terminals' rails, piers, and fire-protection system as well as 325 pieces of equipment, including vehicles, trucks, off-road construction and grounds-maintenance equipment, trailers and vessels, and the port's cranes.

Handling a variety of cargo, the Port of Baltimore is ranked first among 360 U.S. ports in quantity of roll-on/roll-off farm and construction equipment, trucks, and imported forest products, gypsum, iron ore, and sugar. The MPA's Intermodal Container Transfer Facility handles containers, which comprise most of the port's cargo. The remainder is specialized cargo of all shapes and dimensions.

The Port of Baltimore is the Atlantic port closest to the midwestern United States, and is within an overnight drive of two-thirds of the nation's population. Its convenient location, which is served by two U.S. Class I railroads, combines with its access to major interstate highways to enable advantageous shipping rates. Supporting more than 120,000 jobs, 16,500 of which are supported directly by its activities, the Port of Baltimore is a major contributor to the Maryland economy. In 2007 the amount of general cargo handled at MPA public marine terminals reached 8.7 million tons, a sixth-consecutive all-time annual tonnage high, with the total dollar value of an annual record $41.9 billion. In addition to supporting Maryland's shipping trade, the MPA promotes Baltimore's expanding cruise business at the South Locust Point Cruise Terminal, which was opened in 2006 and is specifically designed for passenger safety and convenience.

The MPA is committed to preserving a balance between economic development of the port and protection for the Chesapeake Bay's marine environment, to provide safe, navigable channels for shipping as well as clean, safe water for recreation, tourism, fishing, and agriculture and other commercial activities.

The MPA's environmental stewardship comprises many programs, such as reseeding oyster beds and converting its diesel-fueled vehicles and heavy equipment from low-sulphur-diesel fuel to a blend of ultra-low-sulphur-diesel and bio-diesel fuel.

The MPA works with federal, state, and local law enforcement and uses the most advanced technologies to make the Port of Baltimore secure. A leader in this endeavor, the port was one of the nation's first to inspect 100 percent of its imported containers for radiation.

Supporting the economy of the state, the marine environment of the bay, and the security of the port, the Maryland Port Administration is an important asset of Maryland. It provides additional information about its services and activities on its Web site at www.marylandports.com.

Baltimore/Washington International Thurgood Marshall Airport

Recognized as a low-delay, low-fare airport, Baltimore/Washington International Thurgood Marshall Airport (BWI Marshall) is strategically located, just 11 miles south of Baltimore and 25 miles north of Washington, D.C. BWI Marshall—ranked as the 24th-busiest airport in the United States—efficiently serves the fourth-largest metropolitan area, one of the fastest-growing regions in the nation.

About 20 million passengers pass through the gates of Baltimore/Washington International Thurgood Marshall Airport (BWI Marshall), which offers service by most major airlines. Just over half of the airport's traffic comes from Southwest Airlines, and fast-growing AirTran Airways is BWI Marshall's second-largest carrier. Also at BWI Marshall, international travelers can fly nonstop to London's Heathrow Airport and then connect to cities throughout Europe, the Middle East, and Africa. In addition, nonstop service is offered from BWI Marshall to destinations in Canada, Mexico, and the Caribbean.

Right: The single-terminal design of Baltimore/Washington International Thurgood Marshall Airport (BWI Marshall) means finding gates and making connections is easier and more efficient since no trains, trams, or people movers are needed. Shown here is the Southwest Airlines gate area in the terminal's A/B Concourse.

One of BWI Marshall's prime advantages is its ease of access. Traveling to and from the airport could not be easier by using major roadway systems I-95, I-97, and MD-295, or using a variety of convenient and efficient ground transportation options. As the only international airport in the region with train service, BWI Marshall is served by Amtrak and the Maryland Area Regional Commuter (MARC), which together operate more than 100 trains per day from the BWI Marshall Rail Station. Baltimore's Light Rail service also brings patrons to the door of the international concourse. Bus service from the terminal links the Washington Metropolitan Transit Authority's Metro system in Greenbelt, Maryland, to destinations in the Washington, D.C., area.

Once inside BWI Marshall, navigating through the airport is also simple. BWI Marshall's single-terminal design makes finding gates and making connections easy without needing to use trains, trams, or people movers. BWI Marshall continually receives high marks for providing good customer service and offering many advantages to patrons such as easy access, price, and location. As such, BWI Marshall continues to be recognized for passenger satisfaction in areas such as terminal facilities, security checkpoints, immigration and customs control, the airline check-in process, and the airport's ever-growing food and retail concessions program.

A major employer, BWI Marshall supports nearly 100,000 total jobs, based on the most recent economic data available. And overall airport activity produces an estimated $475 million in tax revenue for state and local governments and $165 million in federal tax revenue. Furthermore, the airport produces $3.2 billion of personal wages and is responsible for $5.1 billion in business revenue to the state annually.

Baltimore/Washington International Thurgood Marshall Airport provides additional information on its Web site at www.bwiairport.com.

Cherbo Publishing Group

Cherbo Publishing Group's business-focused, art book–quality publications, which celebrate the vital spirit of enterprise, are custom books that are used as high-impact economic development tools to enhance reputations, increase profits, and provide global exposure for businesses and organizations.

Both pages, all:
Cherbo Publishing Group
produces custom books for
historical, professional, and
government organizations.
These fine publications
promote the economic
development of America's
cities, regions, and states by
chronicling their history—the
people, enterprises, industries,
and organizations that have
made them great.

Cherbo set out to succeed—and continues to do just that.

Cherbo Publishing Group (CPG) is North America's leading publisher of quality custom books for commercial, civic, historical, and trade associations. Publications range from hardcover state, regional, and commemorative books to softcover state and regional business reports. The company is headquartered in Encino, California, and operates regional offices in Philadelphia, Minneapolis, and Houston.

About CPG Publications

CPG has created books for some of America's leading organizations, including the U.S. Chamber of Commerce, Empire State Development, California Sesquicentennial Foundation, Chicago O'Hare International Airport, and the Indiana Manufacturers Association. Participants have included Blue Cross Blue Shield, DuPont, Toyota, Northrop Grumman, and Xerox.

Jack Cherbo, Cherbo Publishing Group president and CEO, has been breaking new ground in the sponsored publishing business for more than 40 years.

"Previously, the cost of creating a handsome book for business developments or commemorative occasions fell directly on the sponsoring organization," Cherbo says. "My company pioneered an entirely new concept—funding these books through the sale of corporate profiles."

Cherbo honed his leading edge in Chicago, where he owned a top advertising agency before moving into publishing. Armed with a degree in business administration from Northwestern University, a mind that never stopped, and a keen sense of humor,

CPG's series range from history books to economic development/relocation books and from business reports to publications of special interest. The latest series, Going Green, discusses a region's efforts toward environmental sustainability and the way green industry is contributing to the area's economy. The economic development series spotlights the outstanding economic and quality-of-life advantages of fast-growing cities, counties, regions, or states. The annual business reports provide an economic snapshot of individual cities, regions, or states. The commemorative series marks milestones for corporations, organizations, and professional and trade associations.

To find out how CPG can create a custom publication for you, or for information on how to showcase your company or organization in one of our publications, contact Jack Cherbo at 818-783-0040, extension 26, or visit www.cherbopub.com.

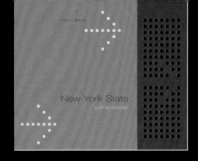

Select CPG Publications

VISIONS OF OPPORTUNITY
City, Regional, and State Series

ALABAMA *The Progress, The Promise*

AMERICA & THE SPIRIT
OF ENTERPRISE
Century of Progress, Future of Promise

AURORA, ILLINOIS *A City Second to None*

CALIFORNIA *Golden Past, Shining Future*

CHATTANOOGA *The Renaissance of a City*

CINCINNATI *Bridges to the Future*

CONNECTICUT *Chartered for Progress*

DELAWARE *Incorporating Vision in Industry*

FORT WORTH *Where the Best Begins*

GREATER PHOENIX *Expanding Horizons*

JACKSONVILLE *Where the Future Leads*

LEHIGH VALLEY *Crossroads of Commerce*

MICHIGAN *America's Pacesetter*

MILWAUKEE *Midwestern Metropolis*

MISSOURI *Gateway to Enterprise*

NASHVILLE *Amplified*

NEW YORK STATE *Prime Mover*

NORTH CAROLINA *The State of Minds*

OKLAHOMA *The Center of It All*

PITTSBURGH *Smart City*

SOUTH DAKOTA *Pioneering the Future*

TOLEDO *Access. Opportunity. Edge.*

UTAH *Life Elevated*

WEST VIRGINIA *Reaching New Heights*

WISCONSIN *A Tradition of Innovation*

LEGACY Commemorative Series

ALBERTA AT 100 *Celebrating the Legacy*

BUILD IT & THE CROWDS WILL COME
Seventy-Five Years of Public Assembly

CELEBRATE SAINT PAUL
150 Years of History

DAYTON *On the Wings of Progress*

THE EXHIBITION INDUSTRY
The Power of Commerce

IDAHO *The Heroic Journey*

MINNEAPOLIS *Currents of Change*

NEW JERSEY *Crossroads of Commerce*

NEW YORK STATE ASSOCIATION
OF FIRE CHIEFS
Sizing Up a Century of Service

ROCHESTER, MINNESOTA
Transforming the World: Rochester at 150

VIRGINIA
Catalyst of Commerce for Four Centuries

VISIONS TAKING SHAPE
*Celebrating 50 Years of the Precast/
Prestressed Concrete Industry*

ANNUAL BUSINESS REPORTS

MINNESOTA REPORT *2007*

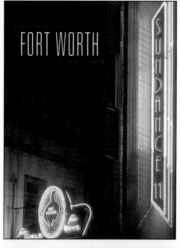
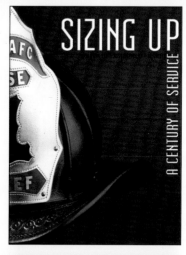
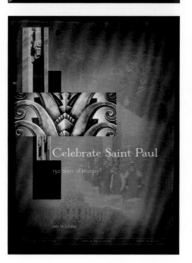
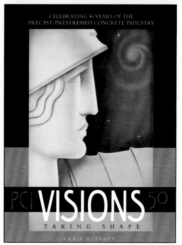

PHOTO CREDITS

cherbo publishing group, inc.

TYPOGRAPHY

Principal faces used: Adobe Jenson, designed by Robert Slimbach in 1996, which was derived from a previous design by Nicolas Jenson in 1470; Univers, designed by Adrian Frutiger in 1957; Helvetica, designed by Matthew Carter, Edouard Hoffmann, and Max Miedinger in 1959

HARDWARE

Macintosh G5 desktops, digital color laser printing with Xerox Docucolor 250, digital imaging with Creo EverSmart Supreme

SOFTWARE

QuarkXPress, Adobe Illustrator, Adobe Photoshop, Adobe Acrobat, Microsoft Word, Eye-One Pro by Gretagmacbeth, Creo Oxygen, FlightCheck

PAPER

Text Paper: #80 Luna Matte

Bound in Rainbow® recycled content papers from Ecological Fibers, Inc.

Dust Jacket: #100 Sterling-Litho Gloss